AFFORDABLE SOLUTIONS FOR CLIMATE CHANGE

THAT ARE ACHIEVABLE AND ASPIRATIONAL

Daniel D. Watch

AFFORDABLE SOLUTIONS FOR CLIMATE CHANGE

———

Book Design by Readz
275 E. Hillcrest Drive Suite 160–276
Thousand Oaks CA 91360
USA
www.Readz.com
sales@readz.com

Printed by BookBaby Publishing, in the United States
7905 N Crescent Blvd.
Pennsauken, NJ, 08110
www.bookbaby.com
info@bookbaby.com

Disclaimer: Although the author and publisher have made every effort to ensure that the information in this book was correct at press time, the author and publisher do not assume and hereby disclaim any liability to any party for any loss, damage, or disruption caused by errors or omissions, whether such errors or omissions result from negligence, accident, or any other cause.

ISBN 978-1-66787-518-7

It is frustrating to hear "it costs more money". Many times, this statement is made because of a lack of knowledge, not having the latest thinking on the topic, or simply opposed to solutions to address climate change. **This document will inform on the recent costs, paybacks, savings and opportunities as we reduce carbon. This book is intended to help people, companies and governments make decisions today to IMPLEMENT NOW to reduce carbon and save money.**

I am advocating to do as much as possible now that has a seven-year payback or less while addressing climate change. Some ideas will save money immediately. I have focused on mainstream solutions that can be implemented quickly. Success stories and lessons learned are shared. The most technically feasible, cost-effective and socially acceptable ideas are proposed in this book. My intentions are to show data that is accurate and easy to understand. Positive change needs to happen at all levels, in the U.S. and across the world.

There are over 40 solutions documented with proposals for the government, private industry and citizens to implement. Each solution is discussed in a way that anyone should be able to understand and make decisions on. The latest data, lessons learned, and research are provided.

Intended Audience is for everyone, with focus on three groups:

1. Government at all levels in the U.S.,

2. Private Industry and Academics, and

3. Citizens.

Each of the three groups has an important role in addressing climate change and the book clearly documents how each can contribute.

Daniel D. Watch

Contents

Introduction

The primary goal of this book is to help individuals, businesses, and governments make decisions today to IMPLEMENT NOW to save money and also help reduce greenhouse gases.

OPPORTUNITIES

Much of the modeling by researchers indicates that we are behind in reducing Greenhouse Gases (GHGs) based on goals the U.S. agreed to. We need to implement solutions quickly and at a very large scale. **I am advocating for a plan that will do as much as possible NOW that has a seven-year payback or less**. There are 40+ specific solutions that are smart financial investments organized in six main categories: food, renewable energy, transportation, cities, buildings, and carbon sequestration. An overview of each issue is discussed with data explaining the cost and potential savings. About 50% of the solutions presented will save money immediately or within one year. The other 50% have paybacks within seven years, which is considered by most as a good financial investment. **Making these policies and incentives aware to the general public and investors in a timely manner is critical.** Success stories are shared. Positive change needs to happen at all levels. I have focused on mainstream solutions that can be implemented across the world.

The pace of change over the past 50 years has been unprecedented in human history. The human population has doubled, the global economy has expanded four-fold, and more than 1 billion people have been lifted out of extreme poverty. We produce more food, energy, and materials than ever before. The global middle class, currently 3.5 billion people, continues to grow by about 160 million people a year, 70% of whom are in China and India. This remarkable growth and prosperity have come at a heavy cost to the natural systems that underpin life on Earth.

My desire is for this book to continually inform and educate. Ideas are provided to help governments set policies, encourage private companies to invest, support innovation with research, and help individuals' decision-making contributes each day to reduce carbon. Ideally the goal is to get to zero carbon emissions as soon as possible, by or before 2050. **There should be the opportunity, one day, to have a world that is regenerative, that provides more back to nature than what we have taken.**

There are many articles, books, documentaries, and webinars with different solutions. There is very little clear information on what solutions to act on now that are also financially justified. This book simplifies the information from many sources to support leaders in making smart and timely decisions. Most of the numbers presented in this document reflect data within the last 12-24 months. This book is written assuming the reader understands the urgency of addressing climate change, based on all the information that has been presented by the media, governments, advocacy groups, researchers, publications, and other sources over the past few years. Also, we hear about a serious natural disaster somewhere almost every day.

There are many other issues that are very important to address alongside the climate crisis, such as education, diversity, hunger, poverty and job creation, to name a few. As you choose your next steps forward, incorporate as many of these important initiatives as possible to support the "Global Good."

The Intergovernmental Panel on Climate Change (IPCC) reported key points in 2022:

Global surface temperature was 1.09C higher between 2011 and 2020.

The past five years have been the hottest on record since 1850.

Human influence is "very likely" (90%) the main driver of the global retreat of glaciers since the 1990s and the decrease in Arctic sea-ice.

It is "virtually certain" that hot extremes including heat waves have become more frequent and more intense since the 1950s, while cold events have become less frequent and less severe.

Recently temperatures reached 118°F in the Arctic Circle!

Most alarming is that the U.S. creates far more carbon dioxide emissions that any other country! This is more than the next three countries combined (China, Russia and Germany). This is based on data from the Union of Concerned Scientists.

2020 U.S. Greenhouse Gas Emissions by Gas:

78.8% Carbon dioxide (CO_2): Fossil fuel use is the primary source of CO_2. CO_2 can also be emitted from direct human-induced impacts on forestry and other land uses, such as through deforestation, land clearing for agriculture, and degradation of soils. Likewise, land can also remove CO_2 from the atmosphere through reforestation, improvement of soils, and other activities. CO_2 makes up the vast majority of greenhouse gas emissions from the sector, but smaller amounts of methane (CH_4) and nitrous oxide (N_2O) are also emitted. **These gases are released during the combustion of fossil fuels, such as coal, oil, and natural gas, to produce electricity.**

10.9% Methane (CH_4): Agricultural activities, waste management, energy use, and biomass burning all contribute to CH_4 emissions. Researchers discovered that methane leaking from gas-burning stoves inside U.S. residences has a climate impact comparable to the carbon emissions of about 500,00 gasoline-powered vehicles.[1]

7.1% Nitrous oxide (N_2O): Agricultural activities such as fertilizer use are the primary source of N_2O emissions. Fossil fuel combustion also generates N_2O.

3.1% Fluorinated gases (F-gases): Industrial processes, refrigeration, and the use of a variety of consumer products contribute to emissions of F-gases, which include hydrofluorocarbons (HFCs), perfluorocarbons (PFCs), and sulfur hexafluoride (SF_6). HFCs have 1,000 to 9,000 times greater capacity to warm the atmosphere than carbon dioxide. The estimated net cost to eliminate any leakage is at $629.25 billion.

The social cost for releasing a metric ton of **carbon dioxide is $51**.

A metric ton of releasing **methane costs $1500**

Releasing a metric ton of **nitrous oxide costs $18,000,** according to the Selective Credit Control (SCC) measure in finance.

TOTAL U.S. Greenhouse Gas Emissions by Economic Sector in 2019[2]

Transportation	29%
Electricity	25%
Industry	23%
Commercial & Residential	13%
Agriculture	10%

Top Options for Reducing Your Carbon Footprint

The average carbon footprint of a person in the United States is **16 tons**, which is one of the highest in the world. Globally, the average carbon footprint is closer to 4 tons.[3] U.S. citizens have a responsibility and the opportunity to have a very positive impact to reduce Greenhouse Gases (GHGs).

Top 10 lists to reduce the carbon footprint:

1. Live Car-free
2. Driving an electric car
3. Flying one less plane flight per year
4. Using renewable energy
5. Using public transportation
6. Refurbishing or renovating your home
7. Eating a vegan diet
8. Installing an electric heat pump
9. Improving cooking equipment
10. Using renewable based heating

SOLUTIONS THAT COST LESS TODAY AND REDUCE CARBON

The research in this book is based on hundreds of articles, dozens of books, and research from several organizations. All the references are enlisted in the Resources and Credits. I have used Bill Gates book, *How to Avoid a Climate Disaster*, *Drawdown: The Most Comprehensive Plan Ever Proposed to Reverse Global Warming* published 2017 and 2020 authored by Paul Hawken, and Mark Jacobson's research as a professor of civil and environmental engineering at Stanford

University and director of its Atmosphere/ Energy Program, as a few of the important resources for this book. Also, much of the data is from various government research agencies, with some providing peer reviews. With all the research I have accumulated, I have found information to be very helpful and confusing at the same time. What I have done is put the information in simple terms. **There are many great ideas but how does an average citizen, CEO, or politician determine what are the best investments now that also will work for decades?** According to the book, *Drawdown*, the overall **net operational savings for changing to more sustainable solutions exceed the net implementation costs four to five times over**.

"Fundamental changes don't happen because they're virtuous. They happen because they make economic sense. We've got to make the right outcome the profitable outcome, and therefore, the likely outcome." — John Doerr from his recent book *Speed & Scale*. **Mr. Doerr** is an American <u>investor</u> and <u>venture capitalist</u> at <u>Kleiner Perkins</u>.

There is affordable technology and behavioral solutions that are available today in the United States that can help the country reach net zero by 2050.

There is a problem today when most decision makers do not know the full cost of solutions to address climate change. It is frustrating to hear the phrase "it costs more money" or "we lack the finances." This book will inform readers about the recent costs, paybacks, savings and opportunities we have to reduce carbon.

There are 40 documented solutions that will save money. There are six solutions listed in this book that will add cost, require more than seven years for a positive return, if there ever is a positive return. These items need to be improved with more research, competitions, and innovations:

Direct Air Capture (DAR)

Carbon sequestration

Aviation

Ocean shipping

Nuclear- Generation IV

High Speed Rail

HEALTH

Carbon from car emissions creates air pollution, which is the cause of an estimated 1 million people dying globally each year.[4] **Using data from the Environmental Protection Agency, researchers at the University of Wisconsin–Madison estimate that about 50,000 premature deaths would be avoided every year if microscopic air pollutants called particulates were eliminated in the U.S. The study estimates that eliminating such air pollution would save about $600 billion each year.** This new study, December 2021, is the latest reminder that climate change and public health are intimately related, and that cutting greenhouse gas emissions doesn't just reduce long-term risk from global warming, it can also save lives immediately by cutting pollution.[5]

Many solutions to restore and preserve the natural environment support reducing the carbon footprint as well as supporting the health of the overall population.

EDUCATION

Many more jobs are projected for many of the ideas presented. There is a shortage of people available and the right skill sets for the new technologies. **Governments can help close the skills gap by funding in-person vocational education** to support the growth in transitioning to a climate-focused world. The government, private institutions, and individuals can work together to create **virtual classes available for free to everyone.** People can learn on their own schedule and pace. Experts can be made available to answer questions. Using technology to educate and accelerate learning is critical. The new training usually will require a few months, not years, and then will provide a very qualified workforce.

The National Science Foundation, the Department of Labor, and the Department of Energy have programs that support training for jobs in energy and manufacturing related workforce programs. The link: Energy & Manufacturing Workforce Training Topics List Version 1.7 (02.11.14) provides a searchable list of the training programs in areas and shows the subjects being taught, grantee, project title, and state. In some cases, the list also shows the certificates provided by the courses. The Department of Labor's new online database allows individuals to search for all programs of study, courses, and find details about grant funded programs of study, institutions, projects, and courses funded by the U.S. Department of Labor's Trade Adjustment Assistance Community College and Career Training (**TAACCCT**) grant program.

The government pays for the education of people to support solutions that address climate change. There is also financial support for people to transition from jobs in fossil fuels to electric technology by providing comparable wages, benefits and maintaining existing pensions.

Businesses provide time to employees for their education and create a culture that encourages continuing education now and throughout their career.

Citizens invest their time to educate themselves and others now as technology changes quickly. Focus on continuing education as technological improvements happen.

SCALING UP MANUFACTURING

Manufacturing is a critical issue now to make sure there is the infrastructure built to support the need and demand for the amount of new products required globally. Governments should provide tax incentives and subsidies to private investors for the construction and expansion of facilities that are necessary to manufacture green technology. This includes the purchase of more equipment as well as upgrading existing equipment for more efficiency to improve the supply chain.

This book is organized into two main categories over 10 chapters:

REDUCING GREENHOUSE GASES

1. FOOD
2. RENEWABLE ENERGY
3. TRANSPORTATION
4. CITIES
5. BUILDINGS
6. CARBON SEQUESTRATION

DECISION MAKERS

7. GOVERNMENTS
8. PRIVATE INDUSTRY
9. CITIZENS
10. GLOBAL
11. SUMMARY

It was estimated and presented in the book *Drawdown* that over 500 gigatons of carbon needs to be removed globally. The U.S. should be responsible for approximately 25% of that total based on the amount of energy it uses (125 gigatons). The solutions represented in this book add up to over 1000 gigatons globally. Most items should become more cost-effective and efficient with improvements in technology, growth in the marketplace that should bring prices down, improvements in manufacturing and supply chain delivery developments. With today's technology, the U.S. should be able to reduce the carbon footprint by at least 125 gigatons, and save money, if all decision makers make the right choices.

The federal government has incredible purchasing power to drive clean energy deployment across the market by purchasing 24/7 clean power for federal buildings. **The federal government spends more than a half-a-trillion dollars buying goods and services each year.** The state and local governments have purchasing power and money to invest in affordable green solutions. The government, at all levels in the U.S., can accelerate growth with smart, timely policies that businesses and citizens can support now.

THE MOST TECHNICALLY FEASIBLE, SOCIALLY ACCEPTABLE AND COST-SAVING TOP 10 ACTIONS FOR THE UNITED STATES TO FOCUS ON NOW:

1. Reduce food waste
2. Build & generate renewable energy (wind, solar, storage)
3. Promote ALL Electric Vehicles (EVs) including cars, trucks, buses, and bikes
4. Cities share amenities
5. Upgrade existing buildings to be more energy-efficient
6. Preserve land (mangroves, trees, farming)
7. Government support accelerating the market for green solutions
8. Businesses innovate, invest and lead
9. Informed decision making and behavioral changes by individuals
10. Global focus

In 1986 and '87, expeditions to Antarctica confirmed a hole in the ozone above Antarctica that left the world on edge. Chemicals called chlorofluorocarbons (CFCs), found in many personal hygiene products, aerosol sprays, and air conditioners had caused a hole in the ozone layer that was only getting bigger. The news was dramatic enough to spur the signing of the <u>Montreal Protocol</u> by the end of 1987, kicking off the global phaseout of CFCs. The hole does not exist today.

It will take all governments, businesses, and people to do their part in order to make substantial lasting changes. The ideas provide hope that we can address climate change responsibly.

FOOD
REDUCE CARBON

When most people think of solving the climate crisis, they think about generating more electricity and minimizing fossil fuels. **The reality is that the way we make, distribute, manage, eat and waste food has a very significant impact on the environment. People need to be focused on food more in the U.S. to reduce our global carbon footprint and live healthier. There are many ways individuals and families can help reduce their carbon footprint based on the right choices of food to eat.**

Sunlight passes through the atmosphere and heats the Earth's surface before it radiates back into space. (NASA) Green House Gases (GHGs) in the atmosphere naturally trap some of the heat before it escapes back. This is called the greenhouse effect, and it's what makes Earth habitable. However, human activity through the burning of fossil fuels has led to an increase in GHGs in the atmosphere, which is thickening the blanket and trapping excess heat[1].

More than seventy billion tons of GHGs could be prevented from being released into the atmosphere if we can cut down on food waste[2]. Methane in landfill is roughly twenty-eight times more potent (traps more heat in the atmosphere) than CO_2 over its twelve-year lifetime[3]. About 25 percent of artificial global warming is caused by methane emissions[4].

The world's top five meat and dairy corporations are now responsible for more annual GHG emissions than Exxon, Shell, or BP[5].

Overview

The following chart provides an outline of the main drivers in the food industry. The Food supply chain is focusing more on local access to food, reducing carbon caused by transportation, and creating less food waste. Consumer behavior is critical to get people to make better choices and reduce their waste.

FOOD SYSTEMS FRAMEWORK

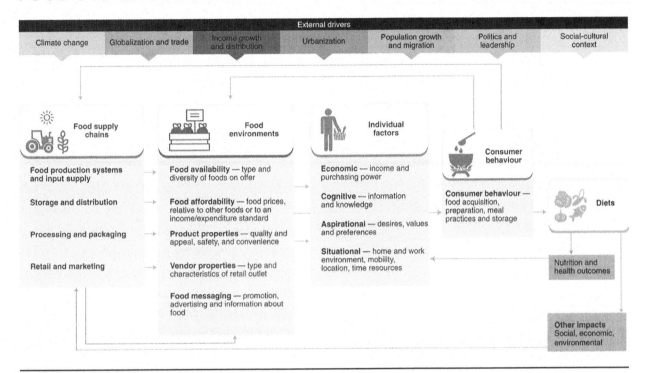

1.1

Key points that can be addressed now in the food industry to reduce carbon:

1. Reduce Waste to Zero

2. Sell and Buy Almost Perfect Food

3. Reduce Food Imports and Exports

4. Grow Local, Eat Fresh & Healthier Food

5. Eat Fewer Animals and More Plants

6. Roof Top Gardens

7. Support Vertical Farming

8. Refrigerant Management

9. No Waste Plastics

Reduce Food Waste

40 percent +- of the food in the U.S. becomes waste. Households are responsible for the largest portion of food waste (40 to 50 percent). One way to reduce waste is to give away or sell at a discount "almost perfect food," as well as damaged cans and packages to families. An additional way to cut much waste out of the system is to transform the farming system. The roofs of buildings and even the walls can use soil-less, hydroponic systems to grow food right on or near the consumer's doorstep. Another way to reduce waste is to import and export less. **Creating food locally and making sure all food is eaten would be a significant improvement, especially in the U.S., where we waste the most per capita by far. Local food reduces carbon with less transportation and less waste, as well as provides healthier food to the market.** Food systems consume about 30 percent of available global energy; out of this, 38 percent is utilized to produce food that is either lost or wasted[6].

It is estimated that, on average, an American meal travels around 1,500 miles from growth to plate. Two-hundred-fifty thousand tons of greenhouse gases are distributed into the atmosphere every year due to importing food products. Understand how far the food is being shipped, then buy and grow locally to keep the carbon cost and waste down. **After twenty-four hours of not eating food, you lose up to 30 percent of the nutrients which that food provides. After one-week, food loses over 70 percent of its nutrients. Buying local food will have less waste and be healthier.**

The USDA explains food loss as the edible amount of food after harvest or available for human consumption but not consumed for any reason. Food loss includes loss from mold, pests, inadequate climate control, cooking loss and natural shrinkage (for example, moisture loss), and food waste (food left on a plate).

Retail-level food loss occurs when grocery retailers remove dented cans, misshapen produce items, overstocked holiday foods, and spoiled foods from their shelves. Estimates of the average supermarket loss rate were 11.6 percent for thirty-one fresh vegetables[7].

ERS (Economic Research Service for USDA) estimates that in 2010, a total of 133 billion pounds, or 31 percent, of the 430 billion pounds of available food supply at the retail and consumer levels went uneaten, with an estimated retail value of $162 billion. On a per capita basis, this totaled roughly 1.2 pounds of food per person per day, with a retail value of over $1.40.

U.N. Environment Program's (UNEP) recently launched 'Think.Eat.Save' initiative with groups around the world to develop and coordinate projects to prevent the environmental problems that can result from food loss and food waste. These initiatives cover a wide range of sectors: private businesses, universities, and nonprofit organizations. **Most food waste is perfectly edible.** For instance, if white rice is mislabeled basmati rice, it's food waste. If a vegetable is misshapen, it's food waste, if a cereal box has a tear, food waste.

A can with a ripped label, also food waste. A bruised fruit, yup, food waste.

"The U.S. is the largest agricultural exporter in the world, exporting **$150 billion worth of agricultural products in 2020**," Texas A&M researcher Ribera said. "These exports account for about one-third of agricultural income. In the same year, the U.S. imported $146.8 billion in agricultural products."

When **food** is disposed of in a landfill, it rots and becomes a significant source of methane – a potent greenhouse gas with twenty-one times the global warming potential of carbon dioxide. The agricultural sector now accounts for 16 to 27 percent of global greenhouse-gas emissions. **Wasted food is responsible for 8 to 10 percent of greenhouse gas emissions**. According to the U.N. Food and Agriculture Organization, food waste globally is responsible for about 3.3 gigatons of greenhouse gas annually, which would be, if regarded as a country, the third-largest emitter of carbon after the U.S. and China[8]. There are different ways of cutting back on food waste. For example, you can start from the end of the chain by banning food in landfills.

Reducing waste is an opportunity for households to improve the environment and strengthen their financial position. Families with higher income generate much more waste than low-income households.

An average U.S. household spends about $5,850 per year on food, according to the Agriculture & Applied Economics Association. The average U.S. household loses **$1,866 on wasted food per year**, according to a recent Penn State study. Another study showed that simply **cutting waste in half for a US household (family of four) could**

save $77.75 per month! Reduce food waste by buying "almost perfect" food that is perfectly healthy and tasty. Blemished fruits and vegetables being discarded on a daily basis, often damaged from improper storage, transportation mishaps, or simply their shape and how they look, become almost perfect food.

1.2 Stop Food Waste Day should be every day.

People check the food donations from a grocery store which are distributed to people in need.

Giving leftover food to charity is no longer just an act of goodwill. It's a requirement under **a 2016 law in France that bans grocery stores from throwing away edible food**. Stores can be fined $4500 for each infraction. Across France, 5,000 charities depend on the food bank network, which now gets nearly half of its donations from grocery stores. The new law has increased the quantity and quality of donations. There are more fresh foods and products available further from their expiration date.

People changing eating habits can improve the health of the individual as well as the environment. Any food provided by the government, at federal, state, and local levels should be required to be healthy based on federal guidelines. Then there is the need to feed the poor and hungry population. Globally, food insecurity is an increasing problem. Up to 811 million people (around 10 percent of the world's population) faced hunger in 2020, according to the UN, **an increase of more than 100 million people from 2019.** The amount of food needed to feed the world's population by the end of the century will increase by almost eighty percent.

SUCCESS STORIES

Fresh Hub, with the help of a smartphone app and automated messaging service, was able to alert residents when fresh food was available. Fresh Hub, since 2017, has led a total of twenty-three events, mobilized a team of 100 high-school volunteers, saved 15,200 pounds (6,900kg) of food from landfill, and served 1,900 Houston residents.

Second Servings, a Houston-based non-profit, has the vans, the equipment, and the expertise in rescuing food, which it donates to non-profits, soup kitchens, homeless shelters, and other places of need. It has expanded to doing events at community centers to help more people.

Bright Sparks, the sustainability series, sets out to find the young minds who are finding new and innovative ways of tackling environmental problems.

Starbucks, the company said it would expand its FoodShare donation program to all 9,000 of its company-operated locations in the U.S. The program initially launched in 2016 and since then has donated some 33.7 million meals to local food banks. This equates to 10 percent of the U.S. population for one meal.

Starbucks also said it is donating $1.7 million to Feeding America to provide equitable access to nutritious food to underserved communities. The grants will be distributed to sixteen food banks across the U.S. where the company has its Starbucks Community Stores or locations in underrepresented neighborhoods[9].

TORONTO FREE IT FORWARD GROCERY STORE

The world's first pay-what-you-can grocery store opened up in 2018 in Toronto, and the shelves are stocked entirely with food that was destined for a landfill. The 'Feed It Forward' store "sells" food and ingredients that are donated by larger grocery supply chains that aren't allowed to sell the products. Customers are free to fill up their baskets and pay whatever they can afford. If they don't have any money, they are still free to take whatever they want, although families are only allowed to take home one day's worth of food in order to ensure that the store remains stocked. The concept behind the store is to showcase how Canadians can utilize the food that's destined for landfills: perfectly edible food that shouldn't be thrown out and can be filling the empty bellies of our citizens. This is the brainchild of Chef Jagger Gordon, a renowned Canadian advocate for reducing food waste and feeding the hungry.

These are just a short list of organizations contributing. There are many more around the U.S. and globally. There are many negative things we hear related to climate change, but there are also many positive stories from people and organizations rising to the challenge.

1.3

World's First Pay-What-You-Can Grocery Store! It Saves Food Otherwise Destined for Trash

1.4

Reduce Food Imports and Exports

The Ellen McArthur Foundation found that forty-five of perishable vegetables grown in Europe are wasted before they reach the table; much of this is due to long and inefficient supply chains. Avoiding food that is flown in and buying food that is both local and seasonal avoids many of these issues. Transport has been estimated to account for about 11 percent of the food emissions associated with an average American diet and 6 percent of an average global diet. If exports and imports can be reduced by 10 to 20 percent, the carbon footprint will be reduced, there will be less food waste, and people will eat healthier local produce.

Anthony Myint, the cofounder of the Perennial in San Francisco, establishes sustainability as a culinary virtue through his Zero Foodprint non-profit. The organization aims to help fellow chefs and restaurateurs achieve carbon-neutral operations. His view is that it's a simple concept for diners to grasp and can thus have a big impact. This year, 178 restaurants joined his initiative and went carbon-neutral for Earth Day[10].

RESOURCES AVAILABLE

Reducing Food Waste/ EPA.gov

Think.Eat.Save

Apps: Too Good To Go and Food Rescue Hero

To reduce waste, many places are looking at technological solutions that improve yields and resilience to climate change that are sustainable. Precision farming uses drones, satellites, and GPS to map out conditions in a field. The technology can precisely calculate what nutrients or other agricultural additions are needed in specific small pockets of land, helping farmers to do things in a smarter, more efficient, and more informed way. It can also reduce negative environmental impacts, such as runoff from nitrogen fertilizer.

Buy Local

Locally grown food can produce fruits, vegetables, dairy products, eggs, and locally raised meats. Local food producers can grow certain types of foods year-round in greenhouses, vertical gardens, and orchards.

Much local food is seasonal. Buying food locally keeps money circulating throughout the community since the farmer can make more profit and, in return, can support other local businesses.

1.5 Buy from local farms: fresher, healthier food with much less waste.

POLICIES

- Support local farmers and food markets with government grants, subsidies, and tax breaks.

- Sell to everyone "almost perfect" food at all grocery stores.

- Provide "almost perfect" to the low-income and homeless at minimal or no cost.

- Subsidize farms in lower-income areas by including solar to generate their electricity.

- Tax incentive for companies that contribute food to Apps like: "Too Good To Go" and "Food Rescue Hero" and others to reduce food waste.

- Each country reduces imports of food by 10 percent and exports by 10 percent.

RECOMMENDATIONS

- Enlist well-known chefs to inspire less wasteful kitchen habits at restaurants by writing books and being on TV shows.

- Encourage the development of Agrihoods: single-family, multifamily, or mixed-use communities built with a working farm as the focus.

- Food-centric residential developments: single-family or multifamily developments built around community gardens and restaurants.

- Next generation urban markets: food halls that **employ innovative food sourcing concepts to encourage food entrepreneurship**.

- Food hubs and culinary incubators: Regional processing and distribution centers that give food-based entrepreneurs access to commercial kitchen space, connect them to retail and institutional customers, or both.

- Have media share information to help communication and education to the public.

Local foods represent a small (less than 4 percent of total farm sales) but growing share of the U.S. food system. Local foods include products sold directly to consumers, retailers, institutions, schools, hospitals, and intermediaries such as food hubs, processors, and wholesalers. Local foods are an important sales component of local food producers, accounting for 76 percent of their gross value of agricultural product sales. An ERS report showed most local foods were sold through intermediate markets and institutions (39 percent) followed by direct-to-consumer (34 percent) and retailers (27 percent)[11].

FOOD PRICES

For a typical dollar spent in 2020 by U.S. consumers on domestically produced food, including both grocery store and eating-out purchases, 27.9 cents went to food service establishments such as restaurants and other eating-out places. The food service share of the food dollar decreased after nine years of gains as households shifted to food-at-home consumption during the first year of the COVID-19 pandemic. For the remainder of the food dollar, transportation (4.1 cents) and wholesale trade (11.9 cents) rose to their highest shares reported in the series, which provides statistics back to 1993[12].

1.6 2020 nominal food dollar by industry group:

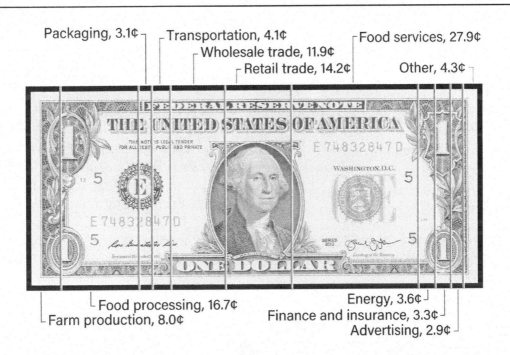

Packaging, 3.1¢
Transportation, 4.1¢
Wholesale trade, 11.9¢
Retail trade, 14.2¢
Food services, 27.9¢
Other, 4.3¢
Food processing, 16.7¢
Farm production, 8.0¢
Energy, 3.6¢
Finance and insurance, 3.3¢
Advertising, 2.9¢

Note: Other includes two industry groups: Agribusiness, and Legal and accounting.
Source: USDA, Economic Research Service, Food Dollar Series data product.

Many studies show little difference between the price of local versus mass-produced food prices. One hundred years ago, most food was grown and purchased locally. To get to net zero, many solutions need to go back to when the earth was much more sustainable. The next time you shop for food, remember that purchasing cheaper, mass-produced commodity food comes at a cost to the local economy and the planet.

Eat More Plants

"Eating healthy food may be the single most important way of contributing to saving the planet." —David Attenborough.

A 2018 Oxford University study found that the single biggest way to reduce your environmental impact is to avoid or reduce animal products. This is largely because more than 80 percent of farmland is dedicated to livestock animals raised for meat and dairy, yet these food products only account for about 18 percent of calories, and 37 percent of protein consumption. The study created a huge dataset based on almost 40,000 farms in 119 countries covering forty food products that represent 90 percent of all that is eaten. It assessed the full impact of these foods, from farm to fork, on land use, climate change emissions, freshwater use, water pollution, and air pollution[13].

The study explained that beef cattle raised on deforested land result in twelve times more greenhouse gases and use fifty times more land than those grazing rich natural pasture. But the comparison of beef with plant proteins such as peas is stark, with even the lowest impact beef responsible for six times more greenhouse gases and thirty-six times more land.

The percentage of vegetarians in the U.S. in 2022 is estimated to grow, considering that more and more people have been reducing their animal product consumption. More than a third of participants in the State of the Industry Report: Plant-Based Meat, Eggs, and Dairy said they were mostly vegetarian or were actively reducing their meat consumption. What's more, 80 percent believe the shift toward plant-based diets is a long-term change. Thirty-two percent of people in the U.S. identify themselves as "mostly vegetarian."[14]

1.7 A plant based diet reduces the risk of heart disease death by 40 percent.[15]

A plant-based diet reduces the risk of heart disease death by 40 percent[15].

Vegetarians show a 10 to 12 percent lower incidence rate for all cancers[16].

Vegetarians are 50 percent less likely to develop Type 2 diabetes than non-vegetarians[17].

At least $500 billion is spent every year on agricultural subsidies, and probably much more. "There is much money there to do something really good with," said Joseph Poore, at the University of Oxford, UK, who led the research. Given the global obesity crisis, changing diets—eating less livestock produce and more vegetables and fruit—has the potential to make both us and the planet healthier. We should interpret these results, not as the need to become vegan overnight but rather as to moderate our meat consumption, especially beef. The bigger the animal, the more harm is done to the climate. Cattle alone account for 4 percent of global emissions.

Consumption of meat and dairy, as well as overall calories, usually exceeds nutritional recommendations. Encouraging plant-based foods reduces demand, land clearing, fertilizer use, and greenhouse gas emissions. Embracing a vegetarian diet would save around half a ton of carbon on average per person each year.

It takes more calories to feed animals that are then used to provide calories to people.

Beef requires six calories to produce one calorie of beef eaten by a person.

A pig eats three calories to be able to produce one calorie for consumption.

A chicken eats two calories of grain for one calorie of poultry it produces.

This means we need to plant more to feed animals than humans. More meat requires more land, which means fewer trees and more emissions. Destroying forests to make room for agriculture is a significant problem in the Amazon and other developing areas of the world. We can not lose our carbon sinks.

Forty percent of plant protein that's grown is used as feed. Currently, the most popular alternative to meat is a plant-based protein, often derived from ingredients such as soy, peas, chickpeas, chia, and quinoa, and it's rapidly going mainstream as more people adopt vegetarian, vegan, or flexitarian diets. As awareness of the impact of meat production grows alongside recognition of the health benefits of eating less meat, diets are shifting towards plant-based protein. China has pledged to halve its meat consumption by 2050[18].

Some opportunities include shopping at ethnic markets that usually cost less than grocery stores. Buy food whole, not pre-cut. Use digital store coupons. Use Apps like: "Too Good To Go" and "Food Rescue Hero" to reduce food waste. The finding of a new study published by Sous Vide Guy titled "Exploring Opinions on Plant-Based Eating" found that meat eaters spend $23 more per week on groceries than vegetarians, vegans, or those who don't eat meat for any reason. **If each person could reduce their meat consumption by at least 20 percent, that would significantly reduce emissions.**

VEGAN DIET

The vegan population is growing in the U.S. and is very common in many developing countries. According to Global Market Research Company, Ipsos, there are currently over 9.7 million American vegans (3 percent of the U.S. population.) In 2014, only 1 percent of the population was vegan. A report by market research firm, Nielsen, shows that a whopping 39 percent of Americans claim that while their diets are not fully plant-based, they eliminate as many animal-related food products as possible, and strive to one day be completely vegan. The plant-based meat market is predicted to register a compound growth rate of 18.9 percent by 2026. Vegan "meat" sales grew 72 percent between 2018 and 2020. Plant-based meat accounted for 2 percent of the total US meat market in 2018. Vegans do not support any animal products.

The global plant-based milk industry revenue was worth $16,130.9 million in 2019 and is expected to exceed a staggering $41,061 million by 2025[19]. The US consumption of plant-based milk increased by 61 percent in 2017, while the consumption of cow's milk declined by 22 percent. The most popular plant-based milk is soya milk.

A 2020 study, by Total Food Service, showed there are more than 1,474 plant-based restaurants in the U.S. There are more restaurants for people to enjoy. People are beginning to understand the benefits of eating vegan. Many famous people, including Tom Brady, Natalie Portman, Venus Williams, Beyonce, Corey Booker, and many others, are vegan.

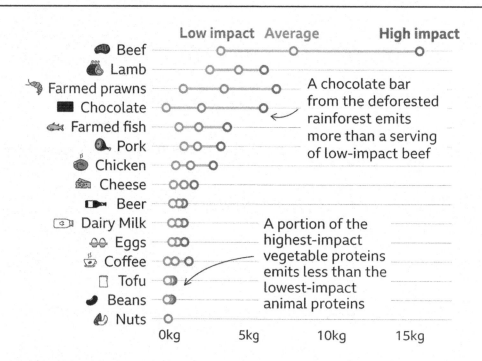

Note: The figures for each food are based on calculations from 119 countries. Serving sizes are from the British Dietetic Association (BDA) and Bupa.

1.8 Kilograms of greenhouse gas emissions per serving.

The figures for each food are based on calculations from 119 countries.

MEAT ALTERNATIVES

People eating meat alternatives is working in the U.S. market today and is growing globally. Demand for **plant-based foods is growing fast in the U.S., with a 27 percent increase in sales of plant-based products in 2020**, according to one report.[20]

By 2030, **meat alternatives will be of higher quality than today and will cost less to produce than the animal products they replace.** The cost of meat alternative proteins will be cheaper by 2030 than existing animal proteins. The number of cows in the US has dropped and will continue to fall as people eat less meat. From the peak in 1975 at 45,000+ cattle to where we currently are at 31,000 cattle, is a drop of 32 percent.

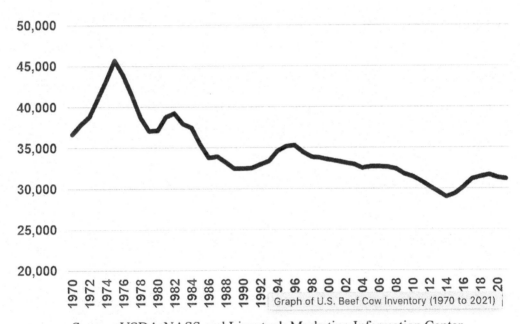

Graph of U.S. Beef Cow Inventory (1970 to 2021)

Source: USDA-NASS and Livestock Marketing Information Center

1.9 U.S. Beef Cow Inventory (1970–2021)

USDA Economic Research Service (ERS) data reveal the U.S. per capita cow's milk consumption has been trending downward for over seventy years and continued to decrease at an average rate of 1 percent per year during the 2000s and a faster average rate of 2.6 percent per year during the 2010s. **People in all age groups are drinking less milk and dairy beverages**. Per capita daily consumption of milk and milk drinks among children was down

26 percent. Some dairy farmers are struggling as demand for milk in America gradually decreases, with alternatives like oat, rice, coconut, almond, cashew, and soy milks taking huge chunks out of the milk market share.

There are several benefits with the development of food alternatives:

- The meat alternative food system will be far more localized, with shorter supply chains and local procurement.

- With the production of alternative meats, unused animal products will be eliminated.

- Fewer cows will mean less waste from the cows. The US greenhouse gas emissions from cattle will drop.

- Water consumption in cattle production and associated feed cropland irrigation will fall.

- Less land will be needed to raise the cattle.

- Many American families could save approximately 8 percent of their income each year, equivalent to $700.

- The average US family will save more than $1,200 a year in food costs. This will keep an additional $100 billion a year in Americans' pockets by 2030.

- Trade relations will shift because decentralized food production will be far less constrained by geographic and climatic conditions than traditional livestock and agriculture[21].

Research by the Plant Based Foods Association showed that sales of plant-based foods grew by 23 percent when supermarkets positioned in the meat aisle[22].

1.10

Vegan burgers are now in many restaurants and fast food chains. I have enjoyed many meat alternative meals.

Burger King will sell vegan nuggets across the UK as part of a pledge to make its menu 50 percent meat-free by 2030. The fast-food giant said the nuggets, made from soy and plant proteins, had been certified by the Vegan Society. Burger King said it's 50 percent meat-free target would help it reduce greenhouse gas emissions by 41 percent. According to the Vegan Society, there were about 600,000 vegans in Great Britain in 2019, four times more than there were in 2014[23].

Farmers and ranchers can reduce their operations' GHG emissions by making changes that are both effective and economical:

- **Increase animal productivity** to produce more output per unit input, such as meat, milk, and eggs.

- **Improve feeding practices** such as feeding more highly digestible foods to reduce methane from enteric fermentation. The longer the feed remains in the rumen, the more carbon is converted to methane.

- **Use dietary supplements and additives** such as, edible oils and ionophores to decrease the methane emission rate of forage-based diets. Edible oils can increase feed efficiency with less methane output. Ionophores reduce the number of bacteria that produce methane in the rumen.

- **Properly store and handle manure** by using covered lagoons that prevent methane and other gases from escaping into the atmosphere. These gases can then be used for power generation on the farm.

- **Use on-farm energy generation** by installing solar panels on barn roofs.

- **Improve farm energy efficiency** with structures and purchasing electric equipment.

Adapting to a vegetarian or vegan lifestyle can be challenging. So, a flexitarian approach is an excellent way to start. For example, you can cut down on meat consumption and transition to a plant-based diet over time.

My wife transitioned from being a vegetarian about five years ago to a vegan diet. She talked to a friend, asking for advice on how to plan meals for the rest of our family as she switched to the vegan diet. Her friend, from India, where the vast majority of people are vegan, was very helpful and said that you plan the entire vegan meal and then simply add meat for everyone else. This has worked well and helped me to reduce the amount of meat I eat in a week. I do enjoy the meat alternatives and eat them often. I do not drink any milk and have not for decades. When I was growing up, I had meat for lunch and dinner, and for most dinners, I had beef. I also drank close to half a gallon of milk a day when I was young. I feel healthier and more energized now, and I do enjoy all the vegan food my wife makes and the vegan restaurants we go to.

FINANCIAL COST/ PAYBACK

The finding of a new study published by Sous Vide Guy titled "Exploring Opinions on Plant-Based Eating," took a deep dive into the diets of 1,072 people living in different parts of the country and found that, on average, **meat eaters spend $23 more per week on groceries than vegetarians, vegans**, or those who don't eat meat for any reason.

POLICIES

- Focus on improving soil quality and using water more efficiently.

- Plant-based options must be available, visible, and enticing.

- Provide high-quality meat substitutes as options in all government buildings, including public schools.

- A hundred percent plant-based restaurants should receive a tax incentive, subsidy, and grants to support operations.

- Food sold in compostable materials—not plastics.

- Set a target to reduce the nation's meat consumption by 20 twenty over ten years.

POTENTIAL NEW JOBS

Food-based careers can provide upward mobility with limited barriers related to education, background, capital, or experience.

RECOMMENDATION

Provide "Nutrition" as a class in high school.

All medical schools must have nutrition in their curriculum.

People shop with their own recyclable bags.

HELPING LOW AND MODERATE INCOME FAMILIES

Solutions during the pandemic that should be continued as much as possible:

Publix Supermarkets are buying food from struggling farmers so they can use it to feed families in need. Since 2009, Publix has donated more than $2 billion in food to people with food insecurities, and has pledged an additional $2 billion in food donations over the next ten years. Publix is donating these products directly to Feeding America member food banks in its operating area. The initiative, which is expected to result in more than 150,000 pounds of produce and 43,500 gallons of milk donated to Feeding America food banks during its first seven days, is expected to run for several weeks.

The first program of its kind in the nation, 'Great Plates Delivered', will support struggling restaurants to rehire or retain staff, prepare the meals, and deliver them to those in need. Eligible seniors will be provided with twenty-one meals per week. "In California, it will bring three nutritious meals a day to seniors in need while providing meaningful work to those who have lost their jobs due to the coronavirus pandemic.

All of this will be accomplished through a partnership with the Federal Emergency Management Agency (FEMA) and state and local governments. FEMA will cover 75 percent of the cost, with the state picking up most of the remaining tab. Restaurants will be reimbursed at rates of $16 for breakfasts, $17 for lunches, and up to $28 for dinners."[24]

Rooftop Gardens

1.11 Agripolis – Above Paris Exhibition Center

The largest urban rooftop farm in the world uses vertical growing techniques to create fruits and vegetables right in the center of Paris without the use of pesticides, refrigerated trucks, chemical fertilizer, or even soil. The garden grows on 3.4 acres, about the size of two soccer pitches, atop the Paris Exhibition Center.

For a price of 15 euros, residents can order a basket of produce online containing a large bouquet of mint or sage, a head of lettuce, various young sprouts, two bunches of radishes, and one of chard, as well as a jar of jam or puree. When the project is finished, twenty staff members will be able to harvest up to 2,200 pounds of thirty-five different kinds of fruits and vegetables, every day. The Parisian mayor's proposal to install an additional 320 acres of rooftop and wall-mounted urban farming space could significantly reduce the number of trucks entering the city, easing traffic and reducing pollution[25].

ROOFTOP GARDEN PROS AND CONS.

The longevity of green roofs has the greatest effect on savings, whereas installation and maintenance have the greatest effect on cost (maintenance costs are even greater than the installation premium). The fewer floors a building has, the greater the energy savings are for a green roof compared to a black roof. The greater the surface area, the greater the stormwater management savings are for a green roof.

The GSA (General Services Administration) did a study on their government buildings that had constructed green roofs. Six separate issues were studied based on their relative benefits:

- Installation, replacement, and maintenance

- Stormwater

- Energy

- Carbon

- Community benefits

- Real estate effects

The costs and benefits are experienced by the developer through installation, rent, or operations. The municipality receives reduced infrastructure maintenance and replacement costs. The community benefits from improved aesthetics, biodiversity, and job generation.

COST OF GREEN ROOFS

The following information is based on a GSA study of nearly 2 million square feet of green roofs on federally owned buildings in GSA's eleven regions. Green roof installation costs per square foot decrease as size increases. The installed cost premium for multi-course extensive green roofs (3" deep) ranges from $10.30 to $12.50 per square foot more compared to a conventional, black roof. The installed cost premium for semi-intensive

green roofs (6" deep) ranges from $16.20 to $19.70 per square foot more compared to a conventional black. Annual maintenance for a green roof is typically higher than for a black roof, by $0.21 to $0.31 per square foot.

- Green roofs are relatively heavy, and not all roofs can support the weight.

- Green roofs typically don't make sense in dry climates like the southwest – it is very hot on roofs which leads to high water use, and plants have difficulty growing.

- Owners of buildings need to compare the best use of roofs, either solar panels or green roofs. Use the roof area for either solar panels or green roofs to extend the longevity of the main roof and be more sustainable.

PAYBACK

The installation, replacement, and maintenance of a green roof cost approximately $18 per square foot of roof. Stormwater and energy savings make up for this cost by providing a benefit of approximately $19 per square foot. Benefits to the community have the greatest positive impact at a savings of almost $38 per square foot of roof.

Green roofs will hold water and help with resiliency during heavy rains. The negative is maintaining ongoing maintenance and educating the staff to maintain green roofs properly throughout the years. Protection along the edge of the roof with a parapet or perimeter railing at least 42 inches high must be provided to protect against falling. Having prepared/allocated funding for long-term green roof maintenance will prevent any serious weed problems.

1.12 U.S. Custom House has the second largest green roof in the world, designed by Perkins&Will.

A green roof can save 10 to 15 percent on energy costs. By keeping a rooftop consistently at a lower temperature, you provide a cost savings of 10 15 percent to HVACs, photovoltaic panels, and other systems on rooftops, as well as the floor below. The savings vary depending on the roof insulation level. The savings will be less in buildings that are well insulated and already energy efficient.

Vertical Farming

It will be one of the key new developments that will improve the world within the next ten years. A vertical farm uses approximately:

- Forty percent less power,

- Eighty percent less food waste, and

- Produces 10× more than outdoor fields.

- Vegetables are 45 percent fresher because they are local.

- Use 70 percent less water than traditional practices.

- Less transportation costs, and **produce from harvest to table in hours,** not days.

- Reduces the chance for "UGLY" food to be grown by an estimated 35 percent.

- Takes about twelve to fourteen days for baby leafy greens to grow compared to thirty to forty-five days at an average outdoor farm.

- No more "seasonal crops."

- Less impact on carbon footprint!

1.13

Controlled-environment farming is sustainable and economically feasible. **Fruits and vegetables grown indoors have far greater yields per area than comparable produce grown outside.** Put a roof and walls around produce, and most problems caused by weeds, pests, and inclement weather vanish. Add technology like hydroponics-that will increase the yields even more. Better yet, build a hydroponic rig that is modular, rotates, and stacks-which means you have several "stories" of produce growing atop the same ground.

Vertical Harvest – Jackson Hole, Wyoming

The project finished construction at the end of 2015 and opened in May 2016. The company leaders developed the project after the great recession of 2008. Vertical Harvest is responding to a need to extend the growing season beyond four months in Jackson Hole.

The building is 30' wide and 150' long up against a parking deck and is on an infill lot owned by the city. The facility cost $3.8 million to build. They received a $1.5 million grant to support economic diversity (women-owned businesses). In three years, the business is expected to break even and, in five years, fully pay for itself.

This is a Community Impact Model to serve the population within forty miles. Vertical Harvest serves twelve local restaurants. The building has become the flagship for the town. The town owns the building, and it is leased for $100/month. The City Council votes on all changes.

Top-down approach with three microclimates created to grow:

Six lettuce heads
Eighteen micro greens
Six cherry tomato varieties

This serves 1 percent of the local need. Plenty of opportunities to grow.

The three greenhouses are stacked on each other throughout the building, with the vining plants (cherry tomatoes) at the top. The lettuce heads are on a vertical rack in the middle of the building at the main entry. This portfolio of crops can work with technology. The herbs that grow on the horizontal shelves provide 40 percent of the revenue. The herbs are very healthy to eat. The carousels with the lettuce heads that move up and down perform better than on horizontal racks.

1.14 Donor wall

Labor costs are the next big issue with twenty-six people employed full time. They have minimal management staff to help keep the cost down. **People who are handicapped are hired to support them to be active participants in the community.** The company is very successful and building more facilities. Good Agricultural Practices is certified by the USDA to make sure the produce is safe to consume by the public. As an architect, I was very impressed with the design of the building, the added social value to the community, and the very good quality of the vegetables. It is a very healthy place to work.

'AeroFarms' and 'Plenty' have patented systems with less staff to run the facility and focused on high technology. These facilities then require much more energy and cost to operate.

The facilities can be built almost anywhere. Vertical farms can and should be near cities, which will help cut the emissions produced by shipping food from rural to urban areas. Plenty is an indoor farming company hoping to solve the world's fresh produce shortage by building a massive indoor vertical farm next to every major city worldwide. The vertical farming startup Plenty plans to build 300 organic, indoor farms in or near Chinese cities. Vertical Farms should be built close to the population it serves.

1.15 An aeroponic system– roots exposed

Schematic diagram of an aeroponic system

Plants grow on twenty-foot vertical towers rather than stacks of horizontal shelves most other vertical farms use. The towers are mostly made of recycled plastic bottles, and there is no soil involved. Water and nutrients are fed from the top of the tower and dispersed by gravity to the leafy greens and herbs that grow horizontally off the tower. All water, including condensation, is collected and recycled, and the plants receive all their light from LED lamps.

Smaller companies grow plants in containers that are now seen in grocery stores where you can literally pick your fresh vegetables.

Companies supporting this are Babylon, MicroFarms, InFarm, LG Garden Appliance, Planty Cube, and Rise. Example website: www. babylonmicrofarms.com.

Vertical farming is an energy-intensive system of crop production involving the integration of multiple technologies such as, big data analytics, robotics, the Internet of Things, and Artificial Intelligence. The advances in information and communication technology can make vertical farming a reality. All that is required is to integrate technology from various disciplines together so that crops can thrive indoors in a simulated environment[26].

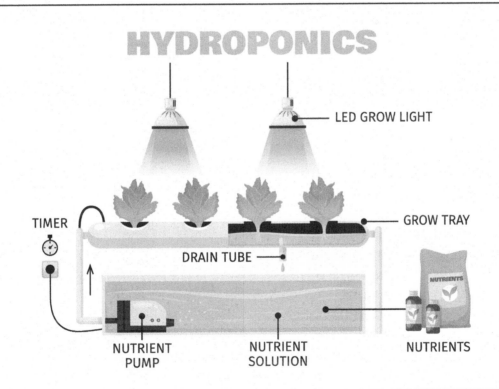

1.16 Hydroponics Farming Concept With Vertical Water Saving

FINANCIAL COST/ PAYBACK FOR VERTICAL FARMING

Three-to-five-year financial payback

POLICIES

- Incentives for building and operating Vertical Gardens.

- Incentives for building and operating community soil-based farms, commercial rooftop farms, and rooftop hydroponic greenhouses.

- Allow one more occupied floor extra in building height to developers for including urban gardens or solar panels on 75 percent+ of the roof.

- Incentives such as reduced permit cost or approval times and tax credits.

The following information is provided from Urban/Vine with a phone conversation with Patrick Kyle:

BUILD COST

- Aerofarms "Model 5" Vertical Farm, set to open in Virginia in 2022, is a 136,000-square-foot facility with a project cost of $52 million to build (includes working capital and tenant improvements but excludes leased real estate). This is equivalent to approximately $382/square foot build cost.

- Aerofarms, according to various sources, spent between $30 million and $39 million to build a 69,000-square-foot facility in 2016. This is equivalent to between $434/square foot and $565/ square foot build cost. This cost outlook was improved by tax credits.

- European Vertical Farming manufacturer CambridgeHOK suggests the following initial build cost guidelines, not including leased real estate:

Size of Vertical Farm	Estimated Build Cost / Sq. Foot ($)
Up to 5,000 square feet	$129 / Sq. Foot
5,000 - 20,000 square feet	$188 / Sq. Foot
20,000+ square feet	$216 / Sq. Foot

- Smaller projects cost less per square foot because less infrastructure is required. Bigger companies and projects have more services and long-term costs to address.

PAYBACK

- In the case of AeroFarms' "Model 5" Farm, it projects an Earnings Before Interest Tax Depreciation & Amortization (EBITDA) of $9 million, including corporate Sales General & Administration (SG&A) allocations and $8 million in gross profit, including depreciation of fixed assets. The EBITDA measures the profitability of operations. **This suggests a payback period of approximately six years.**

- **According to a 2020 survey of 133 commercial indoor farms**, the average yield per pound for vertical farms was 6.89 pounds per square foot, whereas the average yield per pound for container farms (52' long ×10' wide) was 11.72 pounds per square foot. The average revenue per pound was reported to be $7.82 per pound. Therefore, the average revenue per square foot was $53.88/square foot for vertical farms and $91.65/square foot for a container farm.

HARD COSTS

- Fifty-six percent = labor
- Twenty-seven percent = rent, energy, and packaging.
- Six percent = shipping and distribution
- Six percent = growing media
- Three percent = seeds
- Two percent = nutrients

These costs will vary significantly by territory. California Assembly Bill 551 and Washington DC Urban Farming and Food Security Act provide up to 50 percent property tax reduction for urban farming developments. Reports say these regulations are underutilized by companies. Generally speaking, all fifty states in the US give some form of preferential tax treatment to agricultural landowners.

Vertical farming will be a key development in how we produce some of our food much more efficiently to feed large populations while addressing climate change.

Refrigerant Management

It is estimated that 46% of food produced in the world currently requires refrigeration. There is an estimated 13% loss particularly high in developing countries where the available refrigeration capacity is much lower[27]. The chemicals used in refrigeration are potent greenhouse gases, which often leak during use or disposal. We must dispose of the fluorinated gases currently used as refrigerants and replace them with benign alternatives. **HFCs have a 1,000 to 9,000 times greater capacity to warm the atmosphere than carbon dioxide.**

Ninety percent of refrigerant emissions happen at the end of life. **Effective disposal of HFCs currently in circulation is essential.** After being carefully removed and stored, refrigerants can be purified for reuse or transformed into other chemicals that do not cause warming. Alternatives, such as ammonia or captured carbon dioxide, can replace these greenhouse gases. The building codes must accelerate this change because a refrigerator purchased today with fluorinated gases will last for twenty-five years.

Refrigerants are also located in the mechanical equipment that heats and cools our homes. The refrigerants are being phased out. For example, today, you can and should buy heat pumps without fluorinated gases.

FINANCIAL COST/ PAYBACK

Estimated net cost of $629.25 billion to recover the bad HFC refrigerant and provide safe new refrigerants. This is a cost that should be incurred by the government and manufacturers to address the current regulations.

POLICIES

Purchase HFC refrigerants back from consumers and replace them with ammonia or another acceptable chemical at no cost to the consumer. Do not wait for refrigerants to run through their natural course. Remove HFCs as soon as reasonably possible. **Provide consumers with a rebate for returning HFC refrigerants.**

TRANSPORTING FOOD

Amazon scientists developed a model to compare the carbon intensity of ordering Whole Foods Market groceries online versus driving to the nearest Whole Foods Market store. The study found that averaged across all basket sizes, **online grocery deliveries generate 43 percent lower carbon emissions per item compared to shopping in stores**, and smaller basket sizes generate even greater carbon savings.

Shipping food long distances for processing and packaging, importing, and exporting foods are standard practices in the food industry. An apple imported to California from New Zealand is often less expensive than an apple from the historic apple-growing county of Sebastopol, just an hour away from San Francisco. But is it really less expensive in the long run? It is estimated that the meals in the United States travel about 1,500 miles from the farm to the dinner table. The carbon cost of transporting food is very high. **It is estimated that we currently put almost ten calories of fossil fuel energy into our food system for every one calorie of energy we get as food**[28].

Shopping at farmers' markets has begun to make the transition to supporting a local food system. You are able to buy fruits, vegetables, meat, dairy products, eggs, honey, beans, and potatoes that are all grown within a couple of hundred miles of where you live.

The following list shows a representative example of food being delivered from various places around the world in the column on the left to a market in Chicago as an example. The column on the right is food delivered locally to the market in Chicago. The additional miles traveled are staggering and unacceptable.

Install greenhouses outside major cities, where one can purchase land or rent more affordably, get construction approvals in weeks instead of months, and still be close enough to deliver to dozens of metro supermarkets. Encourage major cities to rethink and update their zoning and building codes to support rooftop gardens. New York City, for example, has 14,000 acres of unused rooftops that can support gardens, but zoning does not allow it in residential areas, and where the food can be sold is limited.

The FoodSystemsDashboard.org is an excellent website and community resource that has the capacity to allow policymakers to understand their national food systems and the challenges they face, to prioritize and decide on actions to improve diets for health.

Transformation to healthy diets by 2050 will require dietary shifts. The following information is from the "Summary Report of the Eat-Lancet Commission."

	GLOBAL		CHICAGO
APPLES	1,555 miles	vs.	77 miles
TOMATOES	1,369 miles	vs.	117 miles
GRAPES	2,143 miles	vs.	134 miles
BEANS	766 miles	vs.	101 miles
PEACHES	1,674 miles	vs.	173 miles
WINTER SQUASH	781 miles	vs.	98 miles
GREENS	889 miles	vs.	99 miles
LETTUCE	2,055 miles	vs.	102 miles

Limited intake

Red meat

Starchy vegetables

Optional foods

Eggs

Poultry

Dairy foods

Emphasized foods

Fish

Vegetables

Fruit

Legumes

Whole grains

Nuts

1.17

This includes **doubling the consumption of healthy foods** such as fruits, vegetables, legumes, and nuts and a greater than 50 percent reduction in global consumption of less healthy foods such as added sugars and red meat (primarily reducing excessive consumption in wealthier countries).

Agriculture and fisheries must not only produce enough calories to feed a growing global population but must also produce a diversity of foods that nurture human health and support environmental sustainability. Food systems are intrinsically related to health, environment, culture, politics, and economy.

The Bluehouse intends to be **the world's largest land-based fish farm**. Targeting an initial production of 9,500 metric tons of fish per year, its owner—Atlantic Sapphire—plans to increase that to 222,000 tons by 2031, **enough to provide 41 percent of current U.S. annual salmon consumption**, or a billion meals. Called "Recirculating Aquaculture Systems," or RAS for short, they control everything from the temperature, salinity, and pH of the water, to its oxygen levels, artificial currents, lighting cycles, and removal of carbon dioxide and waste. The latter is filtered out, and treated water is reused.

As it is a closed-loop system, the salmon are not exposed to seaborne diseases and parasites, so unlike sea-based farms, Atlantic Sapphire says its fish do not need to be treated with antibiotics or pesticides. Why did a Norwegian firm choose to build a vast salmon farm in Florida? Firstly so that it can supply the U.S. market without having to fly in the harvested fish from Europe. And secondly, because of the unique nature of the southern state's geology. Florida sits on top of two separate aquifers—freshwater one nearest the surface and then saltwater one lower down. As salmon needs fresh water when it is young and salt water when it is older, Bluehouse has a ready supply of both. People want short, lean value chains with increased traceability, where fewer people are touching your food before you eat it[29].

1.18 The salmon in indoor fish farms swim against an artificial current.

POLICIES

Cities and communities should support local farmers' markets and greenhouses by providing space, tax incentives, advertising, and zoning incentives to developers.

Achieve an overall 50 percent reduction in global food loss and waste as per the targets of the Sustainable Development Goals (SDGs). Actions include improving post-harvest infrastructure, food transport, processing and packing, increasing collaboration along the supply chain, training and equipping producers, and educating consumers.

SUSTAINABLE COOKING

For vegetables, cooking can cause up to 80 percent of the climate impact of the food. Frying is a better option than cooking in the oven. Using a microwave is the most sustainable option for cooking food. Cook efficiently and save ovens for special occasions rather than everyday use. Batch cooking for multiple meals to use less energy[30].

WASTE- PLASTICS

By 2050, plastic in the ocean will outweigh fish. One hundred seventy million tons of plastic already fill the world's oceans.

Nine percent of plastic is currently being recycled. The rest ends up in our landfills, in our streets, and our oceans.

Eight million tons of plastic enter the oceans each year. That's equal to dumping a garbage truck of plastic into an ocean every minute.

"If plastic production continues on a business-as-usual trajectory, plastic will take up about 13 to 15 percent of global emissions by 2050," said Janis Searles Jones, CEO, Ocean Conservancy. Plastic is a massive multi-trillion-dollar global industry. The burden of addressing this issue has historically fallen to municipalities and consumers. It needs to shift to the producers and manufacturers with the intent to solve the problem with better resins and products, recycling and reuse. All plastic made should be able to be recycled and reused.

The British government has announced plans to ban single-use plastic cutlery, plates, and polystyrene cups in England as part of what it calls a "war on plastic." Scotland, Wales, and Northern Ireland already have plans to ban single-use plastic cutlery, as well as the European Union.

We need to rethink how and when we use plastic and perhaps learn to value it more. Plastic keeps our cars and airplanes light and fuel-efficient, and ensures medical devices are affordable and safe. The first step is to limit the flow of "unnecessary" plastic. More than forty countries around the world have begun to ban or tax single-use plastic. One success comes from Saltwater Brewery in Florida, which has come up with E6PR, a biodegradable alternative to plastic six-pack rings. Plastic is now being used in many products, including furniture and clothing. We need to rethink plastic as a precious resource. Companies need to reconsider every element of their products and packaging. Focus on designing materials that are biodegradable and look at better opportunities in manufacturing.

RE-USE OF PLASTIC

India has been leading the world in experimenting with plastic-tar roads since the early 2000s. A growing number of countries are beginning to follow suit. From Ghana to the Netherlands, **building plastic into roads and pathways is helping to save carbon emissions, keep plastic from the oceans and landfill, and improve the life expectancy of the average road.**

Many different types of plastics can be added to the mix: carrier bags, disposable cups, hard-to-recycle multi-layer films, and polyethylene and polypropylene foams have all found their way into India's roads, and they don't have to be sorted or cleaned before shredding.

Adding plastic to roads appears to slow their deterioration and minimize potholes. The plastic content improves the surface's flexibility, and after ten years, Vasudevan's earliest plastic roads showed no signs of potholes. Incorporating waste plastic instead of incinerating it also saves five tons of carbon dioxide for every mile of road. **And there are economic benefits too, with the incorporation of plastic resulting in savings of roughly $1,078 per mile of road. In 2015, the Indian government made it mandatory for plastic waste to be used in constructing roads near large cities of more than 500,000 people.**

In the Netherlands, PlasticRoad built the world's first recycled-plastic bicycle path in 2018. PlasticRoad consists almost entirely of recycled plastic, with only a very thin layer of mineral aggregate on the top deck. The paths are designed to allow rainwater to filter through them, trickling down through a drainage system beneath the path's surface.

RECOMMENDATION

The U.S. and other countries should consider this technology to address plastic waste. Smaller roads can be tested first to see how successful the new road construction performs. Pedestrian and bicycle paths should be made with recycled plastic to keep it out of landfills.

E-WASTE

The amount of e-waste generated is growing by about two million tons every year. Less than 20 percent is collected and recycled.

Tech businesses need to invest in more sustainable manufacturing. Smartphones contain around 30 different elements, some of which the Earth is running out of. Millions of people are unwittingly stockpiling precious elements by keeping old devices in their homes.

The waste electronic and electrical equipment discarded in 2021 will weigh more than 57 million tons, researchers have estimated. That is heavier than the Great Wall of China—the planet's heaviest artificial object. The assessment is by an international expert group dedicated to tackling the global problem of waste electrical and electronic equipment (WEEE) [31].

Summary

IMMEDIATE PAYBACK

Reduce food waste—on average, over $300/person annually—the U.S. will save $120 billion annually.

Sell or donate almost perfect food.

Plant-based meat and dairy alternatives

Eat 20 percent less red meat.

Eat 20 percent less animal meat.

Require Federal Food Programs to provide plant-based foods.

UP TO ONE YEAR

Reduce waste and transportation costs by reducing imports and exports of food.

No plastic packaging

ONE TO THREE YEARS

Use plastic waste for bike paths, sidewalks, and roads.

FOUR TO SEVEN YEARS

Vertical Farming

Roof Gardens

ADDED COST

Refrigerant Management - remove HFCs

1.19
PEOPLE CAN HAVE A SIGNIFICANT IMPACT ON THE ENVIRONMENT BY SIMPLY EATING LESS MEAT, BUYING LOCALLY, AND NOT WASTING THE FOOD. YOU WILL LIVE HEALTHIER, SAVE MONEY AND DO YOUR PART IN REDUCING YOUR CARBON FOOTPRINT.

RENEWABLE ENERGY

GENERATE ELECTRICITY
WITHOUT CREATING CARBON

Any scenario to address the climate crisis will
include a massive ramp up of renewable energies
created by wind, sun, and storage. This ramp up is
occurring now and should be accelerated.

Results from the Renewable Electricity Futures Study showed that **the nation's abundant and diverse renewable energy resources could technically and economically supply 80 percent of U.S. electricity in 2050**—with a significant fraction from wind and solar. The study involved 110 experts from 35 companies[1].

17.7 Terawatts of power globally are needed on an annual basis for all sources of energy. A total of **173,000 terawatts** (trillions of watts) of solar energy strikes the Earth continuously. That's more than 10,000 times the world's total energy use. And that energy is completely renewable. Electricity consumption in the United States totaled **4,146.2 terawatt hours** in 2020 (17.3 percent of world consumption by 4 percent of the global population).

The consensus of recent major global studies is that wind and solar power are the lowest-cost sources of electricity available today. When it comes to the cost of energy from new power plants, onshore wind and solar are now the cheapest sources—costing less than fossil fuels, including coal and gas, geothermal, or nuclear. As electricity is generated by wind and solar, it decreases the cost of energy to consumers. Every $1 million spent on renewables creates 7.5 full-time jobs, compared with just 2.7 jobs for every $1 million spent on fossil fuels.

Mark Jacobson, researcher at Stanford University, has done extensive modeling and studies that show that as a global society, we can reduce the carbon enough to address climate change with wind, solar, and water technologies that currently exist and will continue to improve. **The key is ramping up the existing renewable technologies and implementing them now.** Jacobson projects 2,238,188 construction jobs and 3,020,594 operational jobs produced for a total of 5,258,782 jobs to support the renewable energies. The number of jobs lost by fossil fuel companies is estimated at 2,203,722. Consequently, **the renewable movement will add a total of 3,055,510 jobs to the energy sector. Even after the construction of the renewable equipment is finished, there is a total gain of 817,322 jobs in the U.S.** The government should reduce subsidies to fossil fuel companies over the next ten years, shifting to accelerate the green technologies industry.

For a short period of time around 3pm the electricity for the entire state of California was run from renewable resources sources. When you include hydro and nuclear, which are not fossil fuels, then from approximately 10 a.m. to 5 p.m. the state was generating all its electricity from non-carbon sources. Evening hour demand and battery storage capacity need to be improved. Approximately 65 percent of the state's electrical power comes from renewables, hydro and nuclear. Over the next 10-20 years, California and most states should be running at least 90 percent from renewables with battery storage, hydro and nuclear.

Onshore Wind Turbines

Onshore wind turbines work great on giant wind farms. **The bigger the turbine, the better the efficiency, performance, and investment.** They do not create any air pollution. **Wind turbines can be built and installed in approximately one year. Large solar projects take three months to one year to install.**

Wind is location dependent. The higher the wind, the more energy can be generated- 40 percent capacity factor is a good average for a site; **60 percent+ efficiency is possible if turbines are close to where energy will be used. Remember the most efficient use of energy is to "Deliver the energy locally just in time."** Transmission is difficult for wind with the best location for the turbines far from the highest populated areas in the U.S. and world. Transmission lines must be built to bring the electricity from the wind farm to the city. However, building just a few already-proposed transmission lines should significantly reduce the costs of expanding wind energy. The transmission lines should be underground for much better resiliency.

Wind turbines are less flexible than solar panels. If you install a wind turbine within 500 feet of anything, it will need to be 30 feet taller than the height of that structure. The average wind in a rural area far exceeds the wind in an urban area, so your installation will likely need to be outside of a town.

Wind energy makes more sense at a utility level. That means when you need to generate a lot of power reliably as a group (say, in a town, for example), it makes more sense to do so with a wind farm. Small wind turbines on buildings are not financially viable and produce a minimal amount of electricity. Focus on the biggest wind turbines. On average 3,000 on shore turbines have been built in the U.S. each year since 2005.

Texas now meets 20 percent of its sizeable electricity demand with wind. If it were a country, the Lone Star State would be the fifth biggest in the world in its production of wind energy. In the winter of 2021, the turbines did freeze because the state government decided not to invest in anti- freezing fluids. Turbines can be equipped to deal with freezing temperatures. Turbine blades can be heated, special anti-freeze fluids can be used, along with better insulation of gearboxes. The blades themselves perform very well in sub-zero temperatures, such as those running in Alaska, Canada, and northern Europe. Texas, Iowa, Kansas, Oklahoma, and Illinois generate over 50 percent of the electricity from wind turbines in the U.S.

FINANCIAL COST/PAYBACK

Costs for renewables fell in 2021 as supply chain challenges and rising commodity prices have yet to show their full impact on project costs. The cost of electricity from onshore wind fell by 15%, offshore wind by 13% and solar PV by 13% compared to 2020[2].

INCREASE IN SIZE OF WIND TURBINES OVER TIME

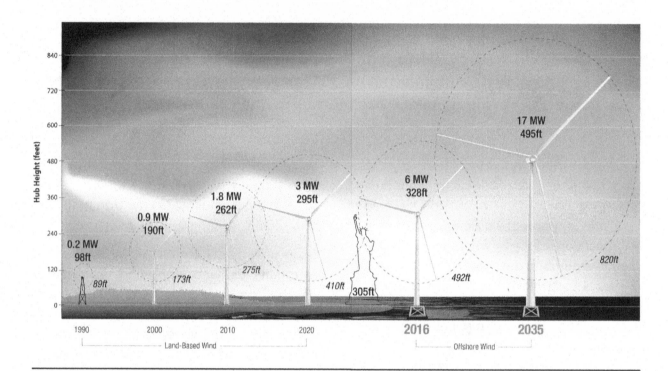

2.1

An average onshore wind turbine rated at 2.5–3 megawatts can produce in excess of 6 million kWh (kilowatts per hour) every year. A 3.6 MW (megawatts)offshore turbine may double that. The typical wind turbine is 2–3 MW in power, and costs in the $2 to $4–million-dollar range. $1,300,000 per megawatt. Operation and maintenance run an additional $42,000–$48,000 per year, according to research on wind turbine operational cost.

One wind turbine can require up to 80 acres of land. Today's typical wind farm towers stand **around 70 meters tall, with blades about 50 meters long**. Their power output depends on size and height, but it generally ranges between one and five megawatts—on the upper end, that's enough to power about 1,100 homes.

As of July 2022, the <u>U.S. Wind Turbine Database</u> (USWTDB) contains more than 72,130 turbines creating 134,362 MW.

POLICIES

Provide tax incentives to landowners for allowing their land to include wind turbines, solar panels, and battery storage.

POTENTIAL NEW JOBS

The U.S. wind sector employs more than 100,000 workers. According to the *Wind Vision Report*, wind has the potential to support more than 600,000 jobs in manufacturing, installation, maintenance, and supporting services by 2050. A wind turbine technician is one of the fastest growing careers in the United States. Wind turbine jobs are well-paying jobs. The median annual wage for wind turbine technicians was $56,230 in May 2020. The highest 10 percent earned more than $83,580.

Onshore wind farms have small footprints, typically using no more than 1 percent of the land they sit on, so grazing, farming, recreation, or conservation can happen simultaneously with power generation. The land around the wind turbines can be used effectively for solar farms. **Using land and buildings for multiple purposes is a smart goal for most developments.** Land-based utility-scale wind is one of the lowest-priced energy sources available today, costing 1–2 cents per kilowatt-hour after the production tax credit. This greatly benefits the economy in rural areas, where most of the best wind sites are found. Farmers and ranchers can continue to work the land. Wind power plant owners make rent payments to the farmer or rancher for the use of the land, providing landowners with additional income.

2.2

Offshore Wind Turbines

The European Union's offshore wind capacity will grow from almost 20 gigawatts (GW) today to nearly 130 GW by 2040. In China, the growth of offshore wind generation is likely to be even more rapid, the International Energy Agency has said. Its offshore wind capacity is predicted to grow from 4 GW to 110–170 GW by 2040. **There are 5,400 offshore wind turbines in Europe, and there are only 7 in the United States**. President Biden wants 2,000 turbines (30 GW) in the water over the next 8–1/2 years.

2.3
Aerial view of wind turbines at sea,
North Holland, Netherlands

Offshore wind turbines can support major urban areas that are typically located near a large body of water. **The offshore winds generally blow more steadily than on shore. Offshore turbines cost 2.8 times more than on shore turbines but generate more electricity according to Energy Information Agency (EIA).** Offshore wind benefits will not be limited to coastal states where the projects are built. While activity will be concentrated in coastal states close to the offshore wind projects, supply chains and service providers across the country will have an opportunity to support this developing industry.

FINANCIAL COST/PAYBACK

Expect the offshore turbines to continue to become more efficient for the same or less cost. **It takes approximately one year to build a wind farm–** quickly producing energy and a return on investment.

Store excess wind power underwater. In 2020, enough electricity to supply more than one million homes was wasted due to a lack of storage, according to a report by KPMG that was commissioned by the power company Drax. Dutch startup, Ocean Grazer, has developed the Ocean Battery, which stores energy below the wind farm.

When there is excess electricity, the system pumps water from an underground reservoir into tough, flexible bladders that sit on the seabed. You could think of them as big bicycle inner tubes. The water in those tubes is under pressure, so when it is released, the water flows quickly and is directed through turbines and on the seabed, generating electricity when needed. The Ocean Battery is effectively based on the same technology as hydro storage. While lithium-ion batteries can last for 5,000–10,000 charging cycles, the Ocean Battery can take up to a million. Though the cost of storage is roughly the same, this extended life makes it much cheaper overall[3].

**2.4
Wind
turbine
storage**

OCEAN GRAZER

POLICIES

At the end of 2020, Congress extended a 30 percent investment tax credit for offshore wind farms until 2025. The Internal Revenue Service also increased the commissioning deadline for offshore wind from 4 to 10 years. This means every project installed by 2030 will receive a subsidy.

POTENTIAL NEW JOBS

With the U.S. stepping closer to installing the first utility-scale wind turbines in U.S. waters, offshore wind energy will be an engine for job creation.

Next year, Danish wind turbine manufacturer Vestas will put up a gargantuan prototype- a 15-MW wind turbine that will be powerful enough to provide electricity to roughly 13,000 homes. Each blade on Vestas' 15 MW turbine is 380 feet long. The turbine itself has a rotor diameter of 775 feet. Very large wind farms at sea must be located carefully to avoid conflict with shipping lanes. The big turbines tend to be positioned far away from land but that means the electricity they generate must travel longer distances.

Chinese firm, MingYang, recently announced plans for an even more powerful device clocking in at 16 MW, for example. Just four years ago, the maximum capacity of an offshore turbine was 8 MW. Guy Dorrell, a spokesman for Siemens Gamesa, explained **that a single offshore wind farm (**from 5 to 150 wind turbines) **can now power a million homes.** Turbines have been tested for a single turn of a 14 MW turbine powering a Tesla Model 3 for 352 km (218 miles). Besides heightened power output, one of the **advantages of bigger turbines is that they are more efficient in terms of installation time and cost**- clearly, you only need one base structure and a set of cables for a 12 MW turbine versus 2 for a pair of 6 MW machines.

Ocean energy, which includes tidal energy, wave energy, and salinity gradient, is gaining major attention as an alternative to fossil fuels. In Europe, marine energy installations reached nearly 40 MW in 2018, and the industry plans to deploy 100 GW of production capacity by 2050, meeting 10 percent of the continent's electricity demand. Underwater turbines could provide renewable energy to off-grid communities that rely on fossil fuels.

In most of the roughly 11,000 inhabited islands around the world, power supply is a big issue. As most of them are not connected to the electricity grid, the 730 million island inhabitants heavily rely on diesel generators to access electricity[4]. Wind and solar resources on most islands are very good; wind and solar electricity on islands is much cheaper than electricity produced by diesel generators.

GE and Veolia announced a recycling plan to turn discarded wind turbine blades into cement. Vestas, one of the world's largest wind turbine makers, is targeting zero waste by 2040.

Solar

The sun produces enough energy every second to cover the earth's needs for 500,000 years. Of that energy, enough energy reaches the earth in one hour to power all of society for one year.

The solar industry is projected to expand exponentially from 2.4 percent of the U.S. electricity mix today to 20 percent of all U.S. electricity generation by 2030. What 20 percent by 2030 will look like:

- Solar will represent the largest source of new power generation added annually.

- 500 GW of photo voltaic panels PV will be installed by the end of 2030, including approximately 77 GW in 2030 alone.

- $345 billion will be invested in solar development over the next 10 years.

- Solar installations will grow annually by roughly 18 percent over the next 10 years.

- Solar will be installed on more than 14 million rooftops by 2030.

- Solar will employ a growing workforce of 600,000 individuals.

- Solar will be responsible for a reduction of over 500 million metric tons of greenhouse gas (GHG) emissions annually by 2030, or roughly 35 percent of all electric sector GHG emissions.

There are several market accelerators that can increase solar energy adoption, including energy storage, carbon reduction goals, and electrification—all of these will be critical to meeting 2030 goals. Climate policy, investment tax credit extension, state net energy metering, building codes, and renewable portfolio standards will all drive solar energy growth. Other factors include regional energy market rules, access to financing and opportunities to further reduce costs.

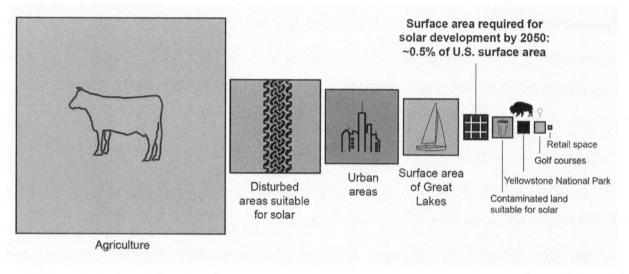

2.5 Solar panels require a very modest amount of space

The level of solar deployment envisioned on land as a single use will require less space than many other current land uses. This calculation does not account for siting of solar on rooftops, on bodies of water, or over farm fields[5].

The Environmental Protection Agency's (EPA) RE-Powering Screening Dataset is a public database that estimates the potential for various renewable energy technologies that includes over 80,000 landfills, contaminated lands, and mining sites. The most promising sites have PV capacity above 500 kilo Watt (kW), with an existing Capped per site PV capacity of 2,000 kW and built within 3 miles of the nearest electrical substation.

One big benefit of solar panels is that they scale up well. This means solar panels on a residential home will generate proportionately similar amounts of electricity as a large solar farm. Solar panels are easy to add to and can

be a smart strategy especially in developing countries. Buy what you can now, buy more later when more funds are available. Just about everyone should be investing in and installing solar panels.

COST OF SOLAR PANELS

A properly sized whole house with solar panels will pay for itself over about 7 years (with federal tax incentive) and will last for at least 25 years or more. Costs are dependent on the size of the system, regional labor rates, the quality of the solar panels and power inverter used, and the complexity of the installation. As technology improves each year, the payback will become shorter.

The trick is that not all solar energy is used when it is created during the daytime. People should consider modifying their habits of washing clothes and dishes from the evening to the middle of a sunny day to take advantage of the electricity generated by the solar panels. Cooling in the daytime with solar works well on sunny days but heating in the wintertime during the evening is an issue. To solve the inconsistency of when solar energy is available, a battery backup system should be considered.

Net metering is an electricity billing mechanism that allows consumers who generate some or all their own electricity to use that electricity anytime, instead of only when it is generated. This is particularly important with renewable energy sources like wind and solar. **Monthly net metering allows consumers to use solar power generated during the day at night**, or wind from a windy day later in the month. Annual net metering rolls over a net kWh credit to the following month, allowing solar power that was generated in July to be used later in the year. Net metering may not require battery storage at one's home, but the storage needs to be accounted for at the local utility provider.

Most net metering laws involve monthly rollover of kWh credits, a small monthly connection fee, and annual settlement of any residual credit. Net metering uses a single, bi-directional meter and can measure the current flow in two directions. Net metering can be implemented solely as an accounting procedure, and requires no special metering, or even any prior arrangement or notification[6]. Net metering should be required by law.

Floating solar panels have been in use for a little over a decade. They have several advantages; they don't take up any valuable space on land, and the **cooling effect of the water makes them more efficient**. In 2018, Japan was home to 56 of the 70 largest floating solar installations.

National Renewable Energy Laboratory (NREL) researchers estimate that installing floating solar photovoltaics on the more than 24,000 man-made U.S. reservoirs could generate about 10 percent of the nation's annual electricity production. It is estimated about 2.1 million hectares of land could be saved if solar panels were installed on bodies of water instead of on the ground. Additional benefits include reduced water evaporation and algae growth.

The cost of acquiring and developing land is becoming a larger part of the cost of a solar project. Los Angeles is getting ready to build solar panels over their waterways that are also built to manage flooding.

2.6 Aerial view of water carrying aqueduct in outer Los Angeles.

The goal for California is to conserve at least 30 percent of land and coastal waters by 2030. California has an extensive labyrinth of canals totaling 4,000 miles. **These canals lose 65 billion gallons of water annually due to evaporation. That's enough to irrigate 50,000 acres of farmland or meet the residential water needs of more than 2 million people.** The State proposed covering the canals with solar panels that would not only safeguard the billions of gallons of water typically lost, but also provide 13 GW of renewable energy capacity. This is about half of the new sources the state needs to add to meet its clean electricity goals: 60 percent from carbon-free sources by 2030 and 100 percent renewable by 2045.

This energy could also be used by local consumers with lower costs and decreased transmission losses. Combining solar power with battery storage can help build microgrids in rural areas and underserved communities, making the power system more efficient and resilient[7].

Because water heats up more slowly than land, the canal water flowing beneath the panels could cool them by 10 degrees Fahrenheit, boosting production of electricity by up to 3 percent. Shade from the panels limits the growth of weeds that block drains and restrict water flow. For large, 100-foot-wide canals in California, it is estimated that shading canals would save about $40,000 per mile. Statewide, savings could reach $69 million per year.

About 4,000 miles of canals transport water to some 35 million Californians and 5.7 million acres of farmland across the state. The first prototypes for both wide-span and narrow-span canals are now in development in California's Central Valley.

But when the co-benefits were included, such as avoided land costs, water savings, aquatic weed mitigation and enhanced PV efficiency, the study found that solar canals were a better return on investment than building ground-mounted systems. Building these long, thin solar arrays could prevent more than 80,000 acres of farmland or natural habitat from being converted for solar farms. This value is significant[8].

2.7 Solar Panels in the center of Shanghai along the Bund.

The 40 MW floating solar power plant at Huainan, China, is the world's largest. Researchers also estimate floating solar farms installed on 24,000 man-made reservoirs could also supply about 10 percent of China's electricity. The solar panels would only need to occupy 25 percent of each reservoir. There are many large warehouse buildings with flat roofs that are perfect to use the air rights to install solar panels. "Air rights" refers to the owner's license over the vertical space extending above their property within the limits of the zoning district. Property owners gain the rights to the land beneath the physical property as well as the airspace above it, which can have significant development opportunities. For example, Germany has many of the barn roofs installed with solar panels by the government to subsidize the electricity for the local farmer and reduce carbon.

2.8 Solar parks can offer plenty of space for cattle

FINANCIAL COST/PAYBACK

The average solar panel shopper pays off their solar purchase in just seven to eight years and earns a strong Return on Investment (ROI), receiving free electricity for the remainder of their solar panel system's 25+ year lifespan. The installation cost typically ranges between $.82 and $1.36/watt—according to the Solar Energy Industries Association's (SEIA) average national cost figures in 2020.

According to Paradise Solar Energy, in 2019, their Utility farms in general had an average return on investment of 15.55 percent and a payback period of 8.1 years across all states.

It's economically better to put solar on a roof and a battery in the garage to create a micro-grid at your home. **It is always better to have your energy generated as close to where it will be used.**

POLICIES

The tax credit extension at the end of 2020 allows solar projects to claim a 26 percent credit for projects starting in 2020–22. This applies to battery storage systems as well and is the only form of tax credit that batteries can access in the current policy environment. **Increase the tax break back to 30 percent for the next five years to accelerate what should be the most cost-effective, sustainable, and the fastest opportunity to generate renewable electricity. Increase and extend tax incentives for inverters.** The Climate Bill (Inflation Reduction Act) will be even better than this!

POTENTIAL NEW JOBS

Many jobs will be added over the next decade, with many of them coming to emerging states and regions that will require training and workforce development. Form partnerships with training providers, community-based organizations and the public workforce system to better educate the public about solar employment opportunities. Develop partnerships with other industries to implement effective workforce and Operations & Maintenance best practices.

Solar Photovoltaic Installers made a median salary of $46,470 in 2020. The best-paid 25 percent made $55,760 that year, while the lowest-paid 25 percent made $37,860. (U.S. News and World Report). On-the-job training usually lasts **between 1 month and 1 year**. During training, PV installers learn about safety, tools, and PV system installation techniques.

Community Solar

Approximately 80 percent of Americans lack the ability to host on-site solar because their properties are not technically suitable for solar (due to shading, roof age, condition, or orientation); they rent their apartment, lease their business properties, or they lack access to capital for up-front solar investment costs. One-third of Americans rent.

Community Solar takes advantage of laws like the ones that give savings to households with rooftop solar panels. Community solar projects are solar developments whose electricity is shared by multiple commercial, municipal, school, or non-profit entities. "Net metering" allows people who produce their own solar energy to sell that energy back into the grid and local utility company. For community solar, utilities use a process called "virtual net metering," which means that when your share the community solar farm produced energy, you get the credit on your utility bill—just as if you had produced it on your own roof.

2.9 Aerial view of many rows of solar photovoltaic panels for producing clean ecological electrical energy and allowing space between for agriculture.

Community Solar can work for many neighborhoods or towns, where citizens go together to commit to a solar farm, which can be located on large, flat warehouse roofs, under power lines, where the land is not being used, over parking lots, or simply in a large open field. If you cannot place panels on your roof or are not sure you will be living at your house for a long period of time, then it may not make sense to instal a rooftop array. **The Community Solar Concept is suitable for a large population, including renters, condo-owners, and homeowners.** You are also able to support local, clean energy. You simply can sign up for short-term (including 1-year) contracts with many offering no cost to cancel.

Encourage your local politicians and businesses to get Community Solar developers in your neighborhood. A few resources:

- Solstice's complete guide to community solar (https://solstice.us/wp-content/uploads/2021/05/Solstice-CS-Guide-High Quality.pdf)

- Vote Solar nicely summarizes the community solar market's potential here.

This white paper on why developers should be considering community solar (More Than Meets the Eye: Why Developers Should Take a Good Look at Community Solar/ Greenbiz)

- Some of the bigger community solar developers to consider are ForeFront Power, NextEra Energy, 38 Degrees North, and Revision Energy, to name a few.

NET METERING

In a perfect world, your solar panels would produce exactly as much energy as you need for your home use. Sometimes you'll produce a little extra, so for every extra kWh you produce that you don't use, your utility will give you a credit that you can use to pay for your future energy use. Whenever your solar panels don't produce enough to cover 100 percent of your energy use (usually in the winter), you can use those banked credits to maximize your savings.

A 1 MW Community Solar farm will need 6–8 acres of land. The rows of panels need to have space for repair and maintenance access and the space is given so that there aren't any shadows from the adjacent solar panel. The national average says that there are four peak sun hours per day, which means that a 1 MW solar farm would make 1,460 Mega Watts per hour (MWh) per year (4 peak sun hours x 365 days = 1,460 MWh per year). The average 1 MW solar farm can make $40,000/year. The cost of a solar panel was $1,000– $1200 in 2021. Overall construction typically takes 4–6 months. The maintenance is very low and only needs to be serviced a few times a year.

Solar panels over the parking will have added cost for the structure compared to on a roof or land but will be helpful creating shade and reducing the heat island effect. The additional cost of a structure to support solar panels, like over surface parking lot is approximately 20 percent. Cars are less efficient when parked in the sun, making shaded parking more important moving forward. Solar panels can be installed almost anywhere.

2.10 Aerial shot of a modern sustainable neighborhood in Almere, The Netherlands.

The New National Community Solar Partnership (NCSP) target is to enable community solar projects to power the equivalent of five million households by 2025 and create $1 billion in energy bill savings. There is enough community solar installed in the U.S. today to power 600,000 households—achieving Department of Energy's (DOE) new NCSP target would mean an increase of more than 700 percent in the next 4 years. The 'Sharing the Sun' report released by NREL in collaboration with NCSP shows that **community solar can lead to substantial bill savings—from 5 percent to 25 percent.**

DOE is offering free, on-demand technical assistance to NCSP partnership members.

Technical assistance provides personalized support to organizations deploying community solar to help them accelerate implementation, improve the performance of their program or project, and build capacity for future community solar development. NCSP has already distributed $1 million for technical assistance and hopes to provide $2 million in the next year.

Flywheel is a company located in Washington D.C. that focuses on community solar projects and pays the building owner to rent their roof. The community solar installer would build a solar array on top of one or more buildings, connect it to the electric grid, and the power it produces would result in savings on electricity bills for residents below. D.C. Green Bank—funded by public dollars—stepped in to provide construction loans for Flywheel to build the solar arrays. Flywheel has done 34 community solar projects till 2021. Once the projects are complete, Flywheel repays D.C. Green Bank's construction loans by refinancing with a longer-term, "permanent" loan from a bank.

But because the primary revenue source for solar installations is still relatively new and highly dependent on political will from governments to keep up with Solar Renewable Energy Credits (SREC) purchasing requirements, longer-term loans are still hard for community solar developers to get, especially those working on smaller buildings or in historically disinvested communities. You earn one SREC for every 1,000 kWh (or 1 MWh) of electricity produced by a solar energy system. These SREC "vouchers" are valuable because many utilities must buy a certain number of them each year to meet sustainability requirements set by the Renewable Portfolio Standard (RPS) in each state. States have created these standards to diversify their energy resources, promote domestic energy production and encourage economic development. As of the end of 2021, **31 states and the District of Columbia** had RPS or Clean Energy Standards (CES).

FINANCIAL COST/PAYBACK

A solar Power Purchase Agreement, or PPA, frees participants of the burden of ownership and maintenance while offering immediate savings and no up-front cost.

Community solar farms have an average ROI of 13.91 percent and an average of 8.21-year payback period. On average, community solar projects would provide a 20 percent utility bill savings.

SUPPORTING LOW- AND MODERATE-INCOME FAMILIES

Local and State governments provide tax incentives and partner with local companies to provide community solar opportunities for all people. Specifically, tie savings into reduced monthly energy bills and profit for companies developing the projects.

Community solar is the key to unlocking 50 million Low to Moderate Income (LMI) households' access to clean, affordable energy solutions. There's an opportunity for community solar to play a critical role in creating an equitable clean energy future. Support can include program carve outs, job training programs, project ownership, siting preferences, and incentives specifically focused on communities, who have been disproportionately impacted by the electric system to date.

'Solar For All' Brings Clean Energy to Low- and Middle-Income DC Residents. Getting started with a community solar project requires a supportive regulatory environment—whether existing laws or a utility, public utility commission, and other stakeholders are willing to set up the structure for each effort to be possible. Washington D.C. has set up a strong framework where community solar is possible and they have a secondary program called "Solar for All" that helps connect developers' solar projects to members of the community, who want to purchase green power[9].

Most solar developers build, then move on. Others manage where margins can be 25-30%. Washington D.C. has Solar Renewable Credits, where the solar must be created within the 70 square miles that makes up Washington D.C. In D.C., the solar is connected to the transformer where there are two meters: one for the utility and one for the developer.

In "Solar for All," the city pre-buys each watt expected from the developer, then offers the cost of the energy to low- and middle-income (LMI) families at 50 percent of the cost. Incomes need to be $80,000 or less, which covers low and moderate families, about half of the U.S. population. The developers get their money up front and can use this to build their project.

Supported by Jubilee Housing, a nonprofit that provides affordable housing for low-income residents. a series of solar panels lie on the roof of the apartments. The electricity gets channeled into a power grid operated by Pepco (the for-profit utility serving Washington, D.C.), and **the value of that electricity is split up among all 100 Maycroft residents, appearing as a credit on their electricity bill.** "Resiliency Center" provides residents with a powered community space, which can last for three days in the event of a city-wide power outage. Through a partnership between Jubilee Housing and New Partners, the Resiliency Center is powered by a battery storage system, paired with solar photovoltaics (PV), funded by the Pepco Foundation. The Resiliency Center provides Maycroft residents with a community space with ventilation, lighting, a refrigerator to store food and medicine, and the ability to charge their phones in times of emergency.

2.11 Solar panels, storage, wind turbines and clean electricity distribution.

The area where there seems to be less interest in cities is with those that have their own municipal utilities, which are controlled by the city. LMI community solar aims to reduce the energy bills for low-and-moderate income renters in the district by 50 percent by the year 2032. This can largely be attributed to the progressive, climate-friendly policies promoted by city leaders.

A revolving fund is another innovative financing mechanism whereby the electricity cost savings from one renewable energy project goes towards paying for another solar project, thereby creating a "pay-it-forward" model for solar energy. Include business energy tax credits, qualified tax credit bonds, clean renewable energy bonds, and qualified energy conservation bonds. Many states offer sales tax incentives for solar facilities in the form of reduced rates and rebates.

RECOMMENDATIONS

1. **Allow developers to receive tax incentives for Community Solar that homeowners would have received if they were able to implement on their own property.**

2. Create Private Partnership Agreement (PPA).

3. Electricity from solar panels is valued at the same cost as electric utility when purchased by the local utility.

4. Contract with local utility over 20+ years with same cost to provide financial resilience.

5. Community Solar projects for LMI families need to be a model focused on across the country.

Roof Top Solar Panels

It is estimated by the NREL (National Energy Renewable Laboratory) that **40 percent of solar needed in the U.S. can be placed on rooftops.** More than 3 million homes and businesses in the U.S. in 2020 had solar systems. **When placed on a roof, they produce energy at the site of consumption, avoiding the losses of grid transmission.** One just needs to add an inverter to tie the electricity generated to go to the home electric panel box, which then distributes electricity throughout the house. Add battery storage and the house can be net zero creating and managing all electricity.

2.12 Apple's new headquarters designed by Norman Foster Associates, has beautifully integrated the solar panels into the entire building design.

POLICIES

- Solar panels on roofs of schools pay for electric load and to help reduce costs of education.

- Require each new flat roof to have solar panels or a green roof.

- Incentives to developers for existing flat roofs to be renovated to add solar panels or vegetation, including farming.

- Incentives to owners to sell air rights on roofs to companies to build solar.

Solar Hot Water

Solar hot water taps the sun's radiation. By supporting conventional energy sources with this clean alternative as a backup option, this reduces carbon emissions and is common in many developing countries. Solar hot water is used during sunny days for the house hot water tank, which provides the hot water for showers, at sinks, and for the dish washer and washing machine. Payback periods are as short as 4–5 years, depending on specifics of the system and location.

Manufacturing

The U.S. **PV manufacturing industry** has the capacity to produce PV modules to **meet nearly a third of today's domestic demand. Increasing domestic PV hardware will keep more value in the U.S. economy and create valuable manufacturing jobs.** It will also decrease the dependence of the U.S. on foreign energy supply, which improves U.S. energy security. Focusing on improvements in domestic solar manufacturing will help the U.S. Department of Energy (DOE) Solar Energy Technologies Office (SETO) reach its goals. Competitions to accelerate the solar industry include:

- American-made Solar Prize: This $3 million prize competition is designed to revitalize U.S. solar manufacturing through a series of contests and the development of a diverse and powerful support network.

- American-made Perovskite Startup Prize: This $3 million prize competition is designed to accelerate the growth of the U.S. perovskite industry and support the rapid development of solar cells and modules that use perovskite materials[10].

Solar in Storms

Politico reported October 7, 2022, that Florida Power and Light Company's 38 solar power farms were located in the path of Hurricane Ian with only 0.3% of the 35million solar panels receiving any damage! Babcock Ranch north of Fort Myers felt 100 mile an hour winds but never lost any power. Power lines to homes are all run underground, where they are shielded from high winds. Giant retaining ponds surround the development to protect houses from flooding. Streets are designed to absorb floodwaters and spare the houses.

When bad weather hits, there are far more solar success stories than failures. Rooftop arrays have survived multiple hurricane hits and panels barely feel hailstorms. Huge sections of California felt the increased intensity of wildfires, and it is unrealistic to expect a solar array to make it through the flames when entire homes are destroyed. The solar panels did not contribute to the fire or be a danger to the surrounding area. Under Writers Laboratory (UL) testing has done a good job making sure panels and mounting systems won't encourage the spread of flames. It's difficult to even find statistics on solar panels involved with fires, let alone starting or spreading them.

2.13 Solar panels after Hurricane Michael in 2018.

While Puerto Rico and other islands saw unbelievable destruction from the 2017 hurricane season, one piece of good news shined through the devastation—a 645-kW array on a medical center roof in San Juan survived and was functioning at 100%. Florida-based contractor Valor Construction installed the system at the VA Caribbean Healthcare System in 2015 using Sollega ballasted mounting systems supported by Anchor Products attachments. Racking manufacturers are adapting racking systems that better accommodate attachments. **When attachments are designed with the proper racking system, wind load capacities can easily exceed 200 mph.** The control electronics and a new high-speed motor design move the tracker from the maximum tilt (60 ʃ to the horizontal position (0 ʃ in less than three minutes for rapid stowing. Hail damage is not a huge concern. NREL analyzed 50,000 solar systems installed between 2009 and 2012 and found the probability of damage from hail was below 0.05 percent.

Improved Permit Process for Solar

Free software that instantly approves permits for rooftop solar systems has been launched by the US Department of Energy (DOE) as part of efforts to cut red tape for households across the country.

The Solar Automated Permit Processing Campaign (SolarAPP) aims to address this challenge by making solar permitting, inspection, and interconnection seamless, while maintaining high quality, safety, and reliability. The goal is to reduce soft costs by $1/W for residential solar and solar plus storage over five years.

The tool has been designed to allow local governments to speed up their review and approval of residential PV installation permits, while also making it cheaper and easier for homeowners to access solar systems. SolarAPP+ aims to solve this problem by providing solar contractors with an automated process for residential installations that reviews PV project applications for building code compliance and instantly approves permits that meet the right specifications.

Direct and Indirect Permitting, Inspection and Interconnection (PII) costs include:

- Direct cost of permit application, site inspection, and interconnection fees,

- Indirect cost related to time spent completing and submitting permitting applications, physical trips for permitting and inspection(s), and high cost of losing customers who grow impatient with delays.

- The best place to get information is on the SolarAPP site hosted by NREL[11]. The results of the pilot testing of the software tool were published[12]. The software is now out of pilot testing and new communities are signing up every month.

Recycling Solar Panels

We need to make solar panels more inherently recyclable and to manufacture a greater share locally around the world in a more distributed way. Solar panels are recycled at general-purpose glass recycling facilities, where their glass — and sometimes their metal frames — are recycled, and the remaining components are thrown away or burned.

According to the NREL, **recycling solar panels in the U.S. costs around $10–20 per module**. Solar panels should be required to be recycled and not placed in landfills. Only about 10 percent of panels in the US are recycled—it isn't mandated by federal regulations but should be. The materials in solar panels coming offline each year could be worth an estimated $2 billion by 2050. The U.S. Department of Energy (DOE) released an action plan to enable the safe and responsible handling of photovoltaic (PV) end-of-life (EOL) materials. The five-year-strategy aims to halve the cost of recycling and reduce the environmental impact of solar energy modules at end-of-life.

Solar Future Study by NREL released on September 8, 2021

- **With continued technological advances, electricity prices do not increase through 2035. 95** percent decarbonization of the electric grid is achieved in 2035 without increasing electricity prices because decarbonization and electrification costs are fully offset by savings from technological improvements and enhanced demand flexibility.

- Compared with the approximately 15 GW of solar capacity deployed in 2020, annual solar deployment is 30 Gigawatts on average in the early 2020s and grows to 60 Gigawatts on average from 2025 to 2030. Similarly substantial solar deployment rates continue in the 2030s and beyond. Deployment rates accelerate for wind and energy storage as well.

- **Storage, transmission expansion, and flexibility in load and generation are key to maintaining grid reliability and resilience.** Storage capacity expands rapidly, to more than 1,600 Gigawatts in 2050. Small-scale solar, especially coupled with storage, can enhance resilience by allowing buildings or microgrids to power critical loads during grid outages. In addition, advances in managing distributed energy resources, such as rooftop solar and EVs, are needed to efficiently integrate these resources into the grid.

- **Expanding clean electricity supply yields deeper decarbonization.** Electricity demand grows by about 30 percent from 2020 to 2035 owing to electrification of fuel-based building demands for heating, charging EVs, and improving industrial processes. Electricity demand increases by an additional 34 percent from 2035 to 2050. By 2050, all these electrified sectors are powered by zero-carbon electricity.

- **Land availability does not constrain solar deployment.** In 2050, ground-based solar technologies will require a maximum land area equivalent to 0.5 percent of the contiguous U.S. surface area. This requirement could be met by using disturbed or contaminated lands unsuitable for other purposes.

- **The benefits of decarbonization far outweigh the initial costs incurred.** Cumulative power system costs from 2020 to 2050 are $562 billion (25 percent) higher, which includes the costs of serving electrified loads previously powered through direct fuel combustion. However, avoided climate damage from storms and natural disasters, with improved air quality more than offset those additional costs, with a very favorable economic payback resulting in net savings of $1.7 trillion[13].

Energy Storage

No other enabling technology will play a more important role in the exponential growth of solar and wind than energy storage. The scaling of energy storage technology, including battery technology, thermal energy storage, pumped hydro and seasonal storage capabilities, is necessary for solar and wind to reach full potential.

Pumped hydropower storage projects account for around 93 percent of installed energy storage capacity in the U.S.

Thermal energy storage in the form of ice-based systems is emerging in North America.

6.6 MW of these systems were installed in 2018 with projections showing a potential 68.8 MW by 2027. **Ice storage systems** have also proven to be cost-effective for commercial and industrial applications under certain rates in some markets[14].

Battery Storage

Putting batteries in buildings can help save money, reduce carbon footprint, and make our energy grids more resilient. Equip buildings with energy storage capabilities. For individual properties, up-front costs can be offset by long-term savings, and clean energy consumption can be optimized. It is time for our buildings to be more self-sufficient!

The cost of lithium-ion batteries has fallen by 85 percent over the last 8 years as manufacturing has scaled up to support both electric grid applications and EVs. Battery energy storage systems for solar and wind are rechargeable battery systems that store energy from solar panels or the electric grid and provide that energy to a home or business as needed.

Co-located solar and storage project pipelines have grown. Developers continued to plan in key regions like the Southwest and California, even as new state markets grew. Texas now has 2 GW of solar co-located with storage, as storage developers look to secure the cost advantage provided by the tax credit.

In 2017, **Tesla used Powerpacks to install in Australia** what it says was at the time the world's largest lithium-ion battery to support local energy grids. **The project reduced costs by almost $40 million during its first year.** Storage has come to account for an increasingly large percentage of Tesla's energy business. The $200 million "Big Battery," installed in South Australia in 2017 by Elon Musk's Tesla company, has almost paid for itself, saving consumers around $116 million in higher power costs in 2019. The project is **on its way to pay back in less than four years.** The 50 MW/ 64.5 MWh expansion finished at the end of 2020 which showcased the complete benefits that grid-scale batteries provide.

Tesla deployed nearly 4 GWh of energy storage in 2021. Tesla is ambitious about growing its energy storage business in 2022, after it reported a 32 percent year-on-year increase in battery storage deployments, executives including CEO Elon Musk have said.

2.14 Solar, Wind and Battery Storage

In December 2020, California's Pacific Gas and Electric Company (PG&E) requested approval for six battery energy storage projects, all using lithium-ion batteries. In March 2021, Apple said it would build a battery capable of storing 240 MWh of energy—enough to power 7,000 homes for one day.

Form Energy, a Boston based start-up, aims to reduce prices to a 10th of what lithium battery packs cost today. Its batteries are designed to store energy for over 6 days. Costs for long storage duration need to fall to as low as $1 per kWh as presented in a study in the journal *Nature Energy.*

The U.S. Army and Ameresco are working together on a 6 MW/6 MWh Battery Energy Storage System (BESS) at Fort Detrick Army Garrison in Maryland. The team estimated **the battery system will provide a cost savings of $125,000 annually for the government.** The Fort Detrick BESS is expected to be completed in early 2023. Ameresco and the Army earlier built the 18.6–MW solar site at the fort. Ameresco completed the work in 2016, installing nearly 60,000 solar panels, 9 central inverters and transformers, as well as overhead and underground distribution. That system supplies close to 12 percent of Fort Detrick's annual electric load requirements. The installed BESS will be microgrid-ready, allowing for future additions at Fort Detrick. **The U.S. Army recently announced a long-term energy plan calling for microgrids at all installations by 2035**[15].

Other Options for Storage

New types of iron-based batteries might be up to the task. Oregon-based ESS, whose batteries can store energy for between 4 and 12 hours, launched its first grid-scale project in 2021. Massachusetts-based Form Energy, which raised $240 million in 2021, has batteries that store power for up to 100 hours. **Both companies rely on batteries that use iron, one of the most abundant materials on the planet**. They will begin installing in 2023.

National storage capacity in the reference case grows to about 200 GW by 2050[16].

Load Shifting

Battery energy storage systems allow businesses to shift energy usage by charging batteries with solar energy when electricity is cheapest and discharging batteries when it's more expensive. Use electricity when it costs the least and more is available. Utilities can begin to manage usage. Companies and people can rethink when and how they use their energy. Many appliances, electric cars, can be programmed to turn on and off at specific times. Reducing the demand for electricity is helpful. Using electricity more efficiently is smarter.

Peak Shaving

In a commercial setting, the most important application of energy storage is **peak shaving**. For businesses on demand charge, utility tariffs, between 30 percent and 70 percent of the utility bill may be made up of demand charges. Solar arrays alone aren't always a sufficient solution for these businesses. Battery energy storage systems can guarantee that no power above a predetermined threshold will be drawn from the grid during peak times.

The California Independent System Operator issued a Flex Alert for June 17, 2021, from 5 p.m. to 10 p.m. urging people to set their thermostats to 78°F or higher and avoid using washers, dishwashers, and other major appliances, said The Associated Press. This type of management of our electricity will become more common and should be very effective in reducing peak loads and the cost of electricity.

Renewable Integration

Energy storage can smoothen the output of renewable power generation from solar and wind. Energy storage allows solar energy production to be available 24/7, like the consistency of fossil fuel energy sources[17].

Distributed Energy Storage

Microgrids, net-zero buildings, grid flexibility, and rooftop solar, all depend on or are amplified using distributed storage systems. Energy battery storage is a safe and seamless alternative to small fossil fuel generators, which are one of the main contributors to carbon monoxide poisoning in America.

Weatherproof construction means energy storage systems can be mounted outside without the added cost of protective structures. Scalable architecture means multiple energy storage units can be linked to form a larger system. Plans should be developed with the desire and understanding that additional units can and will be added later.

EMERGENCY BACKUP — Like the Uninterruptible Power Supply (UPS) under your desk or in your server room, battery energy storage systems can keep operations running during power outages.

MICROGRIDS — Energy storage opens the possibility of building microgrids in conjunction with renewable energy. The scalability and turnkey simplicity of battery energy storage make these systems economically viable. Microgrids can be used in certain large commercial facilities—or even entire communities. The American Samoa island, Ta'u's switch from diesel generation to solar + storage is a good example.

Battery storage and demand-side response are poised to become major sources of flexibility in advanced economies as well as in emerging market and developing economies, together meeting almost a quarter of flexibility needs globally by 2030, on their way to providing around half of flexibility by 2050. **More advanced real-time energy demand visualization, analytics and smart controls are the main technological enablers to support a more effective grid.** Digitally enabled power system transformation should stimulate the development of more innovative business models and new revenue streams.

Tesla and Energy Locals are building the world's largest virtual power plant with the support of the Government of South Australia. Designed to test the technical capacity to provide services to energy markets, it has the potential to connect 50,000 solar and home battery systems.

POLICIES

- Increase tax incentives and rebates when wind and solar are installed with battery storage systems.

- Incentivize battery storage for local utilities as a part of their total portfolio.

RECOMMENDATION

Focus on manufacturing batteries now to support the important transition to wind and solar locally. The government should invest in battery storage now to help drive down costs and improve efficiency.

Battery storage is a key component in addressing carbon and enabling wind and solar renewables to be effective and complete at providing energy 24/7. Incentives, research monies, competitions and other means should be focused on battery storage development, production, and installation.

Nuclear–Generation III
(8 PERCENT OF GLOBAL ELECTRICITY, 20 PERCENT OF U.S. ELECTRICITY)

Nuclear power, which is carbon-free but not renewable, can serve a similar role as renewable energies, although cost, issues with waste, and public perception have limited its deployment. Comparing nuclear power to other power sources is a lot like comparing air travel to car travel. It's safer, but intuitively scary.

Nuclear power produces abundant energy with essentially zero carbon emissions. In fact, nuclear power is our nation's largest source of low-carbon electricity, supplying about 20 percent of electric power. Nuclear energy can also produce reliable electricity around the clock. This positions nuclear power as a key complement to renewables as they are non-carbon solutions to meet the dual challenges of rising global energy demand and mitigating global climate change.

To build a nuclear power plant requires concrete construction with cement and high carbon in that material. Use new cement mixes with lower carbon. Also sequester carbon in the concrete. The carbon simply generated during construction will be significant and needs to be considered. Equipment for construction should be electric to build any nuclear, wind, or solar projects to keep the embodied concrete down.

The United Arab Emirates is looking beyond its fossil fuel history and has just started up the first of four nuclear reactors, which by the middle of this decade will supply 25 percent of its electricity. In the United States, "two new nuclear reactors being built in Waynesboro, Georgia, will produce more carbon-free electricity than is currently generated by the more than 7,000 wind turbines," says John Kotek, at the Washington D.C-based Nuclear Energy Institute, and "will, over a 60–

year lifetime, avoid the release of about 600 million metric tons of carbon dioxide." These two new reactors are the first new reactors to come online in the United States in more than 30 years. The expansion project supported up to 9,000 workers at peak construction and will create 800 permanent jobs at the facility when the new units begin operation in 2023. Unit 3 has taken 9 years to construct, and Unit 4 will require 10 years.

FINANCIAL COST/ PAYBACK

While the cost of virtually every other form of energy has gone down over time, nuclear is 4 to 8 times higher than it was 4 decades ago. Two units being built at Plant Vogtle (Unit 3 by the end of 2022 and Unit 4 by the end of 2023) in Georgia are expected to cost more than $9.2 billion (original construction budget at $7.3 billion). The project has seen some cost increases and schedule delays, which is common for large government projects.

POTENTIAL NEW JOBS

The nuclear industry supports nearly half a million jobs in the United States.

Generation IV Nuclear Reactors

Generation III advanced reactors have been operating in Japan since 1996. **An international task force is sharing Research & Development to develop six Generation IV nuclear reactor technologies. All six systems represent advances in sustainability, economics, safety, reliability, and rapid increase in resistance**. Europe is pushing ahead with three of the fast reactor designs. China is building one molten-salt reactor. Russia and the U.S. are each building one. A separate program set up by regulators aims to develop multinational regulatory standards for Generation IV nuclear reactors. The new developments in IV nuclear technology require most people to be re-educated on the new technology, which is safer, with much less waste than existing

plants. The construction and validation can also happen much faster because **new plants are smaller and simpler to build.**

The original charter members are Argentina, Brazil, Canada, France, Japan, South Korea, South Africa, the UK, and the USA. They have been joined by Switzerland, China, Russia, Australia and, through the Euratom research and training program, the European Union. **The purpose is to share Research & Development to improve the design and construction of the reactors.**

The Department of Energy is also supporting the development of smaller reactor designs (Generation IV), such as <u>microreactors</u> and <u>small modular reactors</u>, that will offer even more flexibility in size and power capacity to the customer. **These factory-built systems are expected to dramatically reduce construction timelines and will make nuclear power more affordable to build and operate.** By using natural circulation, the new designs have 25 percent fewer pumps and mechanical drives than existing active plants.

Selected by the U.S. federal government to demonstrate the viability of nuclear power through its Advanced Reactor Demonstration Program (ARDP), **TerraPower will build a "fully functional advanced nuclear reactor within 7 years**," according to the Office of Nuclear Energy at the U.S. Department of Energy. (April 8, 2021)

TerraPower's cooling system does not rely on any outside energy source to operate in the event of an emergency shutdown of a reactor. Its system works via the hot air rising from natural circulation within the system, called a reactor vessel air cooling system. This prevents accidents like what happened at the Fukushima Daiichi plant. After an earthquake shut down the plant's reactor, the back-up cooling system failed.

Natrium technology can store heat in tanks of molten salt for future use, much like a battery. The technology is like that used in solar plants, which use the technique to store power for when the sun is not shining. That storage capability can increase a Natrium Reactor plant's power output from about 345 MW to 500 MW for five hours. **It is the first nuclear concept to integrate large-scale energy storage capabilities.** One key part of the argument for nuclear is that nuclear power is much safer to use than coal, oil, and gas as documented in the graphic with data on the death rates by energy source.

2.15

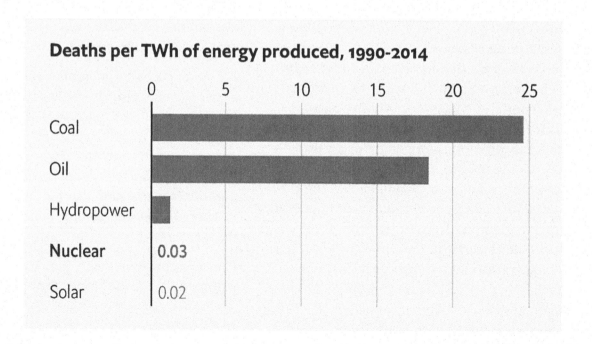

Deaths per TWh of energy produced, 1990-2014

Coal	
Oil	
Hydropower	
Nuclear	0.03
Solar	0.02

Death Rates from energy production per unit of energy generated. Despite some notable disasters, nuclear power is one of the least deadly sources of energy.

Natrium's demonstration plant will be fully operational and connected to the power grid in its as-yet-unknown location by the late 2020s. Its fast-neutron reactor will use high-temperature liquid sodium as its reactor coolant instead of water. **At the other end of this storage system is a set of steam turbines that can take that constant power and generate enough electricity to power somewhere around 225,000 homes[18].**

RECOMMENDATIONS

Countries planning to build coal plants should build nuclear Generation IV plants instead. The U.S. should support other countries interested in the evolution of nuclear technology. Sharing technology to reduce carbon emissions should be encouraged.

Nuclear will be heavily debated in the U.S. and other countries. This will cost time, which will slow down the fight against climate change. Generation IV newer technology is being constructed now and if successful, will jump past Generation III level design for construction and operation. Governments should simplify the permit process to reduce time and cost.

Geothermal Power

Geothermal power plants produced about 0.5 percent of total U.S. electricity generation in 2020. Geothermal power uses heat generated by the Earth's core to provide energy. This heat can be captured and used on both a residential and utility scale. Residential geothermal uses water running through underground pipes (called geothermal heat pumps) to regulate a building's internal temperature. In winter, the water in these pipes carries heat from the Earth into the building. In summer, the geothermal system carries excess heat out of the building.

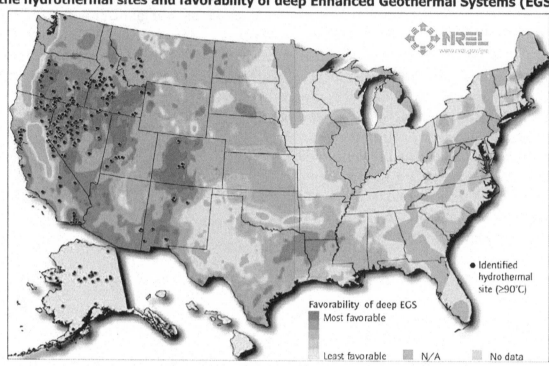

Map 1. Geothermal Resources of the U.S.: Locations of the hydrothermal sites and favorability of deep Enhanced Geothermal Systems (EGS)

[Source: National Renewable Energy Laboratory]

2.16 Geothermal Resources of the U.S.

FINANCIAL COST/PAYBACK

The payback period for a typical geothermal heat pump system is **between 5 and 10 years**, according to the Department of Energy. December 23, 2020.

POTENTIAL NEW JOBS

There currently are approximately 100,000 geothermal jobs in the U.S. Geothermal jobs of all kinds will be most prevalent in the western United States, where geothermal projects are most common. As the demand for clean energy grows, jobs in geothermal energy will be a small but growing potential source of new employment opportunities.

RECOMMENDATION

The focus should be on geothermal where the soil is favorable, which is primarily the western portion of U.S. Geothermal will have a small but positive impact on the national level to reduce carbon.

Hydropower

HYDROPOWER plants produced about 7.3 percent of total U.S. electricity generation in 2020. Hydropower plants use flowing water to spin a turbine connected to a generator and are nearly carbon-free. No energy storage is required. Hydroelectric powerplants are the most efficient means of producing electric energy. The efficiency of today's hydroelectric plant is about 90 percent. The lifetime of hydropower plants is by far the longest of all power generation technologies—on average 80 years and often longer. Some people regard hydropower as the ideal fuel for electricity generation because there are no waste products, and hydropower does not pollute the water or the air.

The Energy Department supports innovations to optimize hydropower production and leads the nation's efforts to advance technologies that harness the power of oceans, waves, and tides. With more than 50 percent of the population living within 50 miles of the coastline, these technologies have big potential in the fight against climate change. For example, extracting just 5 percent of the technical resource potential of oceans, waves, and tides could power several million American homes with clean energy. **The main concern is the cost and ROI has net losses.**

The best location for a hydroelectric station should be along the path of a river. It should be at least at the river canyon or at the place where the river narrows. This enables the collection of the water or the diversion of the river. Environmental impact studies to get approval for construction are typically very lengthy. Concerns are the impact on fish and other wildlife, draughts, and floods, which make future large-scale hydropower plants a low priority in the U.S.

FINANCIAL COST/PAYBACK

Low operational costs with potential payback in or nearly six years. Hydro has the highest average construction cost per kilowatt of any generating technology, including all fossil fuels.

POTENTIAL NEW JOBS

The U.S. hydropower industry employs 200,000–300,000 people in project development and deployment, manufacturing, operations, and maintenance.

RECOMMENDATION

The public's unfavorable view of new hydropower plants, length of approval process, cost of construction, and length of time to build make this technology a low option compared to solar, wind, and storage. Also, the dams would be constructed of concrete and the amount of carbon created in the cement mix as well as the actual construction will be significant. **Focus should be on opportunities to generate energy from the oceans.**

Biofuels

Biofuels have been around for decades and release lower levels of carbon dioxide and other emissions when consumed. Most gasoline sold at gas stations in the U.S. already has a 10 percent ethanol component. Biofuels fit three profiles (from least efficient to most efficient): fuel made from food stock (not recommended), fuel derived from waste and wood, and biofuel made from algae. Ultimately though, the less efficient biofuels are two steps forward and one step back, taking farmland for food out of production to grow subsidized corn for fuel. 4 percent of global transportation fuels will come from biofuels in 2030. Use farmland to grow crops to feed people and/or animals, not for biofuel. Creating biofuels from waste, wood, and algae makes more sense but will take a long time to get a favorable Return on Investment.

ELECTRICITY GENERATED AND PROJECTED IN THE UNITED STATES

Projected by Author

RENEWABLE ENERGIES	2020	2030	2050
SOLAR	2.3%	20%	35%
WIND	8.4%	15%	22%
HYDRO/WATER	7.3%	7.5%	9%
BIOMASS	1.4%	1.5%	3%
GEOTHERMAL	0.5%	1%	1%
Renewable	**19.9%**	**45%**	**70%**
NUCLEAR	20.0%	20%	25%.
Non- Carbon	**39.9%**	**65%**	**95%**
FOSSIL FUELS	60.1%	35%	5%
TOTAL	100%	100%	100%

2.17 Solar panels supporting city night architecture.

The growth of solar, wind, and battery storage is critical from now to 2030. If these renewables hit the 2030 projected percentages, then they should be able to continue and meet the 2050 estimates. The hard part is ramping up now.

Some fossil fuels will be necessary to tackle emissions in sectors with limited options:

- Cement, Steel, and Chemicals Manufacturing.

- The production of synthetic fuels for long-distance transport.

- "On-demand" service to ensure the stable operation of power systems night and day.

To counter the need for fossil fuels in 2050 and after, **carbon sequestration equipment at the plants will be required.** Additional preservation of the natural environment to sequester carbon should also be done to assure a regenerative world.

The Energy Department says solar energy can produce up to 40 percent of the nation's electricity within 15 years. "The study illuminates the fact that solar, our cheapest and fastest-growing source of clean energy, could produce enough electricity to power all of the homes in the U.S. by 2035 and employ as many as 1.5 million people in the process," Energy Secretary Jennifer Granholm said. The U.S. must install an average of 30 GW of solar capacity per year between now and 2025— double its current rate—and 60 GW per year from 2025 to 2030. One GW is enough energy to power about 750,000 homes[19].

The energy sector is responsible for 10 percent of global water withdrawals, used for operating thermal power plants producing energy from a steam boiler. **Unlike thermal power plants, wind and solar plants do not require large amounts of water to operate.**

There have been several major changes in various industries over the past 10 years. Amazon is the new bookstore. EVs are becoming very popular and soon will overtake internal combustion engine vehicles in sales. Spotify, Pandora, and other platforms provide us with our music. Netflix and other streaming sources allow us to watch movies anytime, anywhere. **Switching from fossil fuels to renewable energy is the next big change that is happening now.**

The goal should be to have all electricity generated by renewable energies by 2050 at the latest. This will be primary with solar, wind, storage, and nuclear. The U.S. is not totally independent of other countries for fossil fuels. It is alarming to see U.S. oil companies, that are subsidized by U.S. taxpayers, increase the price of a gallon of gas at the pump due to the Russian war in Ukraine. Other countries across the globe that must import their oil and natural gas have seen significant increases in energy. These oil companies have made record profits in 2022.

Fossil Fuels

The goal is to have 100 percent of United States, and ideally the world, run from no-carbon energy sources. There should be no need for coal and minimal or no need for gas and oil. Some believe we can be running 100 percent on no-carbon sources for our electricity.

From 2010-2019, domestic natural gas production climbed more than 50 percent. U.S. oil and natural gas production boomed, thanks to decades of research, technological innovation, readily available capital, desire to be independent, and entrepreneurship. Today, the U.S. is the world's number one oil and gas producer. The U.S went from being a net importer of natural gas in 2010 to being a net exporter as the decade closed. **Renewable energy by 2030 can make the U.S. fully independent by making all electricity at home.** All countries should try to do the same—energy independence.

The key point here is that renewable energies can see a major increase over the next 10 years with the U.S. as one of the leaders in this effort. The U.S. is second only to China in total installed renewable capacity. In the last two years, projects that pair renewables technologies with large-scale batteries have become economically viable. In particular, **"PV+storage"** projects have under-bid natural gas-fired plants to win power-delivery contracts in certain states, thanks to a 77 percent drop in the price of typical PV module and an 87 percent decline in battery pack prices[20]. Constant innovation, smart regulations, collaborative efforts, and industry initiatives help to ensure that industry is providing affordable and reliable energy to consumers, while reducing its environmental footprint and emissions.

It's estimated that 84 percent of all non-renewable fuels the earth has are found under the ocean floor. The tallest structure mankind has ever moved is a massive oil rig. Production wells are the main source of any given offshore oil platform, and they're what these platforms are put in place to run. Oil platforms have the capability of tapping into tens of different reserves in the same general location. The entire process of installing an offshore oil rig takes roughly 2 to 3 years. The average price for one of these rigs is roughly $650 million[21]. **After three years we could have turbines and solar panels providing electricity for two years because solar and wind require up to one year to build, then operate.**

By 2035, it will be more expensive to run 90 percent of gas plants being proposed in the U.S. than it will be to build new wind and solar farms equipped with storage systems, according to the report from the Rocky Mountain Institute.

Companies and countries that have large portfolios of oil and gas have access to another very important natural resource—the sun and plenty of land. Build large solar farms now in the deserts! We need to transition to making energy from the sun.

Fortunately, there are many choices to generate renewable energy. The decisions will be made primarily on cost, and politics at the national, state and local levels. Decision makers will need to weigh options and make timely decisions that are smart long-term investments. Individuals will need to advocate for decision makers as well as make smart purchases from non-carbon sources energy sources.

A 2020 report by the International Renewable Energy Agency (IRENA) tracked some $634 billion in energy sector subsidies in 2020 and found that around 70 percent went to fossil fuels. Only 20 percent went to renewable power generation, 6 percent to biofuels, and just over 3 percent to nuclear. Legislative approval by Congress would be needed to end most of the subsidies and financial incentives for the US oil and gas industry.

U.S. taxpayers spend tens of billions of dollars a year subsidizing new fossil fuel exploration, production, and consumption. This needs to stop. A conservative estimate from Oil Change International puts the U.S. total at around $20.5 billion annually, including $14.7 billion in federal subsidies and $5.8 billion in state-level incentives. Most of the subsidies are in the form of tax deductions and exemptions.

The permanent tax expenditures alone favor the fossil fuel industry over the renewable energy sector 7 to 1. Most of the tax breaks that renewables get—like the investment and production tax credits for wind and solar—are only temporary. It is estimated $81 billion that the U.S. military spends to protect oil supplies around the globe[22].

Financial Summary

IMMEDIATE PAYBACK

The International Energy Agency urges everyone to turn down the thermostat by a degree during the winter—that could save up to 10% of heating energy costs.

Community Solar

PPAs

4 TO 7 YEARS

PV+ Battery Storage

Wind Turbines

Geothermal (5–10 years)

TRANSPORTATION
REDUCE CARBON THROUGH BEHAVIORAL CHANGES

When you need transportation, try to either walk or bike as the first option, use public transportation as the second option, and use EVs as the third option.

The pandemic has brought new ways to communicate virtually that have reduced actual travel significantly, especially flying and driving—two big carbon problems.

The EPA data for 2019 U.S. Greenhouse Gases Emissions by **Sector**:

TRANSPORTATION	**29%**
ELECTRICITY*	25%
INDUSTRY	23%
AGRICULTURE	10%
COMMERCIAL & RESIDENTIAL	13% (onsite GHG emissions)

* Electricity GHG emissions = x% Commercial & Residential, x% Industry, x% Transportation

Electric Vehicles (EVs)

In 15 years, most vehicles (cars and light duty trucks) will be all-electric, and one will **NOT** be able to buy a new gasoline-driven vehicle. Benefits of electric cars over gasoline-driven cars:

1. They are better for the environment with no carbon emissions

2. Electricity can come from a renewable resource, gasoline is not.

3. EVs require less expensive and less frequent maintenance.

4. EVs are quieter than gas vehicles.

5. There are tax credits available to purchase most electric cars.

6. There are special highway lanes in some places for electric cars.

7. Electric is around 25–35 percent the cost compared to gasoline for a similar-sized vehicle driving the same distance.

8. Much fewer moving parts.

9. Safer to drive based on standard tests.

10. If you have a solar PV system and charge your EV during the day, you can reduce your greenhouse gas emissions even further. I am a proud owner of two EVs and happy to see one of my daughters has purchased one.

Electric vehicles accounted for 4.6 percent of the light vehicle market in 2021 nearly double the EV share in 2019 (GreenCars Blog). **It took Norway only 10 years to move from 1 percent of car sales being EVs to 65 percent. The number in May 2022 was 85.1 percent when you include plug-in hybrids.** Many believe strong demand-side policies kept in place for a long time supported the quick growth of the EVs. The government therefore taxes the sales of new polluting cars but does not tax EVs at all. The Norwegian parliament has also decided that all sales of new cars and vans shall be zero emission by 2025. The key is to start taxing new sales of at least the most polluting car models. This is a fair way to implement climate policies as it is aimed at people buying a new car, not an indiscriminate tax at the gas pump for all internal combustion cars, used and new. Consumers are given an option when buying a new car. **Norway took 2.5 years to move from 2 percent to 10 percent EV market share, UK took 1.5 years and Germany only one.** The U.S. numbers for EV sales are expected to jump significantly with the support from the federal government.

The initial cost for an EV is more than the gasoline car BUT the costs are coming down and are expected to be the same or less than gasoline vehicles within a year or two. In Car & Drivers 2022 EV Car of the Year article they have listed the Chevrolet Bolt, Hyundai Kona Electric below $30,000 after the federal tax break. More cars will follow with a lower initial cost as the development of the lithium battery is expected to drive down the cost of most EVs.

The EVs will last 2–4 times longer and be much more cost-effective to operate. A typical passenger car should last 200,000 miles or more, says Rich White, executive director of the nonprofit Car Care Council. Electric engines are expected to last 300,000 miles or more.

Elon Musk said that they built the Model 3 to last as long as a commercial truck (1,000,000 miles and 5 times more than a typical gasoline vehicle!), and the battery modules should last **between 300,000 miles (22 years) and 500,000 miles (37 years)**. These numbers assume you follow the U.S. average and drive 15,000 miles annually. **The EVs should last at least 2 to 5 times longer than the internal combustion vehicles.** If you replace the old battery with a new one, the average cost is $12,000 in 2021 dollars. That would be more affordable than buying a new car 22 years from now! The electric car should become a generational family vehicle going from the original owner to their child, then to their child. If the EV travels 1,000,000 miles and the driver averages 15,000 miles annually, the car should last 67 years! If you buy the car when you are 18 it should be around when you are 85. The initial electric car will pay for itself several times over the life of the vehicle. Times are changing. On January 6, 2022, a Tesla Model S P85 (the oldest performance version) reached an impressive mileage milestone of **932,256 miles.** The car is used in Germany by Hansjörg von Gemmingen - Hornberg, who is known in the EV world for setting the highest mileage records in Tesla cars[1].

Our Next Energy, Inc. (ONE), a Michigan battery technology company, has demonstrated a proof-of-concept battery that powered an EV 752 miles without recharging. The vehicle completed a road test across Michigan in late December 2021, with an average speed of 55 mph. The results were validated by a third party using a vehicle dynamometer, where the test vehicle, a Tesla Model S retrofitted with an experimental battery, achieved 882 miles at 55 mph[2]. We should see continued improvements in all technologies in the next few years.

TRUCKS

New smaller trucks are now all-electric. The new electric trucks are being marketed as costing similar to gasoline driven trucks. **The Ford-150 Lightning goes 300 miles and starts at $40,000 up to $90,000 and is expected to outsell its gasoline engine counterpart.** The new electric trucks will have as much positive impact on climate change as the electric cars. The Ford-150 Lightning electric truck will be in demand as much as Tesla cars. More than 160,000 buyers have reserved the F-150 Lightning Electric Truck. America's three best-selling vehicles nearly every year are full-sized pickup trucks. Ford has the capacity to build 15,000 trucks in 2022, 55,000 in 2023, and 80,000 in 2024. **There are more orders today than trucks that will be built over the next three years.** In comparison, Tesla is expected to deliver 1.42 million cars in 2022. **Ford and GM should accelerate the manufacturing of their electric trucks, which will increase the population of believers in the U.S.**

As the top-selling model line in the U.S. for 40 years, Ford Motor Co.'s F-Series pickups hold special weight in the auto ecosystem. The lineup, led by the F-150, generates more than $40 billion in annual revenue. Only one other U.S. product—Apple Inc.'s iPhone—tops F-Series sales[3].

Given this, Ford's decision to electrify the F-150 stands as one of the boldest strategic decisions in 21st century business. **An electric F-150, more than any other vehicle, will persuade rural America to go green, leading the way for almost every automaker that finds itself challenged by the electric transition.**

3.1 Ford started deliveries of the Lightning pickup truck this spring. Ford made an announcement on March 1, 2022, about the bi-directional charging station, shown in photo, that will backup home electrical needs.

When Chief Executive Officer Jim Farley announced plans in early 2019 to sell an electric version of the F-150—later called Lightning—he forced the hand of almost every boss in the business. Within months, several rivals—including General Motors, Stellantis, and Tesla—announced a parade of electric trucks and SUVs. "If Ford can pull this off, they'll move the entire EV market," says Dan Albert, automotive historian and author. "This is a cultural moment for America."

Regardless of how many F-150 Lightnings make it off the lot, the truck arguably already has accelerated the adoption of EVs in both the supply side and the demand side[4].

Costs for Lightning owners will be considerably lower than for those owning the F-150. The $39,974 base price (factoring in federal subsidies) is 17 percent less than that of an entry-level F-150, according to Atlas Public Policy.

Electrifying vehicles, especially SUVs and pickups, will help the U.S. reach its goal.

- **2022** First deliveries of the F-150 Lightning are expected. Ford has 200,000 reservations.

- **2026** Date Ford set to reach annual EV production of 2 million. (This will be a challenge).

- **2030** Goal leading automakers set for 40-50 percent of new vehicle sales to be electric. President Joe Biden's target is 50 percent.

- **2040** Sales of new gas-powered vehicles are set to end as Ford, GM, Mercedes, and others will sell only zero-emission cars.

- **2050** The U.S. government's goal for economy-wide net-zero emissions.

"We need to accelerate the adoption of these vehicles and consumers need to respond to get us even close to achieving carbon reduction targets," says Greg Keoleian, director of the University of Michigan's Center for Sustainable Systems and co-author of a recent emissions study Ford commissioned. **"Decarbonization of the auto sector is very critical."**[5]

A GREENER SET OF WHEELS

U.S. greenhouse gas emissions in 2019 totaled 6.6 billion metric tons, with the transportation sector being the worst polluter. Sedans, SUVs, and pickups accounted for 1.1 billion metric tons. According to a study from the University of Michigan's Center for Sustainable Systems commissioned by Ford, over its lifetime, a battery-powered vehicle will cut emissions by:

- **74** metric tons for a pickup

- **56** metric tons for an SUV

- **45** metric tons for a sedan

A study by Bloomberg Green shows taxes and fees to be the same for the 2022 F-150 Lightning and the 2022 F-150 gas powered vehicle. Maintenance and repairs should be much less for the electric vehicle because there only 10 percent of parts compared to the gasoline vehicle. The cost of the operate the electric truck was estimated at .22 cents per mile compared to .33 cents per mile for the gasoline version. **The key point is the electric F-150 Lighting will cost less to purchase and 50 percent less to operate. A clear win/ win scenario for the consumer.**

We Predict, a data analysis company for manufacturers, in the fall of 2021 shared their Deepview True Cost analysis explaining that after higher first year costs, the EV service costs fall 30 percent below gas vehicle costs at 3 years. The study is based on 65 million orders for maintenance and 13 million vehicles of all kinds.

The first three years, the maintenance of an EV is 30 percent less which equates to $1,500 x 30 percent= $450 savings. This is $450 lower each year for the first three years for EVs. From the fourth year on, based on driving 15,000 miles a year, the chart the Internal Combustion Engine Vehicle (ICEV) costs $1,500 compared to $900 for the Battery Electric Vehicle (BEV). **This is a $600 difference annually.** The hybrid electric vehicle (HEV) and the plug-in hybrid electric vehicle (PHEV) are also documented in the comparison chart.

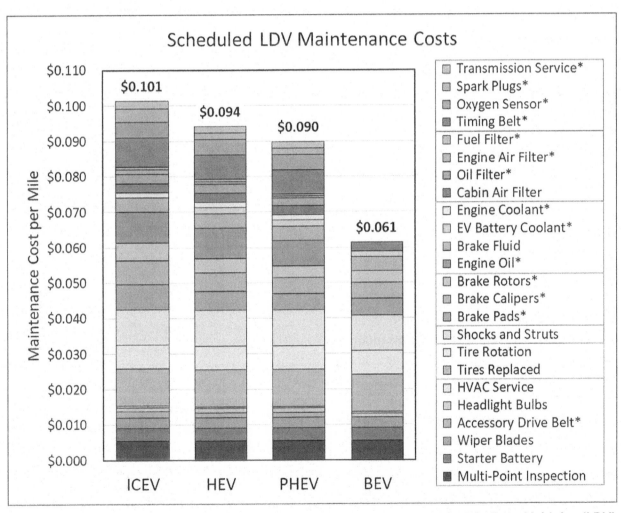

3.2 Light Duty Vehicles (LDV)

Savings on maintenance for EVs compared to combustion engine vehicles:

30 percent for first three years
at $450/year = $1,350

Years 4–7 save $600 annually = $2,400

The 7-year total savings on maintenance for EVs is $3,750.

A recent study (2021) from the Yale School of the Environment published in *Nature Communications* found that the total indirect emissions from EVs pale in comparison to the indirect emissions from fossil fuel-powered vehicles. This is in addition to the direct emissions from combusting fossil fuels—either at the tailpipe for conventional vehicles or at the power plant smokestack for electricity generation—showing EVs have a clear advantage emissions-wise over conventional vehicle. "The surprising element was how much lower the emissions of EVs were," says postdoctoral associate Stephanie Weber. "The supply chain for combustion vehicles is just so dirty that EVs can't surpass them, even when you factor in indirect emissions."

Another study from the University of Michigan's Transportation Research Institute found that EVs **cost less than half as much to operate as gas-powered cars**. The average cost to operate an EV in the United States is $485 per year, while the average for a gasoline-powered vehicle is $1,117. The cost of electricity should continue to go down with further improvements in renewable energies. **Over a 10-year period, the EV operational cost is approximately $6,300 less**, making up the difference from the initial cost to purchase. Gasoline prices are more susceptible to increased costs, which we have quickly seen with the Russia/Ukraine war in early 2022.

In the research study, the operation of EVs assumed the worst-case scenario using fossil fuels to create the electricity to charge the battery. Soon most of the charging will be supported by non-fossil fuel sources so the chart will have very little carbon generated during operations for the EV. Replacing parts and tires would be the primary source that would create the carbon, but that would apply to all vehicles.

A typical gasoline vehicle emits 4.7 metric tons of carbon dioxide every year[6]. Gas vehicles require the gas to be hauled to the gas stations, taking a larger toll on the roads. Installation of the solar panels has an impact, but once it is up and running, it does not require gas to be trucked in regularly, and the impact on the roads is less than the gas stations out there. An EV initially has more embodied carbon to make the vehicle, but much lower carbon in life cycle. Researchers at Argonne National Laboratory estimated emissions for both a gasoline car and an EV with a 300-mile electric range. In their estimates, while Greenhouse Gases (GHGs) from EVs manufacturing are higher, total GHGs for the EV are still lower than those for the gasoline car, even when using fossil fuels to generate the electricity. This is because there are many more parts made of fossil fuels that are in a combustion engine vehicle that need to be repaired and replaced more often. Over time the EV will have created much less embodied carbon because there will be 2-3 gasoline cars required over the same number of miles. If the electric battery is charged by non-fossil fuels, then the carbon created by the EV is dramatically less.

The cost savings on operations are $11.59 to $15.54 trillion for all EVs through 2050[7]. There is also the reduction in carbon. EVs are by far

the best long-term value for taxpayer money in the transportation sector. Also, the resale value is better for EVs. The Tesla cars have been tested to be the safest cars to drive on the road today. **Electric cars cost 31 percent less to service over the first three years than gas cars**, a new study says. Electric cars had both lower maintenance and repair costs, according to We Predict. (October 28, 2021)

Bloomberg NEF's latest lithium-ion battery price index finds the 2020 weighted-average price for lithium-ion storage batteries is $137 per kilowatt-hour. **$100 per kilowatt-hour is the lithium-ion storage battery's magic number. At that point, the up-front cost for an electric passenger vehicle will be the same as—or less than—a similar internal combustion model**. By 2023, average prices will be close to $100/kWh, according to the latest forecast from research company BloombergNEF (BNEF).

Several factors account for the continued decline in EV prices: technology improvements, manufacturing scale, competition among manufacturers, greater product integration ahead of installation, and more overall industry expertise. Another key driver in reducing the cost will be the policies that are set by various governments.

BATTERY CHARGING

As of year-end 2020, there are about 89,000 public EV charging points in the U.S. Most locations in this country have public charging stations within 100 miles. As of February 18, 2021, Tesla operated **over 1,200 Tesla super charging stations** in the U.S. with an average of 9 chargers per station. There are 46,385 publicly accessible EV charging stations

by several companies (Tesla, ChargePoint, EVgo, Pacific Gas and Electric, and Blink to name a few) across the U.S., according to the Department of Energy. Many charging stations, not named Tesla, are found in smaller numbers at shopping malls, public buildings and a part of street parking. The Biden administration has said its goal is to add **500,000 chargers**. Tesla CEO Elon Musk confirmed in July (2021) that Tesla will be making its Supercharger network available to other EVs later in the year, with the Tesla app and using a plug adapter. Those who cannot plug in at their residence need to rely more on public charging stations.

I have found that charging my car at home costs half as much as being charged by a public supercharger.

One significant benefit of EVs is that you can easily charge them at home using a basic three prong 120V outlet. Approximately 80 percent of charging is done at home. A 120V outlet will charge 4 miles an hour and requires only 20-amp service. Overnight for eight hours amounts to 32 miles of charge. The typical roundtrip commute is 30 miles.

A Type 2 charger, requiring a 40-amp breaker at home, will provide 25-30 miles of charge an hour. This totals 200-240 miles of battery charge over eight hours, which should be plenty for most people daily. 120V residential outlets make sense at airport parking, where most people will be gone for at least 24 hours. It is a waste to have fast chargers at airports that can charge a battery in an hour when the driver will be gone for a day or more. The only benefit would be in a short-term parking area. **It is better for the battery to be charged slowly for longer life.** The second option is to install a Type 2 charger that runs out of a 40-

or 50-amp breaker for people who have a day trip planned. Parking decks on campus at universities are another good place to install 120V outlets. Students usually do not drive their car every day when they live on campus and park on campus.

Existing and future construction developments should include outlets for charging. Parking garages should provide standard 120V outlets at every column. Provide Type 2 outlets in designated spaces for approximately 10-20 percent of the total spaces. Private companies that can provide faster charging can be encouraged at shopping areas, restaurants, movie theatres, and other locations, where the person will be there for 1-3 hours. Policy makers and developers need to understand what is the best type of charging EVs based on the building to invest effectively.

The infrastructure for the electric car is much farther developed than the infrastructure for the gasoline engine cars that came out 100 years ago. A 100 years ago, there were **7.5 million cars** and trucks in the United States. The automobile industry was promoting the building of highways and the use of automobiles was beginning to have an effect on railroads. Americans bought **nearly 26 million cars** and 3 million trucks in the 1920s, topped off by superlative sales of 4.3 million new vehicles in 1929. **Now, 100 years later, the electric car is taking over at a more rapid pace with 6.6 million cars sold in 2021. Innovation drives change and the market.**

Jaguar plans to sell only electric cars from 2025, Volvo from 2030. General Motors says it will make only EVs by 2035, Ford says all vehicles sold in Europe will be electric by 2030, and VW says 70 percent of its sales will be electric by 2030. Lotus said it would follow suit, selling only electric models from 2028. Mercedes- Benz also has some great ideas with their electric vans coming out.

The new Mercedes-Benz eSprinter with Electric Versatility Platform
Locally emission-free transport with maximum flexibility in terms of range and body variants

eGrocery transporter   Flatbed truck   People mover   Ambulance

3.3

All major delivery companies are starting to replace their gas-powered fleets with electric or low-emission vehicles, a switch that companies say will boost their bottom lines, while also fighting climate change and urban pollution. Amazon is buying 100,000 electric trucks from the start-up Rivian. Typically vans and smaller trucks—are much easier to electrify, with current battery technology providing enough range for many routes. Companies also have plenty of charging time. The Rivian vans are being used in 10 cities in 2022 and 100,000 vans are expected on the road by 2030. They'll save 4 million metric tons of carbon per year by 2030, according to Amazon, which calls it the largest order ever for electric delivery vehicles. UPS has placed an order for 10,000 electric delivery vehicles.

Technological revolutions tend to happen very quickly. The development of the SMART phone is an obvious recent example of new technology being a disruptor by changing the entire market for phones, calculators, cameras and computers. LMC Automotive expects **General Motors** to surpass Tesla as the country's largest EV seller by mid-decade. GM previously projected its EV revenue to grow from about $10 billion in 2023 to approximately $90 billion annually by 2030 as the company launches new models.

The U.S. is expected to reach almost 160GWh of battery manufacturing by the end of 2023. Growth is expected mainly from the Tesla Nevada Gigafactory, LG Chem's joint investment with General Motors in Ohio, as well as SK Innovation's investment in a facility in Georgia. **EVs are expected to go from around 5 percent of global car sales to more than 60 percent by 2030.** Auto executives say more than half of U.S. car sales will be EVs by 2030[8].

The insurance is basically the same or slightly less for electric compared to gasoline engine cars. The electric cars have been tested to last longer and received the highest grades on safety tests. Replacing some parts is similar because both types of cars have been developed with the latest technology including sensors, cameras, and state-of-the-art lighting. There are many more parts though for the gasoline-driven car, which is added maintenance and cost. The development of all cars with better sensors should reduce accidents as well as the cost of insurance.

The number of electric cars, buses, vans, and heavy trucks on roads globally is expected to hit 145 million by 2030 (the International Energy Agency). These projections exclude 2- and 3-wheeled EVs. Global EV numbers are set to hit 145 million by 2030. The number of EVs may appear high to some, but the reality is the EV numbers in the U.S. are lower than in most countries. The opportunity is available for U.S. businesses and the government to show more leadership in the EV market.

POLICIES

- Support all EVs with tax **rebates**, including used EVs. Programs like the "cash for clunkers" trade-in scheme introduced in the U.S. in 2009, gave people money for their inefficient vehicles, and accelerated a transition to much more energy efficient cars.

- **Make sure all cars and trucks can charge up at all EV stations**. Tesla should allow other car manufacturers to use their electric chargers, which are the best super chargers available along or near main roads located conveniently across the country.

- Promote adoption of vehicle-to-grid electric storage.

- Work with insurance companies to lower rates for EVs.

- Require new gasoline-driven vehicles to increase mileage efficiency to 55 miles/gallon by 2030.

VEHICLE-TO-HOME BI-DIRECTIONAL CHARGING TECHNOLOGY

Soon EV owners will be able to use their vehicles as a backup power source for their homes during an outage. General Motors and Pacific Gas and Electric Company are launching a pilot plan to test the bi-directional charging technology—which includes a vehicle-to-home (V2H) capable EV and charger. Finding ways to store and reallocate energy supplies will become necessary to avoid overstressing the grid. PG&E have had to cut off power for hundreds of thousands of homes and businesses to prevent power lines from sparking wildfires during high-risk weather conditions.

Other companies are investigating ways to give power back to the grid or home via EV batteries, as well. Tesla's Powerwall, for example, uses the same batteries in Tesla vehicles to store solar energy for backup protection, and Ford's new F-150 Lightning electric pickup will also be able to power homes in the event of an outage.

The teams are working to scale the pilot quickly with the goal of opening larger customer trials by the end of the year, GM said. "Imagine a future where everyone is driving an EV—and where that EV serves as a backup power option at home and more broadly as a resource for the grid," said PG&E CEO Patti Poppe. "Not only is this a huge advancement for electric reliability and climate resiliency, it's yet another advantage of clean-powered EVs, which are so important in our collective battle against climate change."[9]

UTILIZING EVS FOR BUILDING BACK-UP

This can be enough to operate a building for days, or longer if rooftop solar is available to recharge the vehicle. There are several variations that can work and will become much more common in the marketplace over the next 3-5 years.

1. **Vehicle-to-grid or V2G** – EV exports energy to support the electricity grid.

2. **Vehicle-to-home or V2H** – EV energy is used to power a home or business.

3. **Vehicle-to-load or V2L *** – EV can be used to power appliances or charge other EVs

* V2L does not require a bidirectional charger to operate[10].

The advent of EVs is expected to increase the demand for electricity, but electric cars can also offer some advantages by controlling the power load. A study showed that EVs could save billions of dollars with controllable load and vehicle-to-grid features, and it would enable the grid to optimize its use of renewable energy.

Controllable load, the ability to control when an EV is charging, is possible with any EV if it is connected to a smart charging station or the vehicle itself has an internet connection. On its own, it can have a massive impact on the grid by reducing peak demand and charging only when demand is lower.

Ford has launched its new Ford Charge Station Pro, a bi-directional home charging station that works with the upcoming F-150 Lightning electric pickup truck. It means that the electric pickup truck can send power back to power a home, another vehicle, or virtually anything it can plug into. In order to use the capacity at home, **Ford-F-150 Lightning owners are going to need a bi-directional charging station into which they can plug their electric pickup. The price of the station is currently $1,310**[11].

There should be support by the government and auto industry to train, build and maintain EVs. The Certified Electric Vehicle Technician (CEVT) certificate program has been designed to train a new generation of EV specialists to work in EV production, repair, and maintenance. The **16-week** training program covers comprehensive topics through lectures and hands-on workshops in advanced electric car theory and practice. **Pay people their full salary to take the training program**.

Some studies have shown that making a typical EV can create more carbon pollution than making a gasoline car. This is because of the additional energy required to manufacture an EV's battery but this is NOT totally correct. The EVs have 10 percent the parts, which means their supply chain produces much less embodied carbon. This is being addressed within the EV industry as the evolution of the battery continues. Over the lifetime of the vehicle, total greenhouse gas emissions associated with manufacturing, charging, and driving an EV are clearly much lower than the total GHGs associated with a gasoline car. They are much lower when the electric car is charged with renewable energy, explained researchers at Argonne National Laboratory[12].

HYBRID CARS

Hybrid cars pair an electric motor and battery with an internal combustion engine. The combination improves fuel economy—more miles on a gallon—and lowers emissions compared to a gasoline engine vehicle. **As the electric cars and infrastructure continue to improve, the hybrid car will not be as beneficial to the environment and is viewed as a short-term transition by consumers.**

Autonomous Vehicles

From 2025-2035 the global car market will be interrupted by **the rise of autonomous vehicles, which greatly reduces the need for private car ownership.** In November 2021, Bloomberg reported that Apple plans to release a self-driving EV as early as 2025. Within this scenario, electric cars will continue to grow, supporting the drive to reduce carbon. Autonomous cars should increase vehicle life expectancy by reducing accidents. The biggest safety flaw in automobiles is human drivers: 94 percent of crashes are due to human error, according to the National Highway Traffic Safety Administration. Autonomous cars are meant to react faster than people and the vehicles' cameras and sensors allow them to see more of the road, all of which could reduce accidents by 90 percent. This will drive car insurance costs down, helping to make autonomous vehicles more affordable. Even today, there are many sensors in new cars to help try to prevent accidents. Car ownership is wasteful because cars are parked for 98 percent of their lifetime, with a third of cars not going out each day[13].

- **3 parking spaces for every car**

- **Congestion stats:** "According to the 2015 Urban Mobility Scorecard, travel delays due to traffic congestion caused drivers to waste more than 3 billion gallons of fuel and kept travelers stuck in their cars for nearly 7 billion extra hours—42 hours per rush hour commuter. The total nationwide pricetag: $160 billion, or $960 per commuter."

Bicycles

Electric bikes are now very popular and growing. The amount of space required for a pedestrian, bicyclist, and commuter on a bus takes up much less area than a person riding in an automobile.

Shifting more trips to walking and biking could cut transportation emissions by 54 million metric tons of CO2 each year. Shifting short trips to walking and biking has the potential to generate $138 billion in economic value annually. U.S. government is promoting an active transportation investment program to make grants to eligible applicants to build safe and connected options for bicycles and walkers within and between communities, and for other purposes.

Information provided by Congress finds the following:

1. Nearly half of the trips taken in the United States are within a 20-minute bicycle ride, and nearly a quarter of such trips are within a 20-minute walk.

2. Approximately 90 percent of public transportation trips are accessible by walking or bicycling.

3. Communities that invest in active transportation infrastructure experience significant increases in bicycling and walking rates over time, and such investments are in strong demand because they lead to a higher quality of life, better health, a stronger economy, and increased mobility in communities where investments are made.

4. The communities that perform best in encouraging active transportation create interconnected systems that make it convenient and safe to travel on foot or by bicycle to destinations on a routine basis.

5. Achieving a mode shift to active transportation within a community requires intensive, concentrated funding of active transportation systems rather than discrete, piecemeal projects.

6. Increased use of active transportation reduces traffic congestion, greenhouse gas emissions, vehicle miles traveled, and rates of obesity and chronic disease associated with physical inactivity.

7. Given the contribution that active transportation makes to national policy goals, and the opportunity active transportation provides to accommodate short trips at the least cost to the public and individuals, funding of active transportation is one of the most strategic and cost-effective federal transportation investments available.

8. The Federal Government is uniquely qualified to facilitate interstate connections necessary to build long distance active transportation spines and regional connections in communities that span state boundaries.

A few years ago, London changed one auto lane going in both directions to dedicated lanes shared by bikes and buses. This has helped significantly the traffic problems in London. Another advantage of the bike/bus lane is they allow emergency vehicles to be used, which provides much faster service because the ambulances, police, and fire trucks do not have to fight through the heavily used auto lanes.

Bicycles are, on average, 40 percent faster during peak hours, more predictable, and less expensive than automobiles. Surveys of cycle commuters show that many consider **10 miles one way** to be a maximum reasonable distance for regular riding. Those living further may drive part way and ride the rest. In a few communities, public transportation accommodates bicycles. An ideal bike route is fast, convenient, and direct.

If you live in a big city, then there's a good chance that you're paying a pretty penny to park your car. Parking your bike is as easy as locking it up outside or bringing it inside the home and office.

The health benefits of regular cycling include:

- increased cardiovascular fitness
- reduced anxiety and depression.
- improved posture and coordination
- strengthened bones
- increased muscle strength and flexibility
- improved joint mobility
- decreased stress levels
- decreased body fat levels

Many insurance companies will reduce the amount that you're paying if you are driving your car less.

LIVE CAR-FREE: The average cost of a car annually is high: For vehicles driven 15,000 miles a year, it was **$9,561** a year, or about **$797** a month, in 2020[14]. This number will vary and includes the cost of the monthly payment, insurance, gas (switch to electric), maintenance and repairs, registration fees, and taxes.

FINANCIAL COST/PAYBACK

Payback would be immediate and annual savings would average about $8,000. This is significant for all incomes but especially low- and moderate-income families.

RECOMMENDATION

Governments and developers should collaborate to renovate major urban areas to pedestrian and bike communities. There are hundreds of great examples at the following website created by Yuval Fogelson **of similar examples and success stories** across the world[15].

Some of the most dramatic transformations are correcting the mistakes of the past. Take these before and after shots of Klyde Warren Park in Dallas. Where there was once a broad freeway dividing sections of the city's downtown into different chunks, there is now a spacious garden full of budding greenery. The park joins spaces that where car-dominated but now focus on the pedestrian.

3.5

3.4 Before and After Photos of amount of cars compared to pedestrians, Warren Park Dallas, Texas

Hamilton, New Zealand's fourth largest city, has taken a slightly different approach to improving their city. The subterranean entry is a parking lot, filled in to create a park and encourage people to drive into the city's downtown[16].

3.6

Street designs that favor automobiles and ignore pedestrians and cyclists is being rethought—a newly updated resource created by the Brazilian urban design collective Urb-i allows you to chart just how widespread and profound the changes are. The **Global Street Design Guide provided by** National Association of City Transportation Officials and Global Designing Cities Initiative is a very helpful resource[17].

FINANCIAL COST/PAYBACK

Investments in a community's walkability typically increase land value by 70–300 percent and retail sales by 30 percent. Shifting short trips to walking and biking by **investing in connected active transportation systems** has the potential to generate $138 billion in economic value annually including new jobs and direct spending across rural, urban, and suburban communities[18].

Aviation

Planes now are being built lighter with better engines that are more energy efficient, but they still create a significant amount of carbon in the atmosphere. The aviation industry has committed to halving emissions by 2050. **With air travel set to double over the next 20 years, this will be challenging.** Travel is expected to grow as the population globally increases and more people move up into the middle class. To counter this growth as much as possible, use Zoom and the latest technologies to communicate with people across geographies for business and pleasure. **The pandemic has now created a way for people to communicate virtually which, to a certain extent, should continue and help reduce some flying.**

There are other options. **France has banned short flights of 200 miles or less. The bill ends routes where the same journey could be made by train in under 2.5 hours.** Connecting flights will not be affected, however. In 2020, Austrian Airlines replaced a flight route between the capital Vienna and the city of Salzburg with an increased train service, after receiving a government bailout with provisions to cut its carbon footprint. **A third opportunity is for smaller aircrafts, covering up to 1,000 miles, to use electrification as a very good opportunity to reduce carbon in the next 10–15 years.**

Boeing's electric autonomous passenger air vehicle just had its first flight[19].

Airplanes emit around <u>100 times</u> more CO2 per hour than a shared bus or train ride, and the emissions of global aviation are around 1 billion tons of CO2 per year. Air travel contributes 4 percent to global warming, more than almost all countries[20].

POLICIES

- A frequent flyer levy—a tax that increases the more you fly each year.

- Tax for each mile flown.

- Ban 200-mile flights or less, except connecting flights. Allow only if planes are flown with electric power.

Public Transit (Subways)

TRAINS FOR LOCAL TRANSPORTATION.

Rail electrification enables trains to be powered by renewables. Electric trains can provide nearly emissions-free transport. The cost to maintain and expand is typically challenging.

BUSES

Electric buses are **safe, reliable, and have similar rates to other technologies**. Their quiet, smooth rides allow passengers to relax and easily have conversations. The lack of a diesel engine reduces noise pollution. **There is great flexibility in creating bus routes to move passengers compared to trains. Buses have more flexible routes than trains, enabling them to serve their customers better.**

FINANCIAL COST/PAYBACK

The U.S. National Renewable Energy Laboratory has found that **the fuel economy of Battery Electric Buses (BEBs) is five times lower than that of diesel buses operated on equivalent routes.** In addition, maintenance costs for electric motors are much lower because they have far fewer moving parts than conventional motors and are far more efficient.

RECOMMENDATION

Provide an incentive program and grants for transit agencies, school districts, and bus contractors to help finance the up-front cost of BEBs and their charging infrastructure. **When purchasing a new bus, buy all-electric.**

Require the purchase of public vehicles, like the U.S. Postal Service, to evaluate based on life cycle costs, not simply initial cost. Taxpayer money should not be spent on short-sighted decisions that the U.S. Postal service is making. Purchase 20 percent of new vehicles each year for five years to provide a logical transition from gasoline delivery vehicles to all-electric. The electric cars should last longer and be a much better investment.

High-Speed Rail

High-speed rail offers an alternative to trips otherwise made by car or airplane. Some countries in Europe are eliminating the 200-mile airplane flight and asking people to take the train. This idea should be implemented wherever the infrastructure is available with a high-speed train system. The northeast corridor of the U.S. should not allow the 200-mile flights, except for connections. China has developed a high-speed infrastructure that is very fast and comfortable.

President Biden made the case for keeping the rail network running. Amtrak says it needs $38 billion just to restore the Boston-to-D.C. corridor to a "state of good repair" as an essential part of the White House's pledge to cut the country's greenhouse gas emissions in half by 2030. **Trains emit 83 percent less greenhouse gas than driving and up to 73 percent less than flying, according to Amtrak's 2019 sustainability report.** According to International Union of Railways (UIC) data, high-speed rail is **more than 4 times as energy efficient as driving in gasoline-driven cars** and nearly 9 times more efficient than flying. According to the Association of American Railroads (AAR), moving freight by **rail** is 4 times more fuel-**efficient** than moving freight on the highway. Private freight companies own 97% of the 21,400 miles of track Amtrak uses across the country.

There are many other benefits to high-speed rail compared to riding an automobile. **People can rest, relax, do some work, and eat safely on a train. People can have a much more efficient and relaxed lifestyle commuting on a train.**

POLICIES

Electric chargers at train stations can be an incentive to support EV owners to also use the train. Build solar panels over the parking to provide electricity locally and minimize the heat island effect.

RECOMMENDATION

Encourage more freight train travel to support growth and keep from adding more trucks on the major highways, or at least the growth of trucks on the highways.

Ocean Shipping

A highly efficient mode of transportation, shipping, enables more than 80 percent of global trade. The big problem is the shipping industry pumps around 3 percent of the world's annual greenhouse gas emissions into the earth's atmosphere, supporting climate change. **If shipping were a country, it would be the sixth–largest emitter globally**[21]. Saving fuel can be as simple as slowing down. If the ships slowed down, the industry could achieve significant emissions cuts with current technologies, better designs and intelligent operations. The problem is that if **food is being shipped, the longer the delivery, the less valuable the food is from a health perspective, and the potential for the food to become waste is much higher**. Support development of ships to be capable of running on zero- emission fuels such as green hydrogen, green ammonia, green methanol, and advanced biofuels.

3D Printing

3D printers reduce shipping, transportation, manufacturing and packaging costs.

3.7

3D printers help reduce greenhouse gases by building locally where needed. Using 3D printing provides **just-in-time availability** of the product locally with minimal transportation costs. 3D printing is revolutionizing everything from wrenches to prosthetic body parts, to transforming large-scale manufacturing. With 3D printing, fewer parts need outsourcing for manufacturing. This equals less environmental impact because fewer things are being shipped across the globe and there is no need to operate and maintain an energy-consuming factory. **3D printing creates less waste material for a single part plus materials used in 3D printing generally are recyclable. The main advantages of 3D printing are realized in its speed, flexibility, and cost benefits**. For small production runs, prototyping, small business, and educational use, 3D printing is vastly superior.

Among the items made with 3D printers are **shoe designs, furniture, wax castings for making jewelry, tools, tripods, gift and novelty items, and toys**. The automotive and aviation industries use 3D printers to make parts. Artists can create sculptures, and architects can fabricate models of their projects.

Speed. One of the biggest advantages of 3D printing technology is Rapid Prototyping. Rapid prototyping is the ability to design, manufacture, and test a customized part in as little time as possible. Also, if needed, the design can be modified without adversely affecting the speed of the manufacturing process.

Cost Savings. For small production runs and applications, 3D printing is one of the most cost-effective manufacturing processes.

Flexibility. Another big advantage of 3D printing is that any given printer can create almost anything that is within its build volume, which can be to the size of a full house.

3.8 SHELTER SOLUTIONS [3D printed]
New Story Charity | 3D printed home in 12–24 hours for $4,000

With traditional manufacturing processes, each new part or change in part design requires a new tool, mold, die, or jig to be manufactured to create the new part. In 3D printing, the design is fed into slicer software, needed supports added, and then printed with little or no change at all in the physical machinery or equipment. The nature of 3D printing allows the step-by-step assembly of the part or product, which guarantees enhancement of the design and better-quality parts/products.

COMPETITIVE ADVANTAGE. Because of the speed and lower costs of 3D printing, product life cycles are reduced. Businesses can improve and enhance a product allowing them to deliver better products in a shorter amount of time.

SUSTAINABILITY

With 3D printing, fewer parts need outsourcing for manufacturing. This equals less environmental impact because fewer things are being shipped across the globe.

Michelin's VISION is a 3D printed airless and organic wheel-cum-tire with several environment-friendly features. With no inflation or rims, the entire structure was designed to be sturdy enough to support the vehicle yet flexible enough to absorb impact and pressure. The tire itself would be made of biodegradable material—rubber compounds derived from organic, recyclable materials—

and have a reloadable 3D-printed tread band, so you could pick new tread patterns for snow or rain, all by yourself.

Airless: a technology that eliminates the risk of flats and rapid pressure loss and reduces environmental impact

Rechargeable: a tread that can be 3D printed on demand.

Connected: for a safe and personalized augmented driving experience.

100% sustainable by 2050: innovation in bio-sourced and recycled materials[22].

3.9 Example of a 3D printed tire

Summary

The EPA data for 2019 U.S. Greenhouse Gases for **Transportation** (29 percent of U.S. Green House Gases).

Light duty vehicles (trucks +cars)	58%
Medium and Heavy-Duty Trucks	24%
Aircraft	10%
Other (buses, motorcycles)	5%
Rail	2%
Ships and Boats	2%

Solutions you can implement today to save money and reduce the carbon:

Immediate Payback

Walking

Live Car-free

Carpooling

Riding a bike

Reduce number of plane flights

Buy local and buy within the U.S. to reduce transportation costs.

A speed limit of 55mph - the most efficient running speed for many cars - could be set during the energy crisis to cut carbon emissions.

Up to 1 Year

Riding an electric bike or motorcycle

1 to 3 Years

Using Electric trucks and some electric cars (with and without federal tax incentives)

Use 3-D printing to reduce manufacturing costs

4 to 7 Years

Using an Autonomous Car

4

CITIES
REDUCE CARBON

By 2050, it is estimated that almost 70 percent of the world's population will live in cities, making the concept of sustainable communities an efficient resolution to the growing population.[1] Cities are already responsible for 70 percent of global waste and consume almost 80 percent of the world's energy[2].

BEST PRACTICES FOR CLIMATE CHANGE IN CITIES

Strong master plans that are holistic are critical. Land use, transportation, management of food, and the design of buildings are key components to developing a successful city. The larger the areas you can implement climate change solutions in the bigger and more positive should be the impact. City and campus planning is critical. Positive change needs dynamic and consistent leadership, but it also needs resilient institutional change that can last beyond a political or business leader's tenure.

Remember the ideas presented are solutions that in most places would have a financial payback of 7 years or less.

City/ Campus Planning

4.1

There are over 700 cities that will have populations of more than one million by 2030. There are only 10 in the U.S. New York City took the distinction of becoming the first city in the world to report directly to the international community on its efforts to reach global benchmarks in addressing poverty, inequality, and climate change by 2030[3].

"Cities are the spaces where all Sustainable Development Goals (SDGs) can be integrated to provide holistic solutions to the challenges of poverty, exclusion, climate change and risks" —UN-Habitat Executive Director Ms. Maimunah Mohd. Sharif.

4.2 United Nations Sustainable Development Goals

AFFORDABLE SOLUTIONS FOR CLIMATE CHANGE

Good Practices for City Planning:

- Promote urban agriculture

- Encourage healthy diets

- Reduce and manage food waste

- Add green spaces for healthier environments and improved lifestyles

- Reconnect cities with surrounding rural areas

- Build compact and well-connected urban areas with dense network of streets and paths

- Prioritize walking, cycling, and public transportation for access to jobs, social services, and environmental amenities

- Foster transit-oriented developments and mixed-use neighborhoods

- Optimize designs of buildings and neighborhoods to suit local climatic conditions

- Renovate and restore existing buildings

This chapter is organized to focus on the biggest issues first on a city scale, then campus, building, and then using safe, no-carbon materials.

APPROACHES CITIES CAN IMPLEMENT

Building codes and standards: Require new buildings to meet net-zero building codes. Subsidize existing buildings to make sure they meet net-zero building codes. Building owners benefit from long-term savings.

Energy-efficiency targets: Municipalities set mandatory energy-reduction goals for city-administered buildings to be within net zero 2050. Also include projects providing some federal funding to support privately owned projects.

Lead by example: Municipal governments can initiate policies and projects that set an example for the community and foster greater acceptance and demand for energy-efficiency solutions. Cities start with government-owned buildings and pursue pilot projects with the private sector. Many of these projects should be renovations and upgrades, not just new projects.

Engagement strategies: Facilitate occupant feedback.

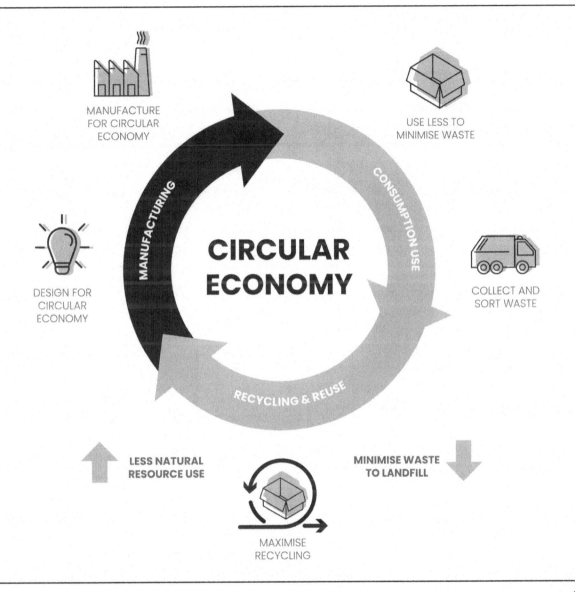

MANUFACTURE FOR CIRCULAR ECONOMY

USE LESS TO MINIMISE WASTE

MANUFACTURING

CONSUMPTION USE

CIRCULAR ECONOMY

DESIGN FOR CIRCULAR ECONOMY

COLLECT AND SORT WASTE

RECYCLING & REUSE

LESS NATURAL RESOURCE USE

MINIMISE WASTE TO LANDFILL

MAXIMISE RECYCLING

4.3

FOCUS ON A CIRCULAR ECONOMY

Understand and plan for the use of a product two, three and more times in a circular economy. Do not simply plan for one time and then throw away as has been done for many products for decades in a linear economy.

Sustainable Cities

CURITIBA: ONE OF THE GLOBAL SUSTAINABLE CITIES ON EARTH

Curitiba's Master Plan limited the growth of the city center and encouraged commercial and service sector development along the transportation arteries. The Master Plan included strategies for economic development and local community self-sufficiency with livable city spaces. The city is public transport-oriented, and its Bus Rapid Transit (BRT) system carries 50 times more passengers than it did 20 years ago. Curitiba's gasoline use per capita is 30 percent below that of 8 comparable Brazilian cities. It has lower greenhouse gas emission levels, less traffic congestion, and more livable urban spaces. **Curitiba adopted an incremental approach to development, whereby the city procured the basic rights of way for critical transport infrastructure systems, then developed the infrastructure when demand justified supply.**

With a population of 1.9 million people, Curitiba is the greenest city in Brazil. This remarkable metropolis has become world renowned for its creative and environmentally conscious solutions to urban planning. The city's environmentally friendly solutions run the gamut from reducing pollution through citywide recycling programs, to maintaining biodiversity in the region by planting 1.5 million trees. There are low carbon emission lanes for buses as well as bike lanes and pedestrian-only streets across the city.

Curitiba, located in Parana State, Brazil, has implemented several innovative systems to create jobs, improve public transportation accessibility, promote housing development, and improve waste management. The city has integrated a "radial linear-branching pattern" to protect density by diverting traffic from the city center and protecting green areas by encouraging industrial development along radial axes. Curitiba has initiated a BRT System and established the Curitiba Industrial City (CIC) on the city's west side, which has strict environmental regulations and does not allow "polluting" industries.

The benefits of the systems are as follows:

- Reduced transportation time: the per capita income loss due to severe congestion is 11 and 7 times lower than in Sao Paulo and Rio de Janeiro, respectively.

- The creation of the CIC has resulted in about 50,000 direct jobs and 150,000 indirect jobs, and about 20 percent of the state's exports are from the CIC.

- Curitiba's fuel usage is 30 percent lower than in Brazil's other major cities.

- Improved outdoor air quality and associated health benefits.

- 70 percent of the city's residents are actively recycling and 13 percent of solid waste is recycled; Property values of neighboring areas have appreciated, and tax revenues have increased.

- Reduced flood mitigation expenditures by promotion of park development in flood-prone areas (the cost of this strategy is estimated to be 5% lower than building concrete canals)[4]. Fast food restaurants in Curitiba serve food on real plates with real silverware for dine-in customers. Most retail stores in Curitiba sell products made from recycled goods. Unrecyclable, single use, and unrecycled products are virtually nonexistent in restaurant industries like the fast-food industry in Curitiba.

The population has doubled since 1974, yet car traffic has declined by 30 percent. The system reduces fuel consumption and air pollution as well as environmental costs of urban mobility. Urban terminals are built at the end of each express bus lane with social services and smaller terminals, which are located every 1,400 meters. The innovative local public transport system is considered as the pioneer of urban development in Curitiba

- 4,000 passengers per day on special bus

- 25 percent less congestion

- public transport is now used by 75 percent of commuters on weekdays

Trinary Roads—Urban growth is also restricted to corridors of growth along key transport routes. Tall buildings are allowed only along bus routes.

4.4

Curitiba's Bus Rapid Transit (BRT) system has the same capacity as light rail but required half the initial investment. Curitiba provides numerous models for undertaking successful, cost-effective sustainability programs that truly reflect the triple bottom line of economics, environment and social equity. The strategic development pattern and BRT system are both relatively easy to implement in existing cities and yield substantive and measurable environmental improvements. This success, however, is contingent upon adhering to a comprehensive master plan that addresses all city functions in a holistic manner, as well as mobilizing the shared interests of city officials and citizens around the city's sustainability initiatives. The original BRT was established as a high-speed transit line that ran through the poor neighborhoods of the city. Over time, this corridor gentrified and pushed out the very people it was intended to serve. It is important to address resiliency and policy making in a holistic manner to make sure as many people as possible benefit and to assure some are not hurt by the changes.

Curitiba, Brazil recycles around 70 percent of its garbage, thanks to a program that allows for the exchange of bus tokens, notebooks, and food in return for recycling. Not only does this protect the environment, but it also boosts education, increases food access, and facilitates transport for the city's poor. Curitibanos recycle **over 70 percent** of their garbage, largely with help from municipal programs that cost no more than the old landfills. Minimizing the landfills reduces methane gases.

The recycling plants are made up of recycled material and employ people who find it hard to get jobs, for example immigrants and disabled people. This makes the employees feel valued and it helps to improve their lives. Color coordinating teams collect the waste that has been separated into inorganic and organic waste. It is then sorted and sent out to other recycling plants to process. Cans are recycled at a fraction of the cost of producing new ones. Nothing is wasted, Books are sent to the public libraries for all to use and artefacts are placed in a museum.

Due to the Free University of Environment located in the middle of Zaninelli's woods, Curitiba became the first city in the world to offer a space to study and transfer knowledge about the environment and ecology to the public. Its architectonic project reveals through rustic materials the four elements: earth, fire, water, and air. Despite the rare beauty, its main goal is to bring about environmental consciousness to the citizens as a way of survival. It was created on June 5, 1991 and inaugurated by the French oceanographer Jacques Cousteau in 1992.

4.5

Curitiba has 28 public parks and surrounded all the urban areas of the city with fields of grass in order to combat flooding. Those fields are maintained using sheep rather than gas-powered lawnmowers. One result is the sheep offset the carbon from gasoline and provide manure and wool for the city and surrounding farms. Many of the smaller parks are dedicated to one of the ethnic groups that have settled in the city. Filled with shrines to the cultures of the world, they are enchanting oases of shade and quiet in the urban environs.

Within the larger tracts of green space, there is a world-class botanical garden and an opera house built in the dramatic setting of an abandoned quarry.

Today, Curitiba is one of the most prosperous cities in Latin America; per capita income is 66 percent higher than the Brazilian average.

Other sustainable cities, according to National Geographic, include London, Frankfurt, Copenhagen, Amsterdam, Rotterdam, Berlin, Madrid, Santiago, San Paulo, Toronto, San Francisco, New Delhi, Wuhan, Mumbai, Manila, Seoul, Jakarta, Dubai and Abu Dhabi. **A sustainable city addresses the environment as well as social and economic issues. Cities do this by improving their infrastructure with environmentally conscious, physical alterations to streets, parks, and buildings.**

SUPPORTING A STRONG PLAN:

1. **Needs**-based—shopping, refreshments, fast track food offers, all within **75m** of each other to reduce excessive walking distances

2. **Wants**-based—welcome facilities, catering/dining and cafes. Each located within **150m** walking distances of each other, located at prominent locations within the site's pedestrian public realm: squares, plazas, gardens, etc.

3. **Destination**-based—interconnecting the needs and wants-based zones within the user journey by introducing museums, interactives, exhibitions, events, and entertainment retail within and along the public realm. Located within **300m** walking distance.

The above 3 types of amenities create a series of overlapping steppingstones. This is intended to link all districts of the campus through visual points along the user journey within a pedestrian emphasis of plazas, squares, lanes, avenues, and passages.

Cities and campuses focus on design and planning strategies for dramatically reducing the environmental impact and exposure of new and existing development. This drawing focuses on a plan to locate renewable energy sources and as well as central plants. This is one effective way to reduce carbon—at a very large scale.

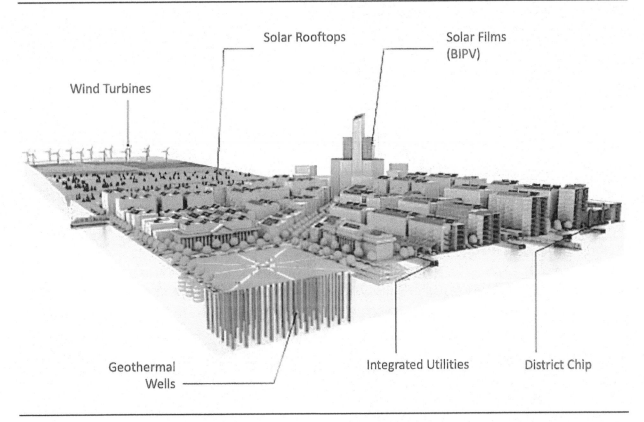

Wind Turbines

Solar Rooftops

Solar Films
(BIPV)

Geothermal
Wells

Integrated Utilities

District Chip

4.6 Sharing City for energy efficient planning.

CITY PLANNING- ENERGY EFFICIENCY

1. Deliver Energy Locally, Just In Time, Just the Right Amount

2. Community Solar Projects- BUY GREEN POWER

3. Battery Storage

4. Minimize Peak Time by Load by Sharing with use distribution to limit peak loads across all utilities and infrastructure.

5. Educate Users and Operators

6. Monitor and Commission Engineering Systems Annually

7. Internet of Things Technology

8. Continued Emphasis on Improvements in Technology and Operations

Vancouver already receives 90 percent of its power from renewable energy sources and is on track to meeting the greenhouse gas reduction targets established in the Kyoto Protocol. The city has already reduced its municipal greenhouse gas emissions to 33 percent below 1990 levels and the city as a whole is close to achieving its goal of 6 percent below 1990 levels. One large contributing factor to the municipal emission reductions was Vancouver's decision to shift its entire taxi fleet to more energy efficient vehicles[5].

Sharing Cities & Citizens

The basic evolution of the city is based on sharing.
People have always shared parks.

Urban design can reduce the average city dweller's carbon footprint by up to 60 percent by shaping lifestyle choices and influencing day-to-day behavior. Compact cities with clustered amenities can shorten average trip lengths. People living in cities on average have less space than those people living outside the city due to a higher density of population and square footage of buildings.

The sharing economy is based on **the exchange, sharing, and collaboration between individuals of goods, services, resources, time and knowledge, with or without monetary exchanges**. McKinsey estimates that in the U.S. and Europe alone, 162 million people or 20-30 percent of the workforce are providers on sharing platforms. June 25, 2019.

The sharing economy is revolutionizing traditional economic models:

Using goods rather than possessing them. No longer do we see it as essential to own a musical recording on a DVD. Equipment is rented more now because people do not want to own it or need it much. Food sharing happens at picnics, potluck dinners, religious and ceremonial events, and street parties many times with the emphasis on ethnic foods.

Putting **service providers in direct contact with consumers** to help them raise concerns for the **environment**. As well as moderating spending and **saving money for consumers**, the sharing economy reduces the environmental impact of individuals by allowing them to minimize waste and excessive consumption.

Some sharing economy companies:

Transport: car sharing (Liftshare), renting between individuals, shared transport vehicles (Uber and Lyft)

Housing: sharing amongst individuals (Airbnb), house sharing (HomeExchange)

Food: catering (Just Eat, Uber Eats is most beneficial when multiple orders to nearby houses can happen.

Used equipment: sale or purchase of secondhand items (Amazon)

Clothing: renting between individuals, selling or buying secondhand clothing (Vinted)

Assistance services between individuals: skills, shopping, childcare

Culture and education: tutoring

Carpooling is a simple way to reduce cost and carbon by coordinating schedules, meeting at a common drop-off or sharing Uber or LFYT rides. Carpooling can help reduce traffic on heavily traveled roads in major cities. Carpool lanes cover thousands of miles of roads across America and make commuting a relative breeze for many drivers every workday. In carpool lanes, only vehicles with multiple occupants are allowed. This allows people who are carpooling to have a lane to themselves, which usually moves at a high speed, even when the rest of the freeway is stuck in stop-and-go traffic. Some cities, like Los Angeles, have two carpool lanes going in the same direction to help with the volume of people that need to move through the city. Many city residents are reducing wasted capacity in commutes by using websites to carpool, or even ditching car ownership altogether in favor of web-facilitated car sharing clubs, which now exist in cities around the globe. A typical car has three parking spaces on average in the U.S. Sharing rides or vehicles will reduce the parking spaces and carbon. Cities with advanced communication technologies make it possible to walk, cycle, or share a ride. Upgrade your commute by carpooling with **the Waze app**. Plan your rides and match with fellow commuters going your way. It's easy, affordable, and eco-friendly.

Websites such as **Streetbank** make it easier for city residents to share other products or pass them on when they are no longer being used. Streetbank puts you in touch with your community, bringing neighborhoods closer and making the world a bit nicer. There are many other options to benefit from.

POLICIES

Companies and governments provide financial incentives for carpools.

Provide free parking spaces for carpooling.

Provide access to specific car lanes without any cost to provide faster and more efficient commutes.

As technology advances on autonomous vehicles use them to maximize carpooling.

City Funding Options

Crowdfunding is the exchange of funds between individuals outside of institutional financing circuits, through a digital platform. Financing can take on the form of subsidies, loans or capital investment. It allows individuals who wish to do business with private funds to connect through platforms such as **Kickstarter, GoFundMe or JustGiving.**

Performance Contracting—make no initial capital investment, decrease energy costs,

and simultaneously reserve available capital for other projects by using an Energy Service Company.

Low Interest Loans—your state energy office can often be the key to funding from other state, federal, and utility programs.

Life Cycle Costing—base decisions not just on initial purchase price, but on the cost of operation over the projected life span or a specific period with a payback.

Public/Private Partnerships—private sector companies can bring capital and expertise to help your city optimize operations and save money.

ATLANTA'S LIFECYCLE BUILDING CENTER sells reusable building materials and home improvement items for the Atlanta community.

Mission: To create environmental stewardship and community resilience by creating a sustainable lifecycle for the built environment.

Vision: To create sustainable communities where the built environment supports the natural environment.

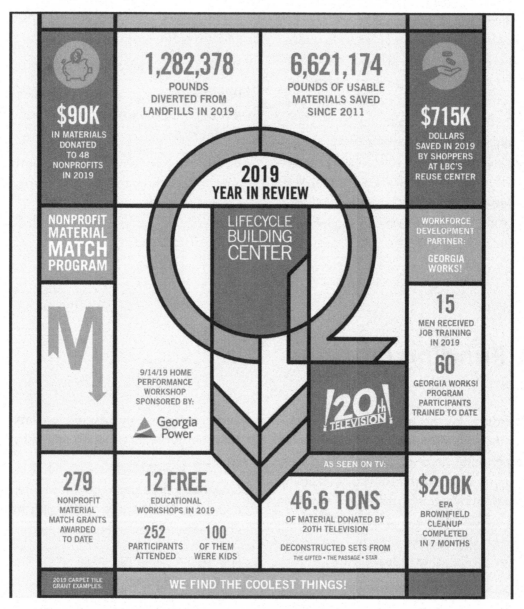

4.7 Every city should have at least one Lifecycle Building Center!

District Heating

District heating is a central plant and pipe network that channels hot water to many buildings. **There is the opportunity to share the heat created from one building to then heat an adjacent building.** For example, a research laboratory building, or hospital generates a significant amount of heat from the equipment it is using. That excess heat generated, sometimes called reheat, can supply adjacent residential and commercial structures, creating a much more energy-efficient and affordable campus.

Getting these two buildings to share the extra heat from the lab building (right) to heat the classroom building (left) **reduced the cooling and heating requirements when combining both buildings**. This project saw a reduction in the carbon footprint of 120 tons each year.

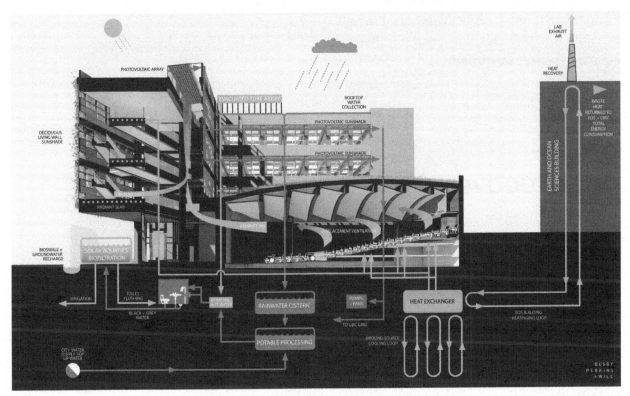

4.8 Sharing excess heat to support adjacent building.

District heating provides thermal energy collectively—and more efficiently than standalone mechanical units at each building. More efficient boilers are often only available or cost-effective in larger sizes. The more space you can manage with the same equipment, the higher, more energy-efficient the solution will be. Look for central heating and cooling plants instead of individual systems for each building. Fat pipes are laid in the ground to supply heat to housing developments, so houses don't need their own boiler.

Project Drawdown defines *district heating* as: a centralized, renewably powered heating system and the distribution of generated heat to the buildings of a defined community, through a network of insulated buried pipes, to satisfy the demand for space heating. Powering renewable district heating systems is possible with biomass, solar, and geothermal energy as well as waste heat.

FINANCIAL COST/PAYBACK

Usually within 1–3 years because you are using waste heat instead of having to cool those spaces.

POLICIES

Tax incentives for using waste heat and creating solutions combining multiple buildings more effectively.

RECOMMENDATION

The buildings should be within a reasonable proximity of the existing heat network, resulting in lower investment in construction to create a good payback as well as using the energy close to the source.

Heat Recovery

The U.S. Department of Energy estimates Americans wash enough energy down the drain every year to power about 30 million homes. Evolving technology is making it easier to harness warm water. Denver is now constructing what is likely the largest sewer heat-recovery project in North America, according to Enwave, a Canadian energy company set to operate the system. It will save on energy costs and avoid greenhouse gas emissions. Enwave's "Sewer Heat Recovery system," an innovative technology that heats and cools buildings with recycled thermal energy from nearby pipelines, will be the largest clean technology system of its kind in North America. Enwave's novel technology will contribute to the city of Denver's climate action plan to reduce carbon emissions. **Using Enwave's system, the 250-acre campus will avoid emitting an estimated 2,600 metric tons of carbon (CO2) per year—the equivalent of eliminating 6.6 million vehicle**

passenger miles driven in Denver annually— and will promote better air quality and health for the surrounding neighborhoods. The benefits of this system include high efficiency, lower capital costs, and a reliable and resilient energy source during outages.

The planned system uses both sewer-heat recovery and a district energy approach. Enwave's system will pull thermal energy from nearby sewer pipes to source nearly 90 percent of the campus's heating and cooling. A heat pump will capture the warmth of wastewater and transfer it to a clean water pipe that enters individual buildings. It is a closed-loop system, meaning the wastewater does not touch the clean water. District energy systems then pump warm water from a central plant to a group of buildings, instead of each building having its own heating and cooling system.

With the advent of large-scale heat pumps, we can cost-effectively use wastewater that is 70°F to heat our buildings and our hot-water systems. **Sewer heat recovery often works best as the heart of a district-size energy system**, where a central plant provides energy to a whole neighborhood or office complex. Ted Smith from the Department of Homeland Security (DHS) explained in his webinar that wastewater treatment can also provide an early warning regarding a virus.

Stanford Energy System Innovations (SESI)

Stanford University has 80 percent of the university's heating demands being met with waste heat that previously was being removed from buildings by the campus cooling system. The waste heat is used to reheat hot water and provide hot air supply to adjacent buildings.

The other 20 percent is covered by purchasing green energy nearby. The university also converted the existing central steam system for heating buildings to a more efficient hot-water system.

Cut total energy required to operate campus in half with:

Heat recovery,

Cold thermal energy storage shifted from ice to cold water,

Heat distribution shifted from steam to hot water,

And heat thermal energy storage added.

50 percent less energy required = 50 percent Greenhouse Gas reduction as a first step,

And 70 percent less water used in energy production = 15 percent total campus water savings.

Shift from gas to electricity

53 percent new renewable electricity = another 25 percent Greenhouse Gas reduction as second step.

Long-term solar PV contracts are at a fixed low cost.

Much flexibility should be preserved for new electricity generation technologies in the future.

Benefits of Heat Recovery

Lower cost.

68 percent Greenhouse Gas reduction and growth.

Flexibility in long-term energy sourcing-electricity can be made in many ways.

Energy Efficiency

If the U.S. invested in energy efficient heating and cooling of buildings, they could fill 20 percent of the urban gap created by today's total emissions. Increasing the energy efficiency of buildings will also speed up and support a higher share of renewables. Less clean energy needed means less investments for grid extension, energy storage, back-up capacities and energy imports. It also means more security of supply[6].

DENSITY

As people live closer together, the average size of their private living space shrinks, their heating and cooling costs decline, and they have less need for individual vehicles. Also, if they are living in housing that is on multiple levels, there is a good possibility that heat is generated from the building to help warm the multiple residents with less energy.

ZERO EMISSION CONSTRUCTION SITES

An important steppingstone is to launch zero-emission construction sites, to bring down CO_2 emissions as well as reduce noise and pollution. Today several pilot projects have been initiated in Copenhagen. The city of Copenhagen plans to enter partnerships with private and public organizations to ensure more zero emission constructions sites.

Do an Energy Checkup on All City-owned Facilities

- Insulate hot water pipes and heaters
- Shut off unused lights and equipment
- Install motion detectors and timers on thermostats and lights
- Clean or replace cooling coils, steam traps, and fans to ensure efficient operation
- Fix broken dampers
- Turn down hot water temperature
- Implement telecommuting and flexible schedules for city personnel
- Purchase energy-efficient office equipment and appliances

Lighting retrofits, steam traps, and LEDs usually pay for themselves in less than 2 years. Most energy efficiency improvements suggested above have a 2– to 5–year payback.

Overland Park, Kansas, replaced 2,023 red traffic lights with LED fixtures, with annual savings of more than $160,000. The investment was paid back in less than 18 months.

Healthy Built Environments

Public Health: All-electric buildings improve indoor air quality and health by eliminating natural gas combustion inside homes. As we move forward to address climate change, we need to make sure all decisions support both energy efficiency and our health. The following is a summary of evidence-based solutions that should be affordable and support health in urban environments:

1. Incorporate a mix of land uses

2. Design well-connected street networks at the human scale

3. Provide sidewalks and enticing, pedestrian-oriented streetscapes

4. Provide infrastructure to support biking

5. Design stairs to encourage everyday use

6. Provide high-quality spaces for multigenerational play and recreation

7. Accommodate a grocery store

8. Host a farmers' market

9. Support on-site gardening and farming

10. Ban smoking

11. Use materials and products that support healthy indoor air quality

12. Facilitate proper ventilation and airflow

13. Maximize indoor lighting quality

14. Minimize noise pollution

15. Increase access to nature, plant trees

16. Facilitate social engagement

17. Adopt pet-friendly policies

For more information, go to ULI Building Healthy Places Toolkit by the Urban Land Institute: http://uli.org/wp-content/uploads/ULI-Documents/Building-Healthy-Places-Toolkit.pdf.

Create Bike/Bus/ Emergency Vehicle Lanes!

The 15-minute neighborhood. In Paris, the mayor is using the Rue de Rivoli as a prototype for a future metropolis in which no Parisian would need to travel more than 15 minutes on foot or by bike to work, shop, or work with a government agency. This is a lifestyle many ideally prefer and expect more cities and towns to focus on this type of planning. This is another idea that goes back several decades to when we had wonderful 15-minute neighborhoods before the cars became dominant.

No matter whether a person has commuted on public transit, parked in a remote lot, walked out the door of nearby student/faculty housing, or come from a long evening practicum at a hospital, every person on the campus is a pedestrian at some point in their day. In many ways, this is the most important movement system on a campus because it provides clarity and safety in finding the shortest paths in addition to offering sunlight, wind, and sun protection, a colorful landscape and access to buildings along the way.

The pedestrian experience is the foremost quality of high-performing communities. When a campus is designed well, pedestrians have priority over automobiles. It is important for people to be able to enjoy the outdoors while walking from place to place. Locate buildings logically near one another that have common programs that people need to use. Allow for spaces outdoors to sit and talk. The walking distances should be studied and minimized to encourage people to walk. For many campus plans, the pedestrian experience is the highest priority.

The pedestrian experience should continue into the building with thoughtful design and way finding. There should be easy transitions from outdoors to indoors.

Urban Trees

"Wherever a tree can grow, we should plant one." — Sir David Attenborough.

Planting many more trees is a big initiative in many places around the world. There are many ways trees can be added to truly add value to our cities and our campuses. **Urban trees that create shade are very important to reduce the heat island effect and can reduce the temperature by 10 degrees or more in many locations** compared to areas that are in direct sunlight. Trees can help drop the temperature through photosynthesis and transpiration.

The masses of concrete, metal, and glass in urban areas can make them warmer than the surrounding landscape due to the way they absorb, emit, and reflect heat. Cities are hotter than the open countryside. With large cement structures absorbing heat and obstructing the natural cooling process, the difference in temperature can be as high as 1.8–5.4°F during the day and a whopping 22°F in the evening.

Therefore, urban trees are very important, and each city should be able to plant more trees along their streets, in parks, in surface parking areas, and on underutilized land. Cars perform better when in the shade during hot days.

Streets with little or no shade need to be repaved twice as often as those with tree cover[7].

- 1 acre of trees produces enough oxygen for 18 people.

- A man of average height and weight would weigh 10 pounds less if he lived in a walkable neighborhood. A woman of average size would weigh six pounds less.

- Strategically placed trees around a home can reduce summer cooling costs by as much as 30 percent, while winter heating costs can be reduced by a similar percentage using trees as windbreaks.

- Trees act as natural water filters and help significantly slow the movement of stormwater, which lowers total runoff volume, soil erosion, and flooding.

On average, low-income neighborhoods have about 15 percent less tree cover and are 2.7°F (1.5°C) hotter than high income areas. A California study found that every $1 spent on tree planting and maintenance in urban areas returns $5.82 in benefits.

Cities have been losing approximately 4 million trees each year, or 1.3 percent of the total urban tree stock[8].

Each neighborhood should have a Tree Committee that helps to identify unhealthy trees in the public domain as well as have a plan to add healthy trees to the neighborhood.

Low- and moderate-income families should try to grow and plant more trees along their streets, in parks, in surface parking areas, and on underutilized land. If **each family was able to contribute one tree to their community each year,** that would help considerably to create a more sustainable and healthier environment. People can volunteer to plant trees. Plant a specific tree on a street to provide a very strong image, like in Philadelphia where there are Chestnut and Walnut Streets, to name a few.

The Nature Conservatory (TNC) combines and analyzes data from a variety of sources, including satellite-based measurements of tree cover, areas where trees can be planted in cities, land surface temperatures, and socio-economic variables.

4.9 Urban trees are critical to successful cities.

In California, an annual investment of **$467 million for urban afforestation using The Nature Conservatory's prioritization pathways will lead to $712 million of net annual benefits and serve 89 percent of the approximately 9 million residents in the lowest income quartiles of the state's cities.**[9]

Lower temperatures can save lives. One recent study estimated that more than 5,000 people die each year in the U.S. from heat-related illness. Other researchers found that in a large majority of American cities, people of color were more likely to live in neighborhoods that suffer from hotter temperatures, driven in part by a lack of tree cover[10].

Heat Island Effect

Elevated temperatures from urban heat islands, particularly during the summer, can affect a community's environment and quality of life. While some heat island impacts seem positive, such as lengthening the plant-growing season, most impacts are negative and include:

- Increased energy consumption
- Elevated emissions of air pollutants and greenhouse gases
- Compromised human health and comfort
- Impaired water quality.

Studies show that increasing a city's green area by 10 percent could compensate for the temperature increase caused by climate change: vegetation helps to block shortwave radiation while also evaporating water, cooling the ambient air and creating more comfortable microclimates. Tree canopies and root systems can also reduce stormwater flows and balance nutrient loads[11].

In Cleveland, a coalition of city agencies, nonprofit organizations, and corporations has endorsed an ambitious plan to expand tree coverage from its current level of 19 percent of the city to 30 percent by 2040.

Urban Planning with Nature-based Solutions for Adaptation

Trees and vegetation shade buildings and surfaces, while water evaporating through their leaves lowers nearby air temperatures.

Locate:

Trees on the east, west, southeast, and southwest sides of a building (east, west, northeast, and northwest in southern latitudes).

Ground cover and shrubs around buildings lower air temperatures and reduce reflected sunlight.

Trees in courtyards, parking areas, and adjacent walkways.

Nations should properly plant and protect as many trees as possible—to absorb carbon dioxide from the atmosphere, provide habitat for animals, restore fragile ecosystems, and provide shade to cool the microclimate. Trees should also be harvested for use in construction and other areas which help landowners get compensation for their trees. People should be advised on the best way to plant, maintain, harvest, then replant to be successful and sustainable.

GREEN ROOFS

Chicago, IL, planted rooftop gardens to reduce energy demand and lower temperatures in the city. The 20,300-square-foot garden on top of City Hall will save an estimated $4,000 annually on the city's air conditioning and heating bill and will reduce ozone pollution and smog.[12]

This system uses a thick layer of soil, often **several inches deep**, spread across a flat roof. Sometimes, a raised garden bed may be used to cultivate a more diverse range of plants. Those can include vegetables. The large amount of nutritious soil people uses there allows for larger plants and trees to flourish.

Intensive green roofs are often on commercial buildings. The structure must be sturdy enough to bear the weight. They often require more maintenance than other types of rooftop gardens. On a macro scale, green roofs help combat the urban heat island effect as well. This is the tendency for the impermeable surfaces in cities—streets, sidewalks, rooftops, walls, parking lots, other cement and asphalt structures—to absorb heat throughout the day and hold onto it at night. That means our cities are as much as 5 degrees hotter than surrounding countryside during the day,

and up to 2-5 degrees Fahrenheit hotter at night.

Rooftop gardens employ some of the best insulation around: **soil and vegetation**. Hot, sunny days can cause the tops of buildings to reach mind-boggling numbers, even as high as 150°F. Without an insulating layer, this heat will naturally pass through the building as its concrete exterior acts as a conductor. It's not uncommon for residents to spend **70 percent** of their electricity bill on cooling costs. By implementing a simple rooftop garden, buildings could save as much as 50 percent on their average electricity expenditure.

One study found the amount of energy saved in the summer by Canadian buildings with rooftop gardens to be 20 percent for the upper floor. This translates into a 6% decrease of energy consumption for the entire building if it is five or more floors, and 10-12 percent if the building only consists of two floors. Green roofs have been found to reduce water run-off by an average of 50 percent, allowing cities to retain healthy amounts of water that can keep them cool when the sun comes out again.

Rooftop gardens can produce food right where the demand for it is at its highest. Growing food in the center of a city reduces transportation costs. That's because customers are in the direct vicinity of the farm. The food produced on these rooftops is often more nutritious than other food on the plate. That's due to its freshness and the lack of processing people need to do to preserve it. Rooftop gardens not only reduce stress and incidents of mental strain, but they increase productivity. Offices that include a considerable amount of greenery have been found to boost the productivity of employees by up to 15 percent[13].

POLICIES

Provide tax incentives to plant 3" round or larger hardwood trees in residential neighborhoods, along streets, in parks, and surface parking lots to create shade to reduce the temperature in the microclimate. Make sure the trees are planted well, protected, have room to grow, and are maintained to assure growth into mature trees.

Resilient Design

Areas of Resilience for both Cities and Buildings:
Engineering + Economic + Social + Resources + Ecological

Resilient design for buildings and communities can survive, recover, grow, and thrive when facing acute shock events or long-term stressors, through a combination of diversity, foresight, and the capacity for self-organization and learning. A resilient society can withstand shocks and rebuild itself when necessary. It requires humans to embrace their capacity to anticipate, plan, and adapt for the future.

Make sure any solutions you move forward with to address climate change should also include resilient design solutions. Focus on "climate resilient development." Between 2010 and 2020, 15 times more people died from floods, droughts, and storms in very vulnerable regions, including parts of Africa,

South Asia, and Central and South America, than in other parts of the world.

Build Back Better.

Hurricane Maria that hit Puerto Rico in 2015 set back their infrastructure by 2 decades. The new infrastructure will focus on clean energy, resiliency, and better policies. Unfortunately, the last governor pushed a very fossil dependent plan for gas, which benefits a bunch of private gas companies. While people in Puerto Rico believe it is necessary to have diversity of resources, most of the population is clearly for renewable energy. **Unfortunately making the wrong decisions after a natural disaster makes addressing climate change at least twice as difficult.**

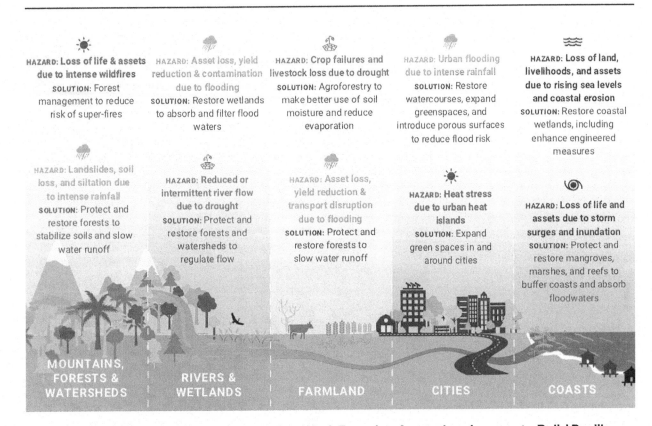

HAZARD: **Loss of life & assets due to intense wildfires** SOLUTION: Forest management to reduce risk of super-fires

HAZARD: Asset loss, yield reduction & contamination due to flooding SOLUTION: Restore wetlands to absorb and filter flood waters

HAZARD: **Crop failures and livestock loss due to drought** SOLUTION: Agroforestry to make better use of soil moisture and reduce evaporation

HAZARD: Urban flooding due to intense rainfall SOLUTION: Restore watercourses, expand greenspaces, and introduce porous surfaces to reduce flood risk

HAZARD: **Loss of land, livelihoods, and assets due to rising sea levels and coastal erosion** SOLUTION: Restore coastal wetlands, including enhance engineered measures

HAZARD: Landslides, soil loss, and siltation due to intense rainfall SOLUTION: Protect and restore forests to stabilize soils and slow water runoff

HAZARD: **Reduced or intermittent river flow due to drought** SOLUTION: Protect and restore forests and watersheds to regulate flow

HAZARD: Asset loss, yield reduction & transport disruption due to flooding SOLUTION: Protect and restore forests to slow water runoff

HAZARD: **Heat stress due to urban heat islands** SOLUTION: Expand green spaces in and around cities

HAZARD: **Loss of life and assets due to storm surges and inundation** SOLUTION: Protect and restore mangroves, marshes, and reefs to buffer coasts and absorb floodwaters

MOUNTAINS, FORESTS & WATERSHEDS

RIVERS & WETLANDS

FARMLAND

CITIES

COASTS

4.10 Different Nature–based Solutions Can Work Together Across Landscapes to Build Resilience

Over the next three decades, the cost of flood damage is on pace to rise 26 percent due to climate change alone. Flooding is the most frequent and costliest natural disaster in the United States. As the atmosphere warms, it holds about 7 percent more moisture for every degree Celsius that the temperature rises, meaning more moisture is available to fall as rain, potentially raising the risk of inland flooding.

POLICIES:

1. **The U.S. government, when assisting other countries and companies, should mandate all monies be invested in sustainable and renewable technologies.**

2. **Require all homeowners who live in a flood plain to purchase flood insurance.**

3. **Discourage any new construction in flood plains.**

4. **Require housing provided after a natural disaster to be built as permanent housing, not temporary.**

4.11 Boston Harbor at a normal water level.

Recommendation: New housing must be built outside the 100-year flood plain.

4.12 A real-life scene of Boston Harbor in the 100-year flood plain

Case Study

Despite the narrow miss of Hurricane Sandy, Spalding Hospital dealt with a different form of devastation just one year later. Having opened its doors just 12 days earlier, the hospital was put into overtime to deal with the shock of the Boston Marathon tragedy. "Sometimes you have to wonder if there's a higher power at work when the city's rehabilitation hospital opens up just as the city needs it most," said Tim Sullivan, director of communications for the Spaulding Rehabilitation Hospital.

The project team researched and tested each component of the design to ensure that the needs of the widest possible audience are addressed, irrespective of ability. And not only is 75 percent of the first floor open to the public, but the design team included a pool, a conference center, and both indoor and outdoor dining that is open to the community. The hospital allows clinicians to have almost unlimited tools to work with patients in novel ways from the gym, the halls and outdoors on the main level.

The Spaulding Rehabilitation Hospital took a holistic design approach that merged both resilience and sustainability strategies to deal with environmental and social issues. The building is designed with vegetated roofs to mitigate storm water runoff and reduce cooling loads and heat-island effect. There are therapeutic terraces on the third and fourth floors to serve as places of respite for patients, staff and families.

Early warning systems save lives and assets worth at least 10 times their cost. Just 24 hours warning of a coming storm or heat wave can cut the ensuing damage by 30 percent and spending $800 million on such systems in developing countries would avoid losses of $3-16 billion per year. **Making infrastructure more climate-resilient can add about 3 percent to the up-front costs but has benefit-cost ratios of about 4:1.** With trillions of dollars in projected infrastructure investments between 2020 and 2030, the potential benefits of early adaptation are enormous[15].

The following are important points to remember when driving in flood conditions:

- Six inches of water will reach the bottom of most passenger cars causing loss of control and possible stalling.

- A foot of water will float many vehicles.

- Two feet of rushing water can carry away most vehicles including Sport Utility Vehicles (SUVs) and pick-ups.

Floods are one of the most common and widespread of all disasters. The following checklist will help your business stay afloat even if the worst happens. Most businesses can save between 20-90% on the cost of stock and moveable equipment by taking proactive action. Warming, rising seas will not only create further disturbances in ocean salinity and pollution levels—they will also force massive shifts in the livelihoods of the nearly 30 percent of the world's population that lives along its coasts. Please review and use the Flood Preparedness Checklist:

BEFORE THE FLOOD

Have a central point of contact.

Have all contact information available and distributed.

Encourage the local population to evacuate the area to safer ground.

Review Emergency Plan with the team.

Take steps to prevent the release of dangerous chemicals. Locate the gas main and electrical shutoffs. Anchor all fuel tanks.

Postpone any deliveries of goods by couriers.

Provide centers for storage of wood, food, and supplies.

Locate Centers for people to go to be safe and provide electric backup systems to allow charging of cell phones.

Establish emergency communication method; identify meeting place and time for crisis team; use smart phones.

Update disaster recovery kits.

Maintain accurate inventory of product on site.

Use plugs to prevent floodwater from backing into sewer drains.

DURING THE FLOOD

Safety is the priority.

Raise the elevators to the 2nd floor and turn them off.

Send unneeded staff home.

Have cell phones, chargers, and emergency kits with you and available to use.

Take critical hardware with you.

Unplug electrical items in home.

AFTER THE FLOOD

Implement Disaster Relief Plan.

Listen to news reports to determine if the water is safe to drink.

Avoid floodwaters.

Clean and disinfect everything that got wet. Mud left from the floodwater can contain sewage and chemicals.

Plan the next steps, then communicate with the team, then the public.

Contact insurance agent.

Get government support to build permanent housing and rebuild as necessary to be more resilient.

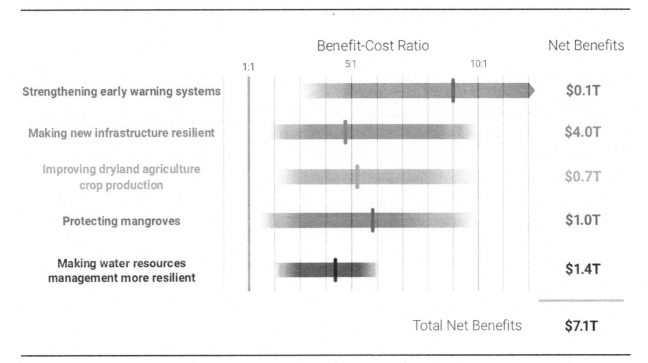

Benefit-Cost Ratio		Net Benefits
Strengthening early warning systems		$0.1T
Making new infrastructure resilient		$4.0T
Improving dryland agriculture crop production		$0.7T
Protecting mangroves		$1.0T
Making water resources management more resilient		$1.4T
	Total Net Benefits	$7.1T

4.13 Benefits and Costs Investments In Adaptation

The graph is meant to illustrate a broad economic case for investment in a range of adaptation approaches. Resilient design has a significant payback when implemented[16].

Food

Subsidize food operators to encourage the use of healthier ingredients. Provide space for farmers' markets. Citywide measures should be managed for recovering safe and nutritious food and redistributing it through charities and food banks. Composting or utilizing discarded food to generate energy can make a huge impact in reducing food waste. Allow rooftops to grow food and then sell locally.

Transportation Models

Think BIG with major urban projects.

Investments in a community's walkability typically increases land value by 70 to 300 percent and retail sales by 30 percent[17].

One of the biggest challenges facing cities is their carbon emissions from transport. Some cities are already trying to reduce these, along with other types of pollution from vehicles, by introducing ultra-Low Emission Zones (ULEZ).

Cities become more vibrant with a focus on people, their health as well as the health of the environment. The following is a great example from Seoul, South Korea called the Cheonggyecheon Stream Restoration Project.

This particular project is about taking down highways and reintroducing parks and other public areas, instead of focusing on cars. This is a great success story and a beneficial operation for cities.

The planning issues to focus on are:

Removal of highways,

Reintegration of beneficial public spaces,

Increased reliance on public transport,

Automobiles are no longer the priority. Pedestrians are the highest priority in great cities.

Cheonggyecheon Stream Restoration in Seoul, South Korea

Performance Benefits

- Contributed to 15.1 percent increase in bus ridership and 3.3 percent in subway ridership in Seoul between 2003 and the end of 2008.

- Increased the price of land by 30-50 percent for properties within 50 meters of the restoration project. This is double the rate of property increases in other areas of Seoul.

- Increased number of businesses by 3.5 percent in Cheonggyecheon area during 2002-2003, which was double the rate of business growth in downtown Seoul; increased the number of working people in the Cheonggyecheon area by 0.8 percent, versus a decrease in downtown Seoul of 2.6 percent.

- Attracts an average of 64,000 visitors daily. Of those, 1,408 are foreign tourists who contribute up $1.9 million in visitor spending to the Seoul economy.

There are hundreds of great examples and success stories across the world at the following website created by urban designer and visionary Yuval Fogelson18.

ELECTRIC VEHICLE (EV) CHARGING

One key issue for city planners and policy makers is addressing EV charging stations. Charging the batteries is easy but misunderstood by most. Eighty percent of the population has the ability to plug in where they live. Superchargers are needed for people traveling more than 300 miles in a day, or do not have the ability to plug in where they live.

The average commute is 32 miles. If one plugs into a standard home outlet that you have throughout your home, it will charge four miles an hour. Charging overnight for nine hours will provide 35+ miles of charge. This is the basis of the design of the Nissan Leaf.

The next level up is a Type 2 charger, which many people install at home, that runs off a 40- or 50-volt breaker and provides 25-30 miles of charge an hour. If you charge your car overnight, then you will be able to fully charge a 30-mile capacity battery.

The Superchargers are Type 3 and can charge 300 miles within an hour. There currently exist superchargers along most federal highways within 100 miles of each other. This works very well for Tesla owners, but Tesla needs to allow others to have an adapter to be able to plug in any electric car to the Tesla superchargers. This is the fastest and most affordable way to grow the EV charging station infrastructure.

The following are recommendations to consider, depending on the building use:

Residential homes: Type 1 and 2 chargers

Airports: Type 1 outlets at each column to allow for cars that will be parked for one day or more to be fully charged. Add 5 percent of spaces for type 2 Chargers for single day travelers. Have Superchargers located in short-term parking.

Hotels: Type 2

Retail/ Main Street/ Malls: Type 2 with some Superchargers

Grocery Stores/ Restaurants: Superchargers

Sporting Venues: Type 1 and 2

Hospitals: Type 2 Chargers with some Superchargers

Parking Decks: Type 1 outlets at each column to allow for cars that will be parked for one day or more to be fully charged. Add 5 percent of spaces for type 2 Chargers for single day travelers. Have Superchargers located in short-term parking.

The various charging stations should be enough to allow the driver to arrive home safely, then charge up as needed. As a driver for five years with my EV, I have never had any problem with the charging. Consider building community solar structures above the charging stations to allow for the electricity in the daytime to come from the sun. Soon, battery storage will be available to allow renewable electricity at many of the charging stations.

4.14 The future of supercharging!

Solutions to Implement

AMERICAN CITIES' CLIMATE CHALLENGE

This is a detailed guide for cities on the considerations and steps involved for a city to procure different types of renewable energy. The procurement guidance provides six business models to help city governments and private developers/companies effectively and efficiently understand associated processes, tools, and best practices in order to facilitate successful implementation of municipal renewable energy projects. **These solutions are critical for cities to focus on and implement!**

1. COMMUNITY SOLAR

This is a local renewable solar energy system that serves many customers. The electric distribution company is usually a partner with the renewable energy developer. The renewable electricity production is directly credited to the building owner's utility bill as if the renewable energy system were located on site. The building owner pays an up-front fee for the program participation. Another option is the building owner subscribes to the program and pays for renewable energy through a premium on the monthly utility bill.

2. RENEWABLE ENERGY INVESTMENT FUND

A monetary account is set up to accept payment from building owners or developers. The managing entity would install renewable energy systems on behalf of the building owner or otherwise invest the proceeds in renewable energy projects with a similar impact. The building owner pays an up-front fee for program participation. The building owner contributes to the program with monthly or annual payments.

3. VIRTUAL PPA

The buyer, building owner, guarantees a minimum price for electricity produced by a renewable energy project, enabling the renewable energy developer to secure funding for construction and operation.

4. SELF-OWNED

A renewable energy system is constructed on a separate property owned and managed by the building owner. I have a net-zero house, where I built a very energy-efficient structure by adding 30 solar panels and two battery storage units.

5. GREEN ELECTRICITY PRICING

A special tariff offered by electric distribution companies or community choice aggregates whereby 100 percent renewable energy is purchased on behalf of participating customers. There are three models: 1. The renewable electricity is purchased from a specific energy generator along with the renewable energy certificates. 2. The obligation is met through the purchase of unbundled renewable energy certificates (RECs) that meet the requirements of the state's renewable portfolio standards. 3. Not applicable in states with Renewable Portfolio Standards (RPS) requirements.

6. UTILITY RENEWABLE ENERGY CONTRACT

A special bilateral contract with the local electric distribution company to purchase 100 percent renewable energy or Renewable Energy Certificates (RECs) on behalf of the building owner. There are three models here also: 1. The renewable electricity is purchased from a specific renewable energy generator along with the RECs. 2. The obligation is met through the purchase of unbundled RECs that meet the requirements of the state's renewable portfolio standards. This is not applicable in states with Renewable Portfolio Standards requirements. 3. The obligation is met through the purchase of non-qualifying RECs.

Ideas for the Future

GREEN DREAMS was a research and design project at Delft University of Technology Why Factory. The following are two very exciting ideas.

4.15 Sunny Water Lilies floating solar thermal power plants.

On each island, our artificial beaches, restaurants, and hotels with the solar flowers generate the energy needed. This project was proposed in Thailand as a potential tourist attraction.

4.16 Food racks in Barcelona by Nicola Placella and Magnus Svensson. The regular city blocks form a base for modular three-story greenhouses and food shelves. Crops are grown inside vertical gardens!

There are great ideas and opportunities for cities to consider!

5

BUILDINGS
REDUCE CARBON

The information presented is in the order that these issues would be typically discussed and decisions made during the initial development of a project and the design process involving the owner, contractors, architects, engineers, cost estimators and other experts.

Embodied Carbon

Can you work with an existing structure, or do you need to build all new construction?

Is it better to renovate an existing structure or to build all new?

Whenever possible, try to work with an existing building. Renovating existing buildings is an excellent opportunity to minimize embodied carbon in a project. If you renovate and reuse existing buildings—typically the structure, foundation and possibly exterior walls are maintained, saving up to 50 percent of your carbon on the project. Embodied carbon, which is responsible for 72 percent of all CO_2 emissions of new buildings, and 11 percent of general emissions worldwide, has already been spent in the initial construction.

As the world builds the equivalent of an entire New York City every month, reducing the carbon emissions of materials is an imperative. While we've made great progress improving the energy efficiency of building operations, the next frontier is reducing embodied carbon in buildings—the emissions from material manufacturing and construction processes.

Buildings consume over 31 percent of global energy use. The global building inventory is expected to double in floor area by 2060. 47 percent of the greenhouse gases are related to the building industry. The manufacture of building materials makes up 11 percent of total annual global greenhouse gas emissions[1].

Embodied carbon represents emissions from building materials and construction and typically represents 28 percent of global building sector emissions. The operational carbon that's inherent in buildings is emitted through the functional use, management, and maintenance of the building, and will escalate over the building's life cycle. Every year, 20 billion square feet of buildings are constructed. The embodied carbon emission of that construction is approximately 3729 million metric tons CO_2 per year. The chart below shows the importance of focusing on opportunities to reduce carbon throughout the building process, not just construction and operations.

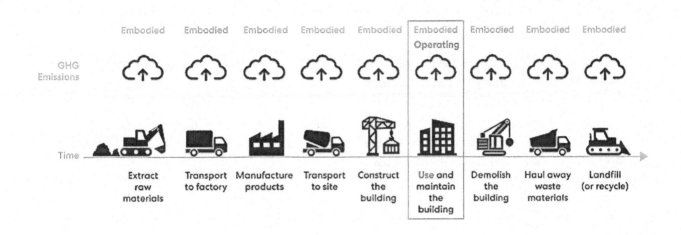

GHG
Emissions

Time

Embodied — Extract raw materials
Embodied — Transport to factory
Embodied — Manufacture products
Embodied — Transport to site
Embodied — Construct the building
Embodied / Operating — Use and maintain the building
Embodied — Demolish the building
Embodied — Haul away waste materials
Embodied — Landfill (or recycle)

5.1 Embodied carbon timeline

Building reuse and incorporation of salvaged building materials can greatly reduce the embodied carbon of construction.

Before a building is inhabited, it has created a huge carbon footprint. One way to get a clear picture of how one material or system compares to another in the context of a building project is to use **Whole- Building Life-Cycle Assessment, or WBLCA**[2]**.** This process looks at multiple impacts of building materials, including global warming potential, over their entire life cycle—from extraction and manufacturing through the landfill or recycling plant. Owners, architects and engineers are focusing on reducing the environmental impact of the built environment. **Life- Cycle Assessment is computer modeled** for project to assist in better understanding the energy for procurement, during construction, operation and decommissioning.

Users can learn more about the **Carbon Smart Materials Palette** on the Architecture 2030 website[3]. The palette includes the material's basic attributes, information about how the material is produced, where its embodied carbon footprint comes from, and design guidance for reducing its footprint.

Key Material Strategies

So one opportunity when looking to reduce the embodied carbon of a project is to focus on the structural system. Concrete, steel, and wood can all be optimized in different ways to reduce impacts. Wood should be the first choice for most new construction. Concrete is about getting cement content down and using only what you need. Getting the structural engineer in direct dialogue with the ready-mix supplier is essential to this approach.

Steel has a much higher embodied carbon footprint than concrete does—with one ton of steel representing approximately a ton of greenhouse gas emissions. Steel production is responsible for 6.6 percent of greenhouse gas emissions globally. **Reducing the embodied carbon of steel on a project by specifying steel produced in North America ideally that has been recycled.**

It has now become even more important to look at the embodied energy; the energy used to produce a building. This embodied energy could account for 45 percent of the environmental impact of the building, considering its total lifespan in a low-energy house. Many building materials used today are also still based on fossil fuels and their derivatives, which means a high level of embodied energy.

Prevention (of waste) is the highest level in the waste hierarchy, followed by reuse, recycling, and recovery, and the lowest level is disposal.

Embodied carbon reduction benefits communities with less areas destroyed by mining, less air pollution, more circular jobs, less fossil fuels used, less heavy transport, and less congested landfills.

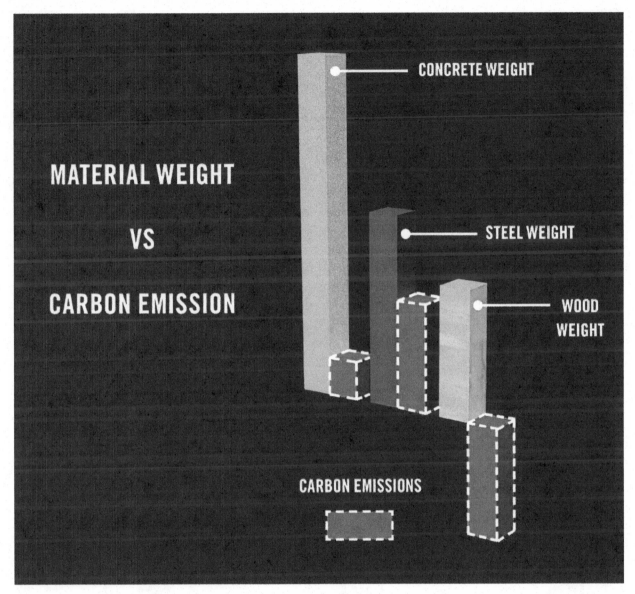

CONCRETE WEIGHT

MATERIAL WEIGHT

VS

CARBON EMISSION

STEEL WEIGHT

WOOD
WEIGHT

CARBON EMISSIONS

5.2 Comparison of carbon for wood, concrete and steel

When you start playing around with window-to-wall ratios, you can have quite a big impact because of glass wall's footprint. The embodied carbon of glass (curtainwall), not to mention the aluminum shading systems that often come with it, is just one more reason to minimize the use of aluminum, since it has operational energy impacts as well[4].

Wood

If 50% of construction switched from steel and concrete to wood construction, that would be a drop in 8 percent of global carbon emissions—and in many parts of the world, there is enough wood that can be farmed and not take away from natural sequestration from preserved forests and other natural sources. The U.S. has more than enough trees to support wood construction.

Wood is produced by solar energy, making it the only renewable building material. One cubic meter of wood sequesters approximately one ton of greenhouse gas as opposed to other building materials that generate greenhouse gas.

Wood is 75 percent lighter than concrete. This allows for taller construction on poor soils, smaller foundations and additions onto existing structures. Wood has a very high strength to weight ratio.

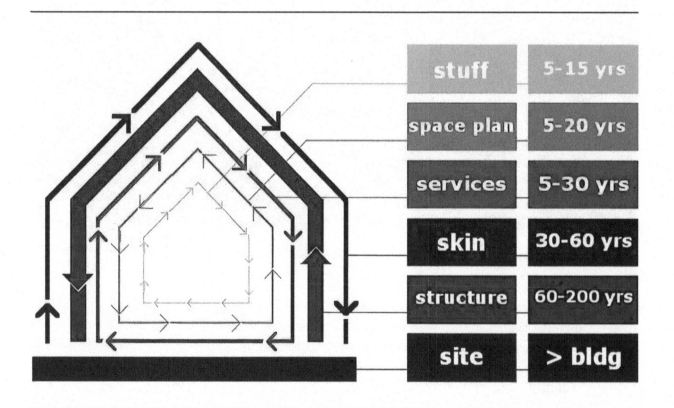

5.3 Different layers of the building and their expected life.

The building codes have been updated to allow for wood structures up to 12 stories with the wood elements exposed. If the wood is enclosed in gypsum board then 18 stories is allowed. Using light-weight gypsum that requires less water in the manufacturing process, and minimizing the waste are impactful ways to reduce the carbon footprint for gypsum board.

Innovative new wood products and building systems are coming into the marketplace that will allow designers, engineers, and builders to expand the range of wood products used in buildings. **Nationally more than 70 percent of commercial buildings could be built with wood.**

PRE-ENGINEERED WOOD

Pre-engineered wood construction is an alternative building material that is carbon neutral for homes and offices. **It is structurally feasible to build mid-rise wood buildings in the range of 4 to 18 stories.**

 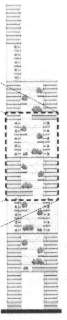 

5.4 Pre-engineered wood design

This relatively new technology has just been approved in the International Building Codes (IBC) 2021 version and includes three new construction types—Type IV-A, IV-B and IV-C—allowing the use of mass timber or noncombustible materials up to 18 stories. This will work for many new construction projects.

Environmental benefits: Wood sequesters carbon and supports a high performing envelope for efficient operation. Using wood responsibly is part of a healthy forest ecosystem. Environmental benefits also include long-term carbon sequestration, reduced greenhouse gas emissions, smaller energy footprint, and shift to renewable resources

Economic benefits: Off-site fabrication, precision cut and fit, significantly reduces overall construction time and simplifies on-site construction. Shorter financing timelines, smaller crews, simple tools, easy delivery to site as flat packed or volumetric components. It's lighter, so foundations and footings require less concrete, enclosure is complete quickly for less exposure to weather. Depending on your location, typology, and product, mass timber product is competitively priced with concrete or steel structure. Landowners benefit by selling their trees. Sustainable communities in rural areas depend on both the economic return from harvesting timber as well as having sawmill and other wood dependent industries operating to provide jobs, taxes, and other revenues.

Now there are many complete or well into design and construction wood structures around the world. You can check them all out on the woodwork's web site, or on RethinkWood.com.

FINANCIAL PAYBACK

Immediately compared to steel or concrete.

POLICIES

Provide tax incentives and grants to support pre-engineered wood buildings.

Most new federal buildings should first consider using pre-engineered wood over steel and concrete.

RECOMMENDATION

Educate the public, developers, and clients as well as architectural and engineering professionals on the benefits of wood construction. The biggest challenge now is changing social perceptions of mass timber, so the industry has a green light to step up development.

Focus on building regional manufacturing facilities across the country.

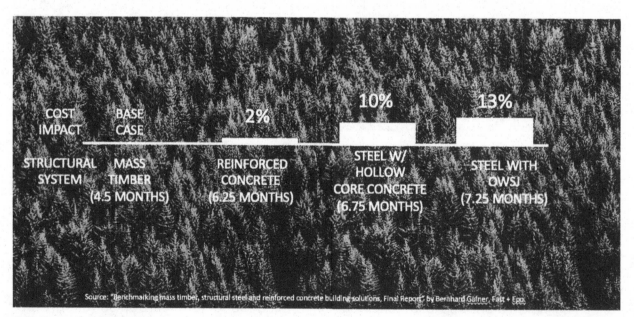

5.5 Construction Time

Concrete

Concrete is the most abundant substance on Earth after water. **Once the concrete is made, the carbon is in the concrete forever.**

- **Cement makes up 12 percent of the concrete but has 95 percent of the carbon in the concrete.**

- **7 percent of the world's CO_2 emissions. (International Energy Agency)**

- **Cement-free, Carbon-negative Concrete.**

- **Improve cement mix and reduce carbon by 40 percent. Fly ash is one option.**

The two most common methods of laying concrete are ready-mix and precast. Ready-mix is manufactured in a plant and then transferred in cement mixers to the building sites. Precast concrete utilizes reusable molds to prepare, cast, and cure the concrete in a controlled environment. Molds reduce any potential errors and make it quicker and more efficient to produce large amounts of identical components, such as wall panels, staircases, pipes, and tunnels. Precast concrete has several advantages, including lower labor and transport costs, and is a growing industry. If the global precast concrete industry switched to the **carbon curing innovation, we could reduce up to 246 million tons of CO_2 a year— equivalent to removing emissions from 53 million cars.**

New technology enables the **production of cement-free, carbon-negative concrete using industrial by-products and captured** CO_2. Companies use an admixture for cement reduction. The cement is replaced with steel slag—a by-product of the steel-making process that is often placed into landfills. Using a process called carbonation activation, CO_2 is injected into the wet concrete to give it its strength. As a result, any product made using this technology permanently sequesters CO_2, while turning industrial waste (steel slag) into a high-quality construction product.

Concrete made using this process meets the same specifications as cement-based concrete, has lower material costs, and possesses better mechanical and durability properties. During curing, the gas becomes a solid, binding together the slag granules, and giving the concrete its strength. **The process can be implemented in any precast concrete manufacturing plant.**

The new cement mixes usually cost less, do not lessen the structural integrity and take the same amount of time to cure. New cement mixes with less carbon should become a new and required standard in construction. Some states are now requiring this and should be adapted by the international building codes.

Supplementary Cementitious Materials (SCMs) are a common feature in mix designs today. The most common are fly ash, a by-product of the coal industry; slag, a by-product of steel production; and silica fume, a by-product of ferrosilicon metal industry. **Fly ash, for example, costs significantly less than cement.** SCMs increase the strength of concrete over time to levels greater than that of traditional concrete mixes. **Longer cure times should reduce carbon in the concrete.** It is critical to address the cement mix in concrete design solution.

Concrete suppliers have found out that by using less cement they can make more money because the cement costs more than fly ash, slag, or other materials. Typically, the cement mix can be reduced 3-7 percent, reducing the carbon in the concrete by that amount. There have been cases where the cement has been reduced up to 40 percent, but this requires a much longer cure time. The schedule then becomes the challenge. This improvement in the cement mix can reduce carbon emissions near 1 percent. That may not seem like a big number, but by doing so, you reduce carbon and save money. Ten more products like this, and they start adding up with the big solutions like solar, wind, and battery storage. Everything counts.

The following is an example specification:

Provide mix designs meeting the requirements of the specification and drawings that have reduced embodied carbon content, compared against industry baseline mix designs. Alternative approaches for reducing the amount of embodied carbon will be considered, including:

1. Use of CarbonCure ® or similar technology.

2. Use of Supplementary Cementitious Materials (SCMs) to reduce the Portland Cement content of the mix.

3. Other approaches that reduce the embodied carbon of the mix designs will be considered provided they meet the structural performance requirements of this specification and of the "Embodied Carbon Mix Design Summary Table" provided within the specification. Further information about CarbonCure Technologies can be found at www. carboncure.com.

CarbonCure: From Carbon to Concrete

1 CarbonCure is installed at an existing concrete plant in one visit, once a CO_2 tank has been installed.

2 Carbon dioxide (CO_2) gas is primarily sourced as a by-product from industrial processes.

3 The purified CO_2 gas is delivered in pressurized vessels by commercial gas suppliers.

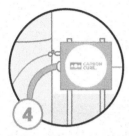

4 CarbonCure's proprietary delivery system, contained in the Valve Box, precisely injects the CO_2 into the concrete mix.

5 CarbonCure's Control Box is wired to the Valve Box and integrated with the batch computer; so adding CO_2 is just like adding an admixture.

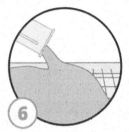

6 Once injected, CO_2 reacts with cement to form a nano-sized mineral that becomes permanently embedded in concrete.

5.6

A key part of the concrete structure to reduce carbon is to have the most efficient design. From a study to find scale factors from different slab types and based on relative stiffness, significant material volumes can be reduced by adopting common slab forms. The lower the number, the more efficient the slab.

FINANCIAL COST/PAYBACK

The cost difference is marginal and depending on the cement mix, it might be more cost-effective than business as usual. The payback is then immediate.

POLICIES

Provide tax incentives to use lower carbon cement mixes.

Provide grants, subsidies and incentives to update equipment to support the manufacturing process.

RECOMMENDATION

Update in the building codes to require better cement mixes with much lower carbon.

Steel

Steel is manufactured in two types of factories. Electric Arc Furnaces (EAFs) are powered by electricity. **Using steel from EAFs is the best way to reduce embodied emissions in steel, because EAFs uses high levels of recycled material and can be powered by renewable energy sources.** EAFs use an average of 93 percent recycled content, where **Basic Oxygen Furnaces** (BOFs) use an average of 25 percent recycled content.

Large steel mills typically use **Basic Oxygen Furnaces** (**BOF**s), which burns coal or natural gas to melt iron ore to extract the iron, and then mixes the iron with scraps of iron and steel to make new steel. Worldwide, 70 percent of steel is still made using BOFs. The U.S. has shifted and has 39 percent BOFs.

EAF+100 Renewables

 MIGHTY EARTH

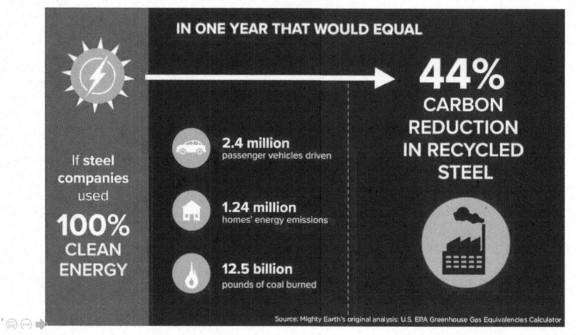

5.7

Today producing a ton of steel using BOF still requires about 20 million BTU (British thermal units) of energy and generates about two tons of CO_2. A ton of steel made using EAF consumes about 10 million Btu and generates about a ton of CO_2, according to the U.S. DOE.

CARBON IMPACTS OF STEEL

BASIC OXYGEN FURNACE (BOF)

BOF INGREDIENTS:
IRON ORE
LIMESTONE
RECYCLED STEEL (~25%)

CO_2

ELECTRIC ARC FURNACE (EAF)

EAF INGREDIENTS:
RECYCLED STEEL (~97%)
OTHER ELEMENTS (3%)

~50% LESS CO_2 EMISSIONS

VS

CO_2

CO_2

or

1. MINE RAW or PROCURE RECYCLED STEEL

2. MANUFACTURING ON EITHER AN EAF OR A BOF FURNACE

3. TRANSIT

4. USE

5. END OF LIFE

MOST STEEL MEMBERS ARE RECYCLED AT THE END OF THE BUILDING'S LIFE

TYPICALLY 25% RECYCLED CONTENT

TYPICALLY 97% RECYCLED CONTENT

71% OF GLOBAL STEEL PRODUCTION

29% OF GLOBAL STEEL PRODUCTION

5.8

DESIGN for adaptability and deconstruction. Due to its metal fasteners and standardization, structural steel framing is well-suited for deconstruction and reuse. Plan to have structural steel members recycled or reused at the end of the building's life.

Concrete buildings contain a lot of steel and steel buildings contain a lot of concrete: rebar and other steel products are used extensively in concrete buildings; and concrete is used for foundations, flooring, and other elements in steel buildings. This holds true for wood also, which typically requires concrete foundations and some elements in steel.

ZERO-EMISSION CONSTRUCTION SITES

In a first of its kind in the world, in Oslo, Norway, **all the machinery used on site–excavators, diggers, and loaders were electric. Norway has the rare benefit of an electricity grid with 98 percent renewable energy**, most from hydropower, which makes Norway an ideal testing ground for zero-emission sites. The city now wants all municipal construction sites to be zero emission by 2025 and all construction work, public or private, to be zero emission by 2030. Since 2019, public tenders for construction work, for example roads, schools, nursery homes, water and sewage pipes, have been awarded to those building with zero-emission machinery and trucks.

Using electric equipment in place of traditional diesel engines meant that everyone in the vicinity **noticed a reduction in ambient noise and pollution.** "We observed shops keeping their doors open towards the street, even when construction work was going on just outside on the pavement," says Philip Mortensen, a senior adviser at the City of Oslo's Climate Agency. "The workers also reported much better communication on site due to lower noise levels, and that as a consequence, the working environment felt safer."

Battery technology is rapidly evolving. The challenges of power storage provide a range of options that are being developed that will apply to buildings and structures. A battery system that's recently been tested in Hong Kong is called the Ampd Enertainer. It's an advanced, compact battery system that can replace the diesel generators that currently power

the world's construction. For the founders of Ampd Energy, which makes the Enertainer, the goal is to provide the infrastructure for the backbone of the electrification of the construction industry. The makers of the Enertainer say it can reduce carbon emissions by 85 percent—for each deployment of a battery system to a construction site, it saves the equivalent of 200–400 cars' emissions. It can also generate 1/30th of the noise pollution of a diesel generator.

The **digitization of construction** sites has been gathering pace. Knowing what's going on at a construction site, capturing data, and digitizing the process is a big development for the construction industry. Any improvement in the construction site process means big savings. Time saved is money saved. Using drones for building inspections of taller buildings is a viable option contractors are using now that is safer, faster, and more affordable.

Another innovation looking to increase efficiency and reduce waste is modular construction. The process is where a building, or parts of it, are constructed off-site, which brings its own advantages. This is a trend that reduces waste. Reduce the waste in the assembly process but also increase the safety for the workers[5].

Adaptable architecture defined theories on how to design buildings with multifunctional use and accessibility without requiring changes or rebuilding. Create a flexible layout of the building to ensure that the usable space can be extended and/or reduced without rebuilding.

Net-Zero Buildings

By 2060, the global floor area is expected to increase by 2.4 trillion square feet or double the current worldwide building stock. Most of this construction is expected to take place in urban areas[6].

Zero Carbon Building is a highly efficient building that uses no on-site fossil fuels and produces on-site or procures off-site enough carbon-free renewable energy to meet building operations energy consumption.

Global architecture firm Perkins & Will, whose commitment to climate action through Living Design has earned critical acclaim, will issue its clients a "carbon forecast" for their projects—a tool to facilitate measurable and meaningful carbon reduction in the built environment.

Carbon forecasts will help clients understand—at the earliest stages of design—their projects' carbon emissions from building design, construction, and operation (known as whole-life-carbon), as well as the impact of those emissions on human and environmental health. Most importantly, the forecasts will identify steps clients and project teams can take to reduce those emissions. These include:

- Strategies for realizing net-zero operational carbon immediately or in the near-term.

- Measures for realizing maximum reductions in embodied carbon.

- Opportunities for enabling circular design.

For developers of multi-story, multifamily residential buildings, adding solar is a good return on investment, and can lower utility bills for residents. Developers can provide this benefit to tenants if they raise the rent less than or equal to the monthly solar benefit, thus solving the "split incentive" issue and allowing the solar panels to repay the developer's investment.

A 2017 University of California study on the cost of constructing **new all-electric buildings** on campuses and powering them with renewable energy found that the **university system could save 14 percent on energy costs for academic buildings and 8 percent for laboratory buildings over 20 years. The return on investment on many projects is getting 20 years or more of free power—moves green building from being a moral issue to a business issue**[7].

In every city the Rocky Mountain Institute (RMI) analyzed, a new all-electric, single-family home was less expensive than a new mixed-fuel home that relies on gas for cooking, space heating, and water heating. **In most cities, the mixed-fuel home (with gas furnace, water heater, air conditioning, and new gas connection costs) has a higher up-front cost than the all-electric home, which uses a heat pump system for both heating and cooling.**

Samsung and Q CELLS entered a partnership for Zero Energy Homes in July 2021. Samsung's SmartThings Energy service is connected to Q CELLS' solar modules and Energy Storage Systems (ESS). This solution allows homeowners to produce and store their own energy. Then they have the capability to benefit from the SmartThings IoT (Internet of Things) platform to monitor and optimize energy consumption in their home appliances and heat pumps. Home appliances will automatically switch to energy-saving mode at night or during cloudy days when solar energy capture is low.

Net-Zero Building Codes

ZERO CODE PROPOSAL BY ARCHITECTURE 2030

New buildings place additional load on the electric grid. The **ZERO Code accelerates progress toward a clean grid** by requiring that new buildings come with additional renewable energy that exceeds what utilities are already required to do. This encourages the performance approach and to go beyond the minimum required by code for energy efficiency.

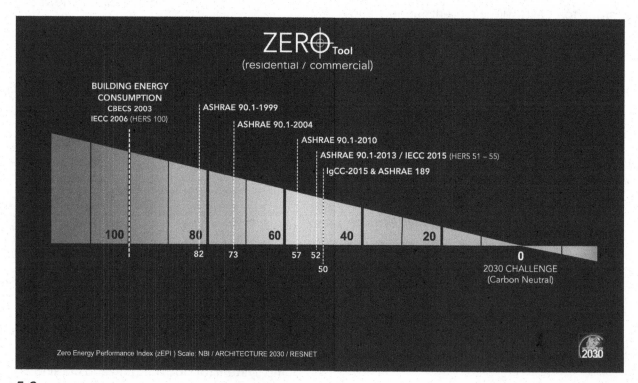

5.9

The electricity used by ZERO Code buildings is clean and carbon-free. For this reason, adopting jurisdictions should consider prohibiting the use of gas appliances in buildings. The ZERO Code expands on the cost-effective 2022 energy efficiency standards adopted by the California Energy Commission by:

- requiring on-site or off-site renewable energy,

- eliminating the direct use of fossil fuels in buildings, and

- specifying beyond-code energy efficiency (optional).

A strong building energy code is one of the most affordable and effective mechanisms for advancing energy efficiency in buildings. The national model building energy codes have increased energy-saving potential by around 30 percent from 2006 to 2018. However, energy savings are only realized when the code is enforced. Although there has been a push to adopt the latest model energy codes in many states and cities in recent years, resources for training and enforcement have been lacking, and code compliance rates in many municipalities remain low. City building departments have many priorities related to life-safety and are often resource constrained. It is challenging for them to maintain a staff of building plan reviewers and inspectors, who are fully educated on and actively enforcing complex and evolving energy code requirements particularly low in building renovations. In order to capture the benefits of more stringent codes during the natural cycle of building upgrades, local jurisdictions should issue clear direction on how and when renovation and retrofit projects trigger the need to bring specific building systems up to code. Most compliance assessments and studies to date have focused solely on new construction, and data on compliance rates for renovations is largely absent. Most major mechanical systems need to be replaced every 20–25 years. This is when the building upgrade from the latest energy codes should occur.

EFFICIENT BUILDING ENERGY CODE STANDARD

Existing Code: ASHRAE 90.1 2016 (minimum) or Title 24-2019

Recommend Upgrade/Adopt Code: ASHRAE 90.1 2016 (minimum) or 2021 IECC

RENEWABLE ENERGY

Establish and adopt Renewable Energy (RE) requirements by ordinance, legislation, or 2021 IECC Appendix to the code. Refer to the ZERO Code Renewable Energy Technical Support Document for guidelines on establishing on-site and off-site RE procurement requirements.

BENEFITS OF AN ALL-ELECTRIC BUILDING CODE:

Fewer Emissions

A 2020 RMI analysis found that in Seattle, a new all-electric home would reduce carbon emissions by more than 93% compared to a mixed-fuel home.

More Efficient

Washington state law already requires that the State Building Code Council (SBCC) update the energy code to reduce 70 percent of the

annual energy consumption from buildings by 2031 compared to a 2006 baseline. The SBCC has calculated that every energy code update (which happens every three years) must achieve a 19 percent reduction in energy consumption in order to reach the 2031 goal. **Heat pumps are at least two to four times more efficient than gas appliances** at providing space and water heating, and they have the added advantage of being able to run on carbon-free electricity, making them perfect candidates for reaching both energy and climate goals.

Economical

Going all-electric in many cases saves money. A recent study found substantial cost savings for small hotels that go all-electric. Accounting for the high costs of connecting new buildings to the gas main, installing gas pipes throughout the building, and carrying out combustion safety testing and precautions, **building all-electric is typically the best financial decision**[8].

Specify materials that naturally sequester carbon. Materials such as wood, straw, clay-straw, hemp, cork, and sheep's wool naturally sequester carbon and store it for their useful life.

SPECIFY MATERIALS MANUFACTURED WITH RENEWABLE ENERGY

Design for durability

Use the appropriate product to withstand the wear and tear of the space to ensure that they'll last the lifespan of the building.

Choose the right materials for your climate

Use the appropriate product for the building's climate by understanding how each material handles heat and moisture, individually and in an assembly, to ensure the durability of the building.

Get to know the supply chain for your specific project

Understand where the materials for your project come from and the carbon implications of their manufacturing and transportation. Design to use the lowest carbon systems and materials.

Understanding your region and source locally

Knowing what materials are available in your region is the key to specifying local materials. Additionally, using local resources and materials reduces transportation emissions.

All-electric Construction costs less to build: In California, developers save an average of $3,300/unit of construction costs by avoiding gas use, or more than $20,000 per 8-plex for gas distribution, laterals, interior piping, appliances, and venting. Piping to gas appliances is usually an additional cost, ranging from $200–$800 per gas appliance.

Energy efficiency alone supported 2.3 million jobs, while natural gas supported roughly 398,000 jobs and solar 345,000 jobs. 78 percent of the 2.3 million employees involved in energy efficiency spent most of their time on energy efficiency tasks. The jobs created to make, sell, and install efficient products such as ENERGY STAR® appliances, build well-insulated homes, or offer energy-saving services such as weatherization. One of every five U.S. construction jobs now deals with products proven to save energy. Of the efficiency jobs, about half (49 percent) are related to heating and cooling equipment. Over one-fifth are related to lighting and appliances (23 percent) and another fifth to building materials (19 percent).

Energy efficiency creates jobs in yet another way. Efficiency reduces energy use and thus energy bills. Customers spend or invest the money they save somewhere else in the economy. Jobs that support energy efficiency grab much less headlines than automotive jobs. A recent report by the department of energy found that **building efficiency employs about twice as many people as the auto industry.**

BUILD ENERGY-NEUTRAL HOUSING

Musk's Tesla Energy is partnering with Brookfield Asset Management and Dacra to create SunHouse at Easton Park in Austin, Texas, the first Tesla Solar neighborhood and the nation's most sustainable residential community. The goal of creating SunHouse is to establish an energy-neutral, sustainable community and a model for the design and construction of sustainable large-scale housing projects around the world. The new community being developed by Brookfield and Dacra will feature solar power and battery installations placed in different housing types in SunHouse. Brookfield's renewable power business will integrate a community-wide solar program to serve broader public use needs and surrounding neighborhoods.

Methane

Huge plumes of the warming gas methane have been mapped globally for the first time from oil and gas fields using satellites. CH4 doesn't last as long in the air as CO_2. It's a very potent gas usually released by leaks created by humans that can be stopped relatively easily. The three countries with the largest plumes identified in the latest research were Turkmenistan, Russia, and the US. By plugging these leaks, countries could save billions—including $6 billion for Turkmenistan, $4 billion for Russia and $1.6 billion for the US, the research suggests[9].

"If you emit a ton of methane today, in a decade's time, I would expect half that ton to remain in the atmosphere," said Professor Peter Thorne, an IPCC author from Maynooth University in Ireland. "In two decades, time, there would be a quarter of a ton, so basically, if we managed to stop emitting methane today by the end of this century, emissions would be down to natural levels, that they were in about 1750."[10]

Residential Natural Gas Methane System Leakage to California Residences: 2.7% - 5.2%

2.2% (1.0-2.9%)
In and Out of State Extraction
(Wentworth 2018)

0.03%
Processing and
Temporary Storage
(CEC 2017)

0.31%
Residential Meter
(CEC 2017)

Extraction

Processing

0.02%
Seasonal Storage
*(CEC 2017)**

Compressor
Station

0.07%
Transmission
(CEC 2017)

Image by:
Emily Higbee of
Redwood Energy

0.3% - 0.9%
Appliance and
Incomplete Combustion
(CEC 2018)

0.68%
Low Pressure
Distribution
(CEC 2017)

Storage

*Aliso Canyon leaked 4.62 Billion cubic feet and alone cost $1.014 billion shared by 5.6 million meters - $181/meter cost (Reuters, Aug 6, 2018)
California Energy Commission. (2017). A Survey of Methane Emissions from the California Natural Gas System. CEC-500-2017-033. <https://eta.lbl.gov/sites/all/files/publications/pdf_5.pdf>
California Energy Commission. (2018). Natural Gas Methane Emissions From California Homes. CEC-500-2018-021. <https://ww2.energy.ca.gov/2018publications/CEC-500-2018-021/CEC-500-2018-021.pdf>
Wentworth, N. (2018). White Paper on the Lifecycle Leakage Rate of Natural Gas Consumed in California. Scripps Institution of Oceanography. June 2018.

5.10

According to Environmental Defense Fund analysis of IPCC data, "**about 25 percent of manmade global warming we're experiencing is caused by methane emissions**," assuming a conservative 2.7 percent lifecycle leakage rate. Some cities have begun exploring a ban on new gas plumbing in buildings due to the fire, explosion, and public safety risks. Earthquake and accidents have broken more than 9,000 pipelines between 1986 and 2016, almost one a day[11].

MULTIFAMILY ELECTRIFICATION BEST PRACTICES POWER AND ENERGY

In multifamily housing, design towards lower power demand using 15amp rather than 30amp heat pumps for both HVAC and hot water. In new development, where each apartment has its own dedicated PV system, a 200amp service panel is required.

New construction for hot water: Multifamily housing has fewer exterior surfaces than single family homes, which then provides a more energy efficient exterior enclosure. Hot water is often the largest energy use rather than HVAC in new multifamily housing. Best practices to consider in new construction of hot water systems include:

- **The least energy use design uses individual tanks per residence**.

- The least cost design is sharing individual 80-gallon tanks at 140°F between two family units and up to 7 senior studios.

Install more efficient domestic hot water uses such as showerheads, faucets, dishwashers, and laundry washers. Insulate accessible pipes, which reduce the heat pump and storage tank costs. This may avoid power upgrade costs and lower utility bills.

Operational Carbon

Both new construction and renovation projects need to focus on reducing the operational carbon. Solutions are listed with cost benefits.

As of 2010, the total U.S. building stock was approximately 300 billion square feet. During normal economic times:

We tear down approximately 1.75 billion square feet of buildings each year (0.6 percent).

We renovate approximately 5 billion square feet (1.67 percent).

We build new approximately 5 billion square feet. Another 1.7 percent to the total building stock each year for a total of 4 percent.

Design to Accommodate Future Change. Designing for flexibility extends the life of the building and provides future generations with further chances to retrofit. Minimize customization to create buildings that can change easily and meet new program needs.

5.11 Renovate/ Reuse/ Retrofit existing buildings

According to a 2018 poll by Dodge Data and Analytics, 94 percent of building owners in the United States believe their properties are worth more after a green retrofit. Today's most common and affordable energy retrofit options can reduce building energy use by 20 to 40 percent. State-of-the-art "deep" retrofits can reduce energy costs by 70 to 90 percent with most of the solutions saving money initially or within a few years.

A comprehensive retrofit of the Empire State Building saved $4.7 million in two years. The project provides an example of what can be achieved in large commercial buildings when owners, managers, tenants, and partners come together to improve energy performance.

In the U.S., that's around 3-6 million buildings per year that need to be fully decarbonized," says Martha Campbell, a principal in the Carbon-Free Buildings program at the energy nonprofit RMI. In Europe, by another calculation, roughly 15,000 houses need to transform every day for the next 30 years.

Energy Efficiency

Energy efficiency can occur by changing the way we operate and work to reduce the carbon footprint significantly with immediate financial payback:

1. Deliver the energy locally, just in time, and just the right amount.

2. Coordination of electric transmission lines at a regional and national scale.

3. Store of electricity.

4. Minimize peak time with load sharing.

5. Delete emails, apps, and digital content you don't need. Storing it takes energy.

6. Right size equipment.

7. Educate users and operators.

8. Monitor and commission buildings.

9. Utility providers encourage net metering.

10. Maintain a continued emphasis on improvements in technology and operations.

If you develop a computer model for energy efficiency, build in a 10% contingency because people typically do not use the building the way it is designed. They tend to use more energy and do not change their lifestyle as much as they initially thought they would.

FINANCIAL INCENTIVES FOR SUSTAINABLE DESIGN

Leadership in Energy and Environmental Design (LEED) for new buildings compared to conventional design and construction:

- Rental Rates Higher by 2 to 17 percent

- Re-sale Value Higher 5.8 to 35 percent

- Occupancy Rates Higher 0.9 to 18 percent

- Operating Expenses Lower by 30 percent

LEED Credit Categories

Sustainable Sites

Water Efficiency

Innovation in Operations & Regional Priority

Energy & Atmosphere

Indoor Environmental Quality

Materials & Resources

5.12

Tenants are demanding greener buildings, so it makes sense to secure green loans to fund energy-efficient projects. LEED designs have become much more standard over the last twenty years.

LEED Certified and Silver rated buildings will not be net zero. Platinum level rating might achieve net zero by purchasing green power on site. The lower the carbon footprint for renovation and construction, will have the opportunity to be considered regenerative design. This means the project gives back to nature more energy than what the building requires. If designed correctly, LEED buildings should cost less than traditional construction. Seventy-four percent of Americans live in a state with a building energy code that promotes energy efficiency. There should be a national code requiring all states to follow the latest energy building codes.

Jobs: Three million jobs that sell efficient (and other) appliances and building materials, four times more than the auto industry.

Building Automation Systems

Because of their large share of energy consumption, residential and commercial buildings now account for one-third of global carbon dioxide emissions. An efficient technology that has historically been common in large commercial buildings is a building automation system (BAS). There are over 85 million "smart meters" in U.S. homes and businesses, up from 9.6 million a decade ago. Thirteen states now have smart meter penetration rates exceeding 80% of homes and businesses[12].

Building Automation Systems can control heating, cooling, lighting, and appliances in commercial buildings. They cut emissions by maximizing energy efficiency and minimizing waste. Some also call this technology "The Internet of Things" or "SMART Buildings," where sensors are managing our buildings, cities, and transportation. The technology provides timely feedback and data to improve operations.

Bring the building automation systems and the IT systems into one network. You will then have:

Access – the network provides access to all these systems,

Analyze – find new ways to harness information, and

Act – continuously improve building operations.

Beyond energy savings and reduced operations and maintenance costs, BAS benefits the well-being and productivity of people inside the building. **Improved thermal and lighting comfort and indoor air quality directly impact occupant satisfaction.** As buildings become more air-tight, dehumidification systems will be needed to keep mold out.

5.13 Internet of Things

A type of building automation is Grid-interactive Efficient Buildings (GEBs) that make buildings into clean and flexible energy resources. GEBs can avoid the high costs and disruptions associated with peak demand and grid stress with clean, on-site power generation and cutting-edge efficiency measures. GEBs integrate three different energy management technologies and approaches: energy efficiency, distributed energy resources (such as solar panels and battery storage), and demand flexibility. Demand flexibility refers to the building's ability to manage when that energy is consumed. The benefits of GEBs include energy cost savings, lower GHG emissions, and resilience to grid disruptions. They also help limit costly peaks in demand.

An example of this, BrainBox's software systems use deep-learning, cloud-based computing to autonomously optimize building systems, like HVACs, in real-time to deliver maximum energy savings and reductions in carbon emissions. The company's AI engine changes HVAC systems from reactive to fully autonomous in three steps. First, it connects to a building through one of three integration options and collects and maps out large volumes of HVAC data. After sorting through the data, the system draws on external sources of information, such as weather forecasts, utility tariff structures, and occupancy rates. Equipped with all this data, the AI engine can then predict with 99.6% accuracy the future state of each HVAC zone in a building, and then it can fully optimize strategies to manage temperature settings. Once the AI engine is up and running, it works 24/7 to autonomously run the HVAC system in real-time, maintaining occupant comfort levels while also reducing energy use and carbon footprint. The AI engine continues to collect data and, over time, becomes even better at analyzing HVAC trends and optimizing the system. It becomes a self-driving system. It is possible to coordinate multiple buildings, maybe even hundreds of them, to perform certain grid-level functions to shift or shed energy loads.[13]

People will need to be trained to install and program the software. As the new equipment is manufactured, it should be tested in the factory and approved before sending to the site. Then the ongoing maintenance will need to be developed to enable the homeowner to maintain most issues that arise throughout the year without having to call or schedule a technician.

FINANCIAL COST/ PAYBACK

Within 1–3 years

POLICIES

Fast-track permits, low interest loans, tax abatements, and rebates

Smart Thermostats

SMART thermostats can manage the temperature and humidity in the house for energy efficiency. The thermostats can be managed by an app from a person's cell phone. This solution is becoming standard for most new construction and should be required. Night setbacks and setbacks when the home is not in use become productive energy-saving measures.

SMART thermostats are relatively easy to install and may simply require removing the old thermostat and replacing with the new. Many homeowners can do this with the thermostats usually requiring only low voltage wiring. SMART Thermostats can be purchased very easily at Home Depot, Lowe's or over the internet.

The original NEST smart thermostat became available in 2011, not very long ago. **The newest technologies also integrate demand response; they can reduce consumption at times of peak energy use, peak prices, and peak emissions.** The net effect is residences are more energy efficient, more comfortable, and less costly to operate.

FINANCIAL PAYBACK

Within one year

POLICIES

Tax incentive for low-income households and landlords to install in existing buildings.

RECOMMENDATION

SMART Thermostats should be required in all new construction. Add to the building codes.

Highly encourage in renovations because the cost is low compared to the savings in energy.

Government should install SMART thermostats for all low- and moderate-income households older than 10 years.

Heat Pumps

Heat pumps are now 2–4 times as efficient as a gas furnace. Heat pumps extract heat from the air and transfer it—from indoors out for cooling, or from outdoors in for heating. **With high efficiency, they can dramatically lower building energy use.** Heat pumps can draw their energy from three main sources—air, the ground, and water. "Water source heat pump" refers to a two-stage process, where there is a central air source heat pump that chills or heats water, then that water circulates through the building instead of air. **The heating and cooling by water is three times more energy-efficient than all air solutions based on research by the Navy.**

Heat pumps give you flexibility in location. This means you can have heat pumps in multiple places to create zones for your heating and cooling. Heat pumps are run with a two or three-pipe system, which carries a liquid to heat or cool. The most common refrigerant for heating and cooling are the

Hydrofluorocarbons but the industry has been moving toward **"natural" refrigerants** like CO_2 (R744), Ammonia (R717), and Propane (R290) that do not deplete the ozone and do not contribute to global warming. **The liquids over the next five years will change to water, which is an environmentally friendly solution.**

As your existing HVAC system needs to be replaced heat pumps should be considered as the best choice moving forward. Retrofitting existing HVAC systems with state-of-the-art heat pump equipment is a very smart option for consumers looking for ways to reduce building energy costs, without having to make major investments or structural changes to the building. The heat pump may require new copper lines from the exterior to the interior "Split Units" that can hang from the wall or set on the floor like a radiator. If these boxes are not desired, you may choose to have a ducted system, possibly use the ducts from the old HVAC system. **Many times, a ducted**

heat pump can use the same ducts as the old HVAC model. If your building already has ducts installed, most contractors will tell you to take advantage of that existing infrastructure and install a ducted system. A major benefit of ducted heating and cooling setups is that they are installed behind walls and in crawl spaces. As a result, you don't need to worry about seeing any indoor units that need to be installed with a ductless system.

DUCTLESS AIR SOURCE HEAT PUMPS

In a ductless heating and cooling system, warm or cold air is pumped directly to several individual indoor units, which can each be controlled separately, like a hotel room. There is no central indoor unit in a ductless system, making it **easy to heat and cool different parts or rooms of a building to your preference**. Ductless systems are often also referred to as "mini-splits."

Ductless systems have many advantages. **They are much simpler to install, more efficient than ducted systems, and allow for fine control of the temperature of individual rooms in any building.** If you are building a new property or an addition, or are retrofitting a home without a ducted system, a ductless air source heat pump system is a simple and efficient option.

Be aware that most heating and cooling systems generate noise, and you want to place the equipment in a location that will support a quiet home like in a separate utility room, in attic space above unoccupied areas, or in a basement below unoccupied space. Do not place near bedrooms. Sound insulated ductwork is recommended and possibly

a vibration dampening material installed between the condensing unit base and the mounting pad.

Utility Providers pay for heat pumps: The utility company would pay for a basic heat pump installation. The cost of the heat pump and installation would then just be built into a special rate paid by those customers participating in this program. This should be a good option for most people.

FINANCIAL COST/PAYBACK

The first costs of **high efficiency heat pumps** are estimated at $9,911 per installation unit, compared to a weighted cost of $7,915 per unit for conventional HVAC systems. **Usually, the payback is within two years.** During hot weather, a heat pump operates identical to an air conditioner, by reversing the pressure and the flow of refrigerant through its coils. This can be a benefit for the homeowners, who would otherwise need to purchase a separate air conditioner.

For a single winter season, heating costs run an average of $1,550 for a propane furnace, $850 for a natural gas furnace, $900 for an electric furnace, and just $500 for a heat pump. The costs to cool your home will run about the same. The cost to install a heat pump is approximately $500 less than installing a gas furnace. (Source Bob Villa)

OPPORTUNITIES FOR REBATES

Mitsubishi Electric systems are so efficient, they qualify for rebates from many local electric utility providers. Go to their website, enter your zip code to see if you qualify for local rebates on heat pump systems installed by a licensed HVAC contractor.

RECOMMENDATIONS

Grants be made available to public- and low-income-housing residents to replace aging systems, including swapping out oil or gas heaters for electric heat pumps that capture and store energy without burning fuel. Grant energy vouchers to low-income tenants or take the cost out of the overall rent.

Contractors should receive a $100 rebate for educating homeowners to purchase heat pumps. Many contractors simply sell to their customers the old standard that they are used to. Incentivizing the contractor will help them provide the customer with the latest information to enable them to make better decisions. Tax credits for heat pumps and other energy efficiency equipment should be made possible for 2022 and future years.

Home Dehumidifier

Using a new **home dehumidifier** to address humidity and cooling your home is a smart option, which may be a cost-effective solution instead of an air conditioner. Climate change has made humidity in many areas more of a problem that needs to be addressed in buildings. Spending time in an environment with too much humidity can make you sick, especially from respiratory infections. The bacteria and viruses that cause illness thrive and grow in air that's above 60 percent relative humidity. You can overheat your body causing exhaustion, headaches, fever, chills, and even disorientation. Heat stroke, the most serious case of overheating, can even lead to death.

I have installed a home dehumidifier that also cools up to 10 degrees designed by Ultra Aire. Over the last five years, this product has evolved in the U.S. market. Most home dehumidifiers generate heat, requiring air conditioning to counter the heat generated. With the Ultra Aire solution, you have one system that dehumidifies, then cools very effectively and works great.

Ceiling Fans

Ceiling fans used in many rooms can cool the space about 4–6 degrees Fahrenheit. This reduces the peak loads for the air-cooling system, while requiring much less electricity to run. Ceiling fans are inexpensive to purchase and install. They also use one-tenth of the electricity that a heat pump uses to cool a space. Fans should be considered in most residential and commercial spaces, as well as most building types.

Chilled Beams

Use chilled beams to supply cooling and heating in commercial buildings. I have installed these in many research buildings over the past 15+ years.

5.14 Chilled beams located in the ceiling

- Energy Benefits
  - Reduces chiller energy
  - Reduces fan energy
  - Reduces reheat
- Other Benefits
  - Requires less maintenance than conventional variable air volume (VAV) systems because there are fewer moving parts
  - Quieter than conventional VAV systems
  - Even air distribution reduces drafty conditions
  - Water carries much more energy than air
  - 50 percent smaller air handlers and exhaust fans
  - Smaller chillers and boilers

Require less ceiling plenum space than traditional ducted HVAC systems, approximately one foot less per floor, which is a big cost savings. The cost savings has been 2-3 percent of the overall construction cost.

Commissioning

Commissioning should happen on an annual basis, usually before the winter. **Commissioning is verifying and correcting the mechanical systems to run at full efficiency. The payback for the cost of commissioning is within one year.** This can have a significant reduction in the carbon by solving an issue before becoming a problem. This is a very proactive and smart approach to building management.

FINANCIAL COST/ PAYBACK:

Within one year. Always a smart investment and the equipment should run at very high efficiency throughout the year.

RECOMMENDATION:

Train people to commission HVAC equipment and building automation systems. Subsidize their education.

Educate homeowners on the benefits of commissioning.

Energy Star Appliances

Current federal taxes support Energy Star appliances for air conditioning and heat pumps. There is plenty of opportunity for more people to buy more energy efficient appliances. Energy Star appliances will **save you 10–50 percent of the energy required**, compared to new non-energy star models—and more if you are replacing an old appliance. Wood burners produce particles that harm people's lungs and need to be replaced everywhere with electric solutions.

Payback: Within 1–3 years. The incentives should more than cover the cost difference between the appliances that do not meet the Energy Star criteria and those that do. Make sure all new appliances meet certain levels defined as energy efficient.

RECOMMENDATION

Incentives for all-electric Energy Star appliances.

Encourage electric stoves. A meta-analysis of health studies examining the link between gas cooking and children's health found that children living in homes with gas stoves have a 42 percent increased risk of experiencing asthma symptoms and a 24 percent increased risk of being diagnosed with asthma by a doctor[14].

Electric heat pumps are typically more cost effective than heat pumps run by natural gas.

HVAC energy use can be a small or large load, and comfortable or not, depending on the design of the building shell and equipment chosen. Energy Star for Homes construction standards for the building shell, appropriate to climate, are thorough and generally cost-effective.

Solar Power: Whenever possible, incorporate on site solar PV systems to provide low cost, clean energy for residents. Recommendations include:

- For a low-cost solar array, design for many continuous panels on an unshaded roof.

- Plumbing vents can be beneath solar panels with a 4" or greater airgap, but gas exhaust vents cannot.

- If appropriate to the building type, a solar array with edge-to-edge panels produces the most energy per square foot of roof. It should be sloped at greater than 5 percent to shed rain and dust.

Insulation

Recently spray foam insulation has become available and is very effective as long it does not have any toxic chemicals. Ovoid extruded polystyrene in spray foam insulation. Spray foam insulation needs to be only about 2" thick, seals the entire house to hold temperature in, and performs like how a thermos works.

Insulation for new homes is addressed well in the building codes and industry in general. The key is to install insulation that does not have Volatile Organic Chemicals (VOCs) that will off gas and be a potential hazard for the

occupants. Be aware of what the insulation is made of and install insulation that does not off gas and create potential health concerns. **Non-toxic Mineral wool can be a good choice. There are formaldehyde-free fiberglass brands. Wool batt and blow-in insulation work very well to insulate the building and are healthy to use. Safe brands of cellulose insulation include Greenfiber sold at Lowes and Home Depot made of 85 percent recycled newspaper.** Studies have shown that the chemicals in fiberglass have been linked to cancer.

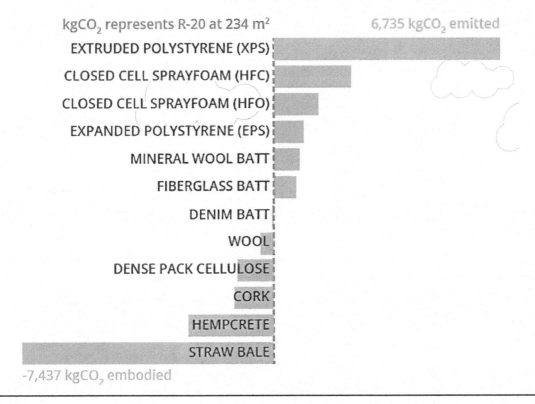

CARBON IMPACTS OF INSULATION

kgCO$_2$ represents R-20 at 234 m^2 — 6,735 kgCO$_2$ emitted

EXTRUDED POLYSTYRENE (XPS)
CLOSED CELL SPRAYFOAM (HFC)
CLOSED CELL SPRAYFOAM (HFO)
EXPANDED POLYSTYRENE (EPS)
MINERAL WOOL BATT
FIBERGLASS BATT
DENIM BATT
WOOL
DENSE PACK CELLULOSE
CORK
HEMPCRETE
STRAW BALE

-7,437 kgCO$_2$ embodied

5.15

One key benefit of the spray foam is you can fill in, then seal up the cracks and openings in the entire house. Make sure to have a home dehumidifier that will remove enough water out of the air in the summer to prevent potential mold that might evolve with a tightly sealed house that has very low air changes.

The roof is the most critical to insulate and will hold the warm air in during the winter and cool air in during the summer. For existing buildings, access above the ceilings and below the roof should be reasonable to allow for insulation to be installed. Existing walls typically are more difficult to add insulation but can be done.

Existing commercial building roof projects should look to pair roof replacements and upgrades with the addition of efficient roof deck insulation. Polyisocyanurate insulation (polyiso) is a rigid foam insulation that delivers both versatility and sustainability in its project implementation. It continues to be the most widely used above-deck insulating roof material in commercial buildings because of its reliability. Polyiso insulation has a high thermal performance of approximately R-6 per inch. With an estimated building service life of 75 years, polyiso insulation is a reliable building application.

Local utility companies in various jurisdictions around the U.S. offer economic incentives to increase building performance. These incentives include rebates to cover the up-front costs of energy-efficient envelope measures, such as upgrades in insulation.

The U.S. Department of Energy's Office of Energy Efficiency and Renewable Energy provide resources for federal tax deductions for envelope energy savings. **The Section 179D tax deduction by the IRS recently became permanent** and allows existing building owners and tenants to take tax deductions for qualifying measures, including energy-efficient envelopes. Insulating the envelope is a critical step towards enhancing its efficiency, and roof applications are successful candidates for lowering a building's carbon footprint.

FINANCIAL COST/PAYBACK

Most insulation will provide an energy savings payback within a few years and is a smart long-term investment now. The International Energy Agency urges everyone to turn down the thermostat by a degree—that could save up to 10 percent of heating energy and costs[15].

POLICIES

Maintain existing tax breaks for installing insulation. **Increase the tax break for roof insulation**.

Federal, state and local governments insulate all public housing projects to meet current building codes.

Governments subsidize low-income families to insulate.

Policies should support landlords of rental properties to upgrade their facilities to be more energy efficient.

Increase tax incentives when multiple solutions are done at the same time.

RECOMMENDATION

Encourage installation of dehumidifiers to address potential health problems with mildew.

LED Lighting

LEDs are the most energy-efficient bulbs available. **LEDs are the most common light bulb sold today and most affordable based on energy savings compared to other type of light bulbs. Most light fixtures support LED lights. This is an easy upgrade for any homeowner or landlord. Most properties should already have LED lights. Just replace them with the latest models when the old ones go out.** LEDs are an excellent example of a product becoming the most affordable option over time.

FINANCIAL COST/ PAYBACK

Immediate

RECOMMENDATION

Maintain existing tax incentive.

Update building codes to require all LED lighting.

Rain Screens

In new constructions, on the exterior wall there is a thin space created one-eighth of an inch to half-inch to allow for air to come behind the wall then continue up to the top and exhaust out. The air space created by the rain screen acts as a type of cushion to reduce impact on the interior air. As a result of temperature differences, a natural convection process, known as the **"chimney effect"**, takes place. This chimney effect **avoids overheating during summer and helps maintain a warm and steady interior temperature during winter**. The cost of the back-up material is less than 1 percent of the construction cost. You cannot see a rain screen and most people are not familiar with this solution. **This type of construction is required in many parts of the world—it is not yet required in the U.S. but is recommended to be required in the building codes.**

BENEFITS OF USING A RAIN SCREEN SYSTEM

Weather-resistant barrier keeps moisture away from the wall assembly.

Water vapor behind cladding and insulation can escape by means of evaporation, avoiding mold.

Helps reduce hot and cold air and thermal movement through the wall, reducing energy costs.

Protects interior walls, increasing longevity.

Roofs

Painting roofs white can help reduce carbon by reflecting the sun and reducing cooling loads. A new, high-reflective white paint has been developed for this use. The average white paint on the market reflects between 80 and 90 percent of the sunlight that hits its surface, absorbing the rest. The new paint reflects 98.1 percent. The research team found that a surface coated with the paint maintained a temperature between 8-18° F lower than the air around it during daylight hours. They estimate that for a 1,600-square-foot building with an average air conditioning system and electricity rate of $0.10 per kilowatt-hour, their paint could result in a savings of $36 per month on cooling. The product should be available by 2023[16].

Ideally you have solar panels(blue) or vegetation(green) on your roof. The added layer to a "Blue" of "Green" roof should lower your home insurance because the main roof is protected and will last longer.

Incentives should be developed to use the air rights of roofs to support sustainable design. The electricity generated can go directly to support the building use like housing, education, manufacturing, and management of food.

Water Management

By 2030, it is estimated that freshwater demand could outpace supply by 40 percent. Currently, the average water loss due to leakage is estimated at 25-30 percent. Smart water management models use sensors in network pipes to monitor flow and manage the entire water cycle, providing sustainable water for human and ecological needs. Addressing leaks in water distribution networks, especially in cities, can curb water loss, energy use, and

emissions. Cleaning, transporting, and heating water requires energy. More efficient fixtures and appliances can reduce home water use significantly, thereby reducing emissions.

The water crisis aligns directly with climate concerns. The availability of water will get worse as climate change gets worse. Carbon is embedded in water. 25 percent of the electricity in California goes to treating the water.

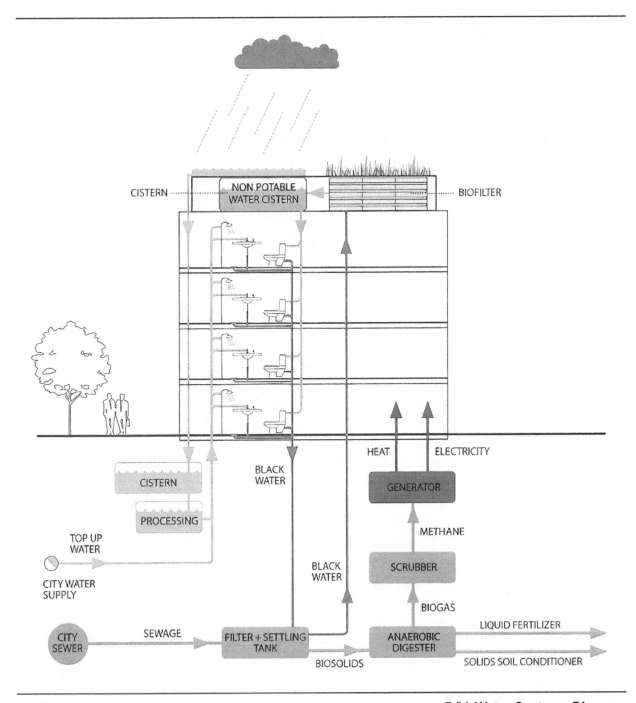

5.16 Water Systems Diagram

Consider grey and black water solutions to preserve water.

Policies: Require water sensors.

The lack of water is the next big issue after climate change. Focus on research, support innovation through competitions, and have smart water management tools available.

Healthy Materials

As we make choices to select materials that help us save energy and carbon, we should also ensure they are healthy for building occupants. A number a of resources exist that share provide information on healthy materials (for example the International Living Future Institute's Red List, and Perkins&Will's Precautionary List).

the **RED**LIST

The Living Building Challenge publishes a "Red List" of materials to be avoided in buildings seeking certification under the Living Building Challenge. What's on it?

● Asbestos ● Cadmium ● Chlorinated Polyethylene and Chlorosulfonated Polyethlene ● Chlorofluorocarbons (CFCs) ● ● Chloroprene (Neoprene) ● ● Formaldehyde ● Halogenated Flame Retardants ● ● Hydrochlorofluorocarbons (HCFCs) ● Lead ● Mercury ● ● Petrochemical Fertilizers and Pesticides Phthalates ● Polyvinyl Chloride (PVC) ● ● Wood treatments containing creosote, arsenic or pentachlorophenol ●

5.17

Nike produced the Material Sustainability Index (MSI). The MSI ranks 80K+ materials based on four key areas: chemistry, energy/greenhouse gas, water/land use, and physical waste. Since its production Nike have advocated an industry-wide approach to innovation and as such have made the MSI publicly available as a MAKING app. The MSI has also been adopted by the Sustainable Appraisal Coalition (SAC) and incorporated into their own Higgs index, which is used by manufacturers to measure the environmental and social performance of apparel and footwear products.

Work with health professionals to expand awareness of health benefits switching to electric appliances: A program to replace gas stoves could succeed by working with air pollution agencies, public health agencies, other health providers, low-income housing agencies, insurance companies, hospitals, and environmental justice organizations.

Other cost-effective ideas to consider for renovating and building new structures that have a small impact but will add up include: North/ South building orientation, shading the sun, low flow plumbing fixtures, and nighttime ventilation by opening windows.

Renovation Case Study

NETHERLANDS RETROFITS- REALIZE- figured out a way to mass-produce home retrofits.

Energiesprong (which translates to "energy jump"), a nonprofit that the Dutch government helped launch a decade ago, is coordinating a system of mass retrofits. In one Dutch factory, the company makes **lightweight insulated panels** that can be popped on the front of existing row houses. The company uses a laser scanning tool to take measurements at the old house; then, at the factory, a machine cuts out windows and doors to match the old facade exactly. When a truck delivers the panels, they're **attached directly to the old wall**. The company also makes insulated panels, **with solar panels attached**, that can be put over an existing roof. The **retrofits are faster** than traditional retrofits, **in some cases happening in as little as a day**, leading to more energy savings.

The goal is to make each home "net-zero energy," meaning that the solar panels on the roof generate enough electricity over the course of the year to equal the power that the house uses for heating, hot water, and appliances. In the Dutch city of Utrecht, for example, **houses and apartments that were retrofitted in 2019 have seen their energy use drop by around 78 percent. The remaining energy use is covered by the solar panels.**

Drachten completed renovation project

Back

5.18

Front

5.19

Many of the first renovations have happened in buildings owned by housing associations, in part because they tend to use a standard design, and that makes it easier to mass-produce the parts needed for a retrofit. Energiesprong helped set up a system that lets **tenants pay an "energy service" bill that partly covers the cost of the renovations; the huge savings in energy that comes with the retrofits also helps cover the cost**. So far, more than **5,700 homes have been retrofitted** in the country through the program, and the concept is beginning to be adopted elsewhere, including the U.K., France, Germany, and the United States[17].

RMI (Rocky Mountain Institute) and others are working with the Department of Energy on a report that lists all the major building types for different regions of the U.S. and will be providing retrofit guidelines for each type in 2022 to consider for all government buildings.

"We know that roughly 70 percent of the buildings that exist today will exist in 2050," says Martha Campbell, a principal at RMI. "And if we're going to hit net zero by 2050 . . . our estimates are that we need to hit a retrofit rate between 4 percent and 6 percent." That adds up to as many as **6 million retrofits each year in the U.S. alone**. The U.S. renovates 2 percent of building stock each year.

The average retrofit cost in the Netherlands is about $94,000 for a family home, typically a row house. In one neighborhood in the city of Utrecht, more than a dozen houses and some 250 separate apartments retrofitted in 2019 saw their energy requirements fall from 225 kilowatt-hours per square meter to just 50 kilowatt-hours per square meter, on average. The remaining demand for energy was met with solar power. **Mass retrofits become affordable if they are done on a large scale.** With thousands of modules at a time, **costs can be cut in half to around $50,000 per dwelling**. This model should be very successful in the U.S.

Engineers have designed a single rooftop module that houses an electric boiler for hot water, heat pump to warm the home, a smart meter, and a solar power hookup. Just days after an order comes into Factory Zero, the firm's installation teams can crane-drop a completed module onto the top of a flat- or pitched-roofed home, or next to one. **The company is making about 1,000 modules a year, and it charges around $16,000 per installation. It claims the typical cost in the Netherlands might be $35,000 if several different suppliers were working separately.** Landlords or governments can finance the retrofit work as part of their regular property maintenance.

5.20 A premade, lightweight, highly insulating material, complete with solar panels, would be installed on the roof.

A 2018 retrofitting project in Longueau, France [Photo: Fabrice Singevin/courtesy Energiesprong]

5.21 Entire buildings can be wrapped in a jacket to save energy.

The new facade is primarily fire-resistant expanded polystyrene with hollow spheres that trap air to create a thick insulation layer faced with hardened clay and sculpted into hundreds of very thin rectangles known as "brick slips." This new building skin is pre-built in a factory. The installation is part of a concerted effort to transform public housing into a set of ultra-low-emission homes, without having to open a wall or remake an attic.

Landlords planning a routine refurbishment of their housing stock can now simply add an energy retrofit to that process, with attractive new facades and roofs. An automated laser device takes precision measurements of a building's entire exterior in a matter of hours. The information is uploaded wirelessly to large factories, where walls, windows, doors and solar roofs are mass-produced and fit together for the target building. Completed facades and roofs are trucked to the site and attached. Often, the building owner or residents see their annual energy costs fall to zero thanks to solar panels that sell excess power to the national grid, at least during the summer.

The group recognized that lower-income owners and affordable housing in particular need technical assistance and capacity (and/or an alternative compliance pathway). It is not enough just to make incentives available. When it comes to incentives, the group proposed that **streamlined programs providing whole-building upgrades would be significantly more effective than traditionally piecemeal utility incentives** (Massachusetts' LEAN Multifamily program as a model). Collect non-compliance fees to create a fund that can support upgrades for disadvantaged communities and building owners. **Limit the ability of building owners to pass through the costs of upgrades to tenants beyond the savings achieved.**

The nation's largest landlord, the General Services Administration (GSA), manages almost 10,000 buildings, including offices, courthouses, post offices, and other commercial buildings. If we were to upgrade all these properties to net zero, the reduction in carbon would be significant.

PACE (Property Assessed Clean Energy) is a financing tool that homeowners can use to upgrade their home's energy performance or install renewable energy systems with no money down but rather repaid on a property's municipal tax bill over time.

While all-electric buildings are generally cheaper to construct than mixed fuel on a fixed cost basis, electrification retrofits typically involve higher first costs than a gas-for-gas retrofit, especially if there are electrical capacity issues. The payback is worth the investment.

The zLab group led by RMI to bring together industry leaders to brainstorm solutions and develop action plans focused on three critical issues:

- Getting consumers to demand electric heat pumps and other electric appliances from their contractors.

- Expanding contractor capacity to deliver electrification solutions.

- Making low-power solutions available and "retrofit ready".

Offer contractor incentives: Contractor incentives could include training incentives. The contractor can be a government-preferred contractor after having gone through the training.

Develop low-power specifications for utilities and manufacturers: It is crucial to develop specifications for electric appliances that are low-power, retrofit-ready, and would not require a house to invest in an electrical panel upgrade[18].

Tax Incentives

In the U.S., there are primarily Federal and State tax incentives for businesses and individuals. State incentives vary greatly.

Residential Renewable Energy Tax Credit includes solar, wind, geothermal, and fuel-cell technology: 26 percent through 2022. There is no upper limit on the amount of the credit for solar, wind and geothermal equipment.

The maximum tax credit for fuel cells is $500 for each half-kilowatt of power capacity, or $1,000 for each kilowatt. For example, a fuel cell with a 5kW capacity would qualify for 5 x $1,000 = $5,000 tax credit.

HOME IMPROVEMENTS THAT MAY QUALIFY FOR FEDERAL TAX CREDITS (verify each year with your accountant and on government web sites):

Windows, Doors, and Skylights - If you replaced any windows, doors, or skylights—or installed new ones that have earned the ENERGY STAR—you are eligible for a tax credit of 10 percent of the cost (not including installation) on up to $200 for windows and skylights and up to $500 for doors.

Roofs (Metal and Asphalt) - Roofing materials that meet ENERGY STAR requirements with appropriate pigmented coatings, and asphalt roofs with appropriate cooling granules, qualify for a credit of 10 percent of the cost up to $500—not including installation.

Insulation - can qualify for 10 percent of the cost, up to $500—not including installation costs.

Products that air seal- Products that reduce air leaks can also qualify, as long as they come with a Manufacturer's Certification Statement, including weather stripping, spray foam in a can, designed to air seal, caulk designed to air seal, and house wrap.

Most government's current efforts to help householders to adapt their homes are "too complicated," and too often things go wrong, say industry and consumer groups. There are the following suggestions that need to be addressed to ensure that plans to decarbonize homes don't fail.

Information: People need more accessible and unbiased information on steps, including installing low-carbon heating and upgrading their insulation.

Costs: Long-term policy framework that **provides certainty for businesses and consumers** and offers financial support such as grants, low-cost loans, and financing.

Simplify: The incentives should be very clear and easy to find. The forms should be simple and easy to fill out.

Help: Provide resources locally and by phone with people that can assist contractors and homeowners.

The Federal and State governments should increase the tax incentives to encourage the homeowner to invest more implementing energy efficiency solutions. **The more bundling of solutions will add up to higher energy efficiency to enable many people to get to or near zero-carbon.**

Summary

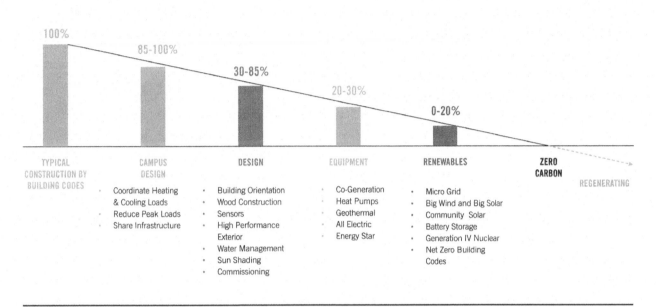

TYPICAL CONSTRUCTION BY BUILDING CODES	CAMPUS DESIGN	DESIGN	EQUIPMENT	RENEWABLES	ZERO CARBON
	Coordinate Heating & Cooling Loads	Building Orientation	Co-Generation	Micro Grid	
	Reduce Peak Loads	Wood Construction	Heat Pumps	Big Wind and Big Solar	
	Share Infrastructure	Sensors	Geothermal	Community Solar	
		High Performance Exterior	All Electric	Battery Storage	
		Water Management	Energy Star	Generation IV Nuclear	
		Sun Shading		Net Zero Building Codes	
		Commissioning			

REGENERATING

5.22

IMMEDIATE PAYBACK

Building Orientation- North/South orientation can reduce mechanical costs up to 10 percent and total costs 3 percent.

Casement or Awning Windows instead of Double Hung or Sliding are 30 percent more efficient.

Cement Mix to Reduce Carbon

Chilled Beam Mechanical System for businesses

District Heating compared to Standalone Solutions

Heat/Cool only spaces that you use

LEED Designed buildings

LED Lighting

Pre-engineered Wood

Reuse

Sharing

Vestibules

UP TO 1 YEAR

Bicycle infrastructure

Ceiling fans

Commissioning

Smart thermostats

Water management

1 TO 3 YEARS

Ceiling fans

Energy Star appliances

Heat pumps

Rain screens

Realize Renovation Model

Solar shading

Spray foam insulation

4 TO 7 YEARS

Battery storage

Plant urban trees

Solar panels

Waste to energy

Most businesses view a payback from their investment in 7 years as a smart decision.

6

CARBON SEQUESTRATION

Sequestration is the active process of removing CO_2 from the atmosphere through photosynthesis.

NATURE

Now scientists and farmers are studying how well cropland and pastures can pull CO_2 from the sky and store it back in the soil. **The IPCC's latest report lists soil carbon sequestration as one of the lower cost, more readily available options for CO_2 removal. Planting seeds without disturbing soil, spreading nutrient-rich compost over fields, and rotating where cattle graze are all considered strategies for trapping carbon.** Although sustainable agriculture methods aren't new, and many trace their roots to indigenous practices, pilot projects and real-world trials are emerging to determine which farming and grazing strategies could be best for storing carbon in soil. Scientists are developing new tools to accurately measure and monitor soil carbon at a massive scale, and policymakers and environmental groups are studying how to set protocols for how farmers should report and verify those measurements. The collection of data should be simple, easy, helpful, and affordable to implement.

"There's a real movement to consider these nature-based solutions as 'shovel- ready,' or something that we can implement quickly as a no-regret strategy," said Giana Amador, co-founder and policy director of Carbon180.

Use imagery from satellites and drones to remotely measure the water and carbon content of cornfields. The idea is to develop sensors that can gather real-time measurements at large scale without collecting physical soil samples. Another novel tool developed by the Soil Health Institute involves 3D-scanning the soil with lasers and using a smartphone app. Cristine Morgan, the institute's chief scientific officer, helped develop this approach to detect the differences in soil health on conventionally tilled and "no-till" farms.

"Virtual fencing" project that uses GPS-enabled collars to guide cattle toward specific pastures —an approach somewhat like invisible fences for pets. The idea is that ranchers can move their herds into new areas without building physical infrastructure and disturbing the land[1].

Collaborating

There are many issues that can help to reduce carbon and reduce the problems associated with climate change. **Some issues primarily apply to specific countries and regions of the world. Countries should support each other to look for creative and accountable solutions.** For example, Canada has a significant opportunity, and responsibility to maintain its peatland. The U.S. may create policies to support Canada's peatlands by limiting or eliminating the use of peat in the U.S. This may require some type of tradeoffs. The U.S. can share technology to help supplement the Canadian budget that would be affected by preserving their peatlands and the loss of sales for the peat.

Design with nature has many benefits. **Nature-based solutions often have more substantial and lasting benefits if deployed at landscape, ecosystem, citywide and country scales. Most countries have the opportunity to restore and maintain much of their natural environment which can have a significant positive impact on reducing carbon and improving health of their population.** Preserving and restoring nature are usually viewed in a highly favorable way.

Most people want natural solutions, like planting trees, before technical solutions. The reality is both are necessary, and the most cost-effective solutions should be implemented now. Tree planting is obviously high on the priority list.

Nothing can make carbon disappear, it can only move from one carbon storage pool to another. We do not want to add carbon to the environment, and we want to store the carbon that exists in the best natural places. Trees near their peak sequestration can be transformed into products that store the carbon for decades and in some cases centuries if we reuse more.

Planting trees is one of the cheapest and most reliable ways we have for reducing carbon at scale today. Forests are powerful carbon storehouses. Protection prevents carbon emissions and enables ongoing carbon sequestration.

The 2019 Edelman Trust Barometer found that more than three-quarters (76 percent) of the population want chief executive officers to lead the way in delivering change rather than waiting for governments to impose it.

There are three ways in which the destruction of biodiversity and ecosystems creates risks for businesses:

1. Dependency of business on nature: When businesses depend directly on nature for operations, supply chain performance, real estate asset values, physical security, and business continuity.

2. Fallout of business impacts on nature: When the direct and indirect impacts of business activities on nature loss trigger negative consequences, such as losing customers or entire markets, costly legal action, and adverse regulatory changes.

3. Impacts of nature loss on society: When nature loss aggravates the disruption of the society in which businesses operate, which in turn can create physical and market risks.

FIGURE 1:
Human activity is eroding the world's ecological foundations

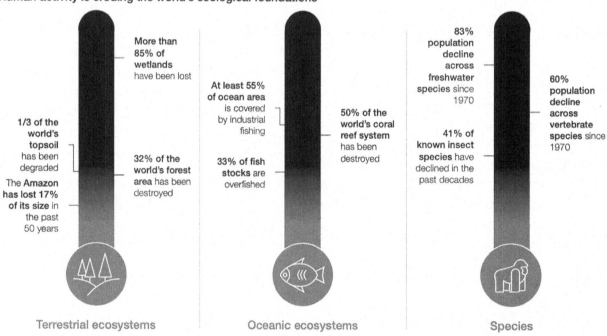

Source: IPBES, 2019, "Global assessment report on biodiversity and ecosystem services"; Maria-Helena Semedo of the Food and Agriculture Organization (FAO) at World Soil Day 2014; The Economist, 2019, "On the brink – The Amazon is approaching an irreversible tipping point"; WWF, 2018, "Living planet report – 2018: Aiming higher"; F. Sánchez-Bayo and K.A.G. Wyckhuys, 2019, "Worldwide decline of the entomofauna: A review of its drivers", Biological Conservation.

6.1 Human Activity is Eroding the World's Ecological Foundations

Forest Protection

The right trees must be planted in the right place if they are to be effective at reducing carbon emissions. Target tree-planting in biodiversity hotspots to protect as many plant and animal species as possible. Work with local organizations to plant trees that target the local community's most urgent needs, like providing jobs, firewood, food and fertile soil.

By reintroducing trees in the landscape, we impact positively humidity, rain capture, soil conservation, and biodiversity preservation. When trees and plants die, whether from fires or logging or simply falling, most of the carbon trapped in their trunks, branches, and leaves simply returns to the atmosphere after several years.

Working Forests

Working Forests are carefully managed to produce a steady, renewable supply of wood for lumber, energy, paper and packaging, and thousands of items that consumers use each day.

Forest products are made of an earth-friendly material that reduces our dependence on fossil fuels. **Almost 3 million Americans have jobs supported by working forests.** There are 514 million acres of working forests in the U.S. which is approximately 3 times bigger than Texas. Working forests vigorously grow trees, which sequester CO_2 from the atmosphere at an impressive rate as they grow. When trees are harvested and turned into solid wood products, they continue to store large amounts of carbon. Over time and scale, working forests are a powerful carbon mitigation tool.

There are more private working forest acres than any other type. **For private working forests, the market keeps the forest land to be continuously used as forest.** Forest products incentivize private landowners to invest in their forests, keep them healthy, and keep them growing—pulling carbon out of the atmosphere and storing it for a long term. **The data clearly shows that the continuous cycle of growing, harvesting, and replanting yields an impressive carbon benefit.**

6.2 Two percent of Working Forests are harvested each year in the U.S.

Private working forests provide 73 percent of our forest's annual sequestration, 54 percent of total carbon storage, all while providing 90 percent of the harvest for forest products. 2 percent of working forests are harvested each year in the United States.

There is the need, and significant benefit of using wood for construction of buildings. It is important that the trees that are removed are replaced to assure the forests are always growing. **Between 1953 and 2017, the total volume of trees grown in the U.S. increased by 60 percent.**

Trees available to harvest in the U.S. today are not a problem. If we can transition from concrete and steel construction to wood, then we may need to add more working forests, but we can start that transition now by planting more trees to be available to harvest later. The U.S. has clearly the opportunity to add many trees in urban areas to reduce the heat island effect and support a more pedestrian environment. **If the U.S. were to focus on planting more trees, we would contribute to help global sequestration.**

6.3 Plant trees for building and energy products.

We replant, regrow, and regenerate, maintaining a never-ending cycle. Today, private forest owners are growing 43 percent more wood than they need to harvest.

There is a recognition that the time has come to give serious consideration to wood products in order to utilize these sustainable resources. Because only by actively managing our forests through harvesting and other practices can we keep them healthy and provide economic opportunities for the landowners. Therefore, **the concept of promoting wood for building and energy products is important to continue to maintain healthy, sustainable forests.** USDA has supported this expansion in recent news releases, grant-funded opportunities,

awards, and competitions. The U.S. Tall Wood Building Prize Competition to Innovate Building Construction is one example[2].

Over $230 billion in wood product revenues are generated annually from 200 million acres of private forestland in the southern United States.[3] Private forest landowners account for 87 percent of forested land in southern U.S.[4]. In South Carolina, the SC Forestry Commission, for example, has determined that it is possible to enhance the forest health and resiliency of the forest and increase the acres of forested land in the state by increasing the number of primary and secondary producers that use wood grown in the state.

In the U.S., there are plenty of trees to harvest to encourage much more wood construction. Trees provide another advantage with the understory growing grasses, herbaceous plants all that absorb CO_2. The harvesting of working forests has been developed over the last 100 years and is self-supporting.

Non-Working Forests

Non-working forests are parks, hiking trails, backyard woods, and urban trees. These are forested lands not managed to produce products. Non-working forests equal 251 million acres, which is approximately 1.5 the size of Texas.

U.S. National Parks contain forested areas that not only protect water sources, but they also help stabilize the surrounding land. This can save lives and infrastructure by preventing landslides, avalanches, and erosion. These areas also reduce floods by keeping natural river basins intact and preserving wetlands. **Parks and protected public lands are proven to improve water quality, protect groundwater, prevent flooding, improve the quality of the air we breathe, provide vegetative buffers to development, produce habitat for wildlife, provide a place for children and families to connect with nature, and a place to sequester carbon.**

6.4 Visit your state park lands and you will feel better!

A 2018 study found that **12 percent** of the country's land area has been conserved as national parks, wilderness areas, permanent conservation easements, state parks, national wildlife refuges, national monuments, or other protected areas. There are currently 63 national parks. About 7.5 percent of the world's forests are in the United States; and all together, U.S. forests cover over 741 million acres.

RECOMMENDATIONS

Protect existing non-working forests first.

Put local people at the heart of tree-planting projects.

Maximize biodiversity recovery to meet multiple goals.

Use natural forest regrowth wherever possible.

Mangrove Protection

Mangrove forests provide more than $80 billion per year in avoided losses from coastal flooding—and protect 18 million people. **We have lost over half of the world's original mangrove forest area, estimated at 32 million hectares (approx. 80 million acres).** It takes 10-15 years for a mangrove tree to reach maturity. For the first 5 years of its life, World Wildlife Foundation (WWF), with the help of local communities will care for your tree to make sure it stays strong and healthy.

6.5 New Mangroves in Batangas in the Philippines.

Mangroves are incredibly effective in naturally combating climate change, thanks to their ability to sequester three to four times more carbon from the Earth's atmosphere than tropical forests.

Mangrove forests are important because they:

- Prevent salt water from intruding into rivers.

- Protect coastlines against erosive wave action and strong coastal winds and serve as natural barriers against tsunamis and torrential storms.

- Retain, concentrate and recycle nutrients and remove toxicants through a natural filtering process.

- Provide resources for coastal communities who depend on the plants for timber, fuel, food, medicinal herbs and other forest products.

- Can be harvested sustainably for wood and other products.

- Are an important breeding ground for many fishes, crabs, prawns, and other marine animals, essential for sustaining a viable fishing industry. About 50 percent of fish landings on the west coast of Peninsular Malaysia are associated with mangroves.

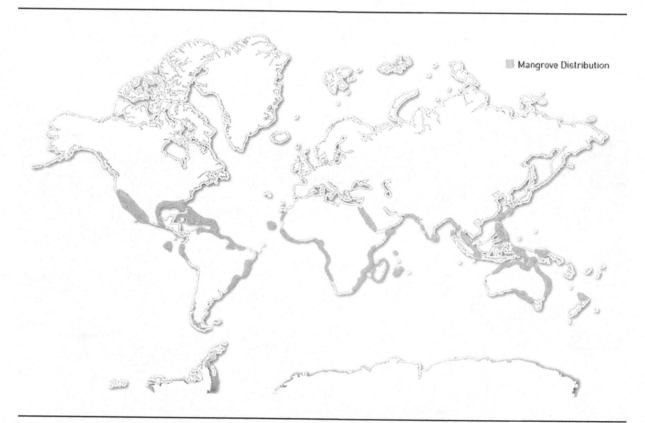

Mangrove Distribution

6.6 Global Mangrove Map

Guidelines for planting trees for social good.

1. As well as planting trees, understand the root causes of loss of trees, protect existing forests and woodlands, and plant more trees.

2. Trees are most likely to thrive in places where they grow naturally. The worst option is to convert other natural ecosystems such as grasslands, peatlands or wetlands to forest. Use native tree species and a mix of species brings more benefits.

3. **Economists estimate that investments in ecosystem restoration can generate multiple benefits for societies worth U.S. $10 for every U.S. $1 invested[5].**

"Planting mangrove forests and regrowing seaweed beds are great ways to engage communities, create relevant jobs, and quickly boost tourism and aquaculture through fast-reviving food and fish stocks." Doug Woodring, Founder and Managing Director, Ocean Recovery Alliance

6.7 Machine learning to distinguish and quantify Mexico's mangroves with drone and satellite imagery.

The University of California, San Diego, is using remote sensing technology and machine learning to better characterize mangroves, guide management of the habitat, and curb mangrove deforestation by increasing the availability of reliable data on mangrove coverage and extent. The Aburto Lab and Engineers for Exploration are developing a methodology that uses machine learning to automatically distinguish and quantify Mexico's mangroves from drone and satellite imagery, resulting in improved understanding of how mangrove distribution changes through time, as well as the ability to estimate mangrove biomass and calculate the carbon storage.

SUMMARY

There are some excellent examples of community-based ecological restoration and protection, with major carbon benefits. Projects such as mangrove defense in Vietnam and watershed restoration in Ghana could set a benchmark for future global initiatives.

The greatest potential for reforestation occurs on former tropical rainforest land that has been cleared for large-scale ranching, palm oil plantations, and timber production.

Farming

The USDA REAP Grant (Rural Energy for America Program) is for renewable energy systems and energy efficiency improvement. Essentially, the program provides guaranteed loan financing and grant funding to agricultural producers and rural small businesses. Agricultural producers may also apply for new energy-efficient equipment and new system loans for agricultural production and processing.

Modern agriculture requires energy input at all stages of agricultural production, whether directly or indirectly:

Direct Energy for irrigation, harvesting and cultivation, processing, storage and transportation.

Indirect energy is the energy required to manufacture inputs such as machinery, equipment, mineral fertilizers and chemical pesticides such as herbicides and insecticides.

12 percent share of global greenhouse gases emissions are from agriculture.

Improving food production on existing farmland will reduce the need to clear more land. In the U.S. in the year 1800, there was a population of 5,308,483 people with 15 percent as farmers (360,000). Today 1 percent of the population comprise farmers (320,000) that feed a population of 330,000,000. The size of farms has increased significantly, technology has enabled farmers to support larger crops, the government funds farming, and there is much more knowledge on getting more crops from the land more efficiently.

While American farming has certainly expanded and increased its value since 1920, there were almost 3 times as many farms 100 years ago than there are today—in 1920, there were 6.5 million farms, while 2020 estimates come in at **2 million. Using the latest best practices for farming increases the productivity of the land and supports carbon sinks that existed 100 years ago and earlier. This is a U.S. success story! Something similar can happen with the change from fossil fuels to renewable energies over the next 25 years.**

But many places are now looking to find new technological solutions that allow them to improve yields, resilience to climate change and sustainability together. **Precision farming** is an interesting example of this. This is a kind of technology we've never had before, which **uses technologies such as drones, satellites, and GPS to map out the conditions in a field.** It can precisely calculate what nutrients or other agricultural additions are needed in specific small pockets of land, helping farmers to do things in a smarter, more efficient, and more informed way. It can also reduce negative environmental impacts, such as runoff from nitrogen fertilizer sprayed on a field that doesn't need it[6].

6.8 Technology for More Productive Farming.

Regenerative agriculture asks us to think about *how all aspects of agriculture are connected through a web*—a network of entities who grow, enhance, exchange, distribute, and consume goods and services—instead of a linear supply chain. It's about farming and ranching in a style that nourishes people and the earth[7].

Farmers could reduce rainfall runoff by up to 20% in flood events, depending on how they manage their crops and fields. These practices often involve up-front costs for new equipment, training, technical assistance, and research to optimize them for different crops, soils, and weather conditions.

Opportunities for farmers to be more successful include:

Silvopasture

Managed grazing

Perennial staple crops

Tree intercropping

Regenerative cropping

Agroforestry

Conservation agriculture

Agrivoltaics

Investments in resilient design solutions are proactive ways to work with nature to benefit the world. When soil is degraded, carbon is released back into the atmosphere as CO_2, while further plant growth is compromised. Better land management, including controlled grazing by animals and tree planting, can boost soil fertility, helping to reduce poverty and boost food security.

Alternative crop and soil practices can improve water absorption during heavy rainfall.

FIGURE 4. Alternative Crop and Soil Practices Can Improve Water Absorption During Heavy Rainfall

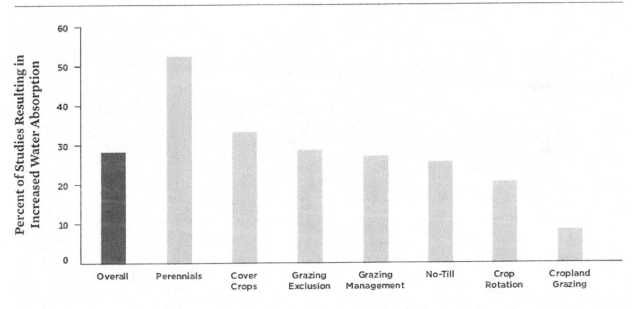

6.9 **The bars show the percentage within each category that improved absorption of rainfall. The red bar to the left represents the average of the 7 solutions in yellow.**

SILVOPASTURE is an old practice of **integrating trees, forage, and the grazing of domesticated animals in a mutually beneficial way.** It utilizes the principles of managed grazing. Silvopasture is an important system to help landowners diversify their operations and add to their income. The system **combines trees with livestock.** The Silvopasture system provides shade and shelter for livestock while growing grass and hay for the animals.

Pastures with trees sequester 5–10 times as much carbon as those of the same size that are treeless, storing it in both biomass and soil. As the impacts of global warming progress, appeal will likely grow, because silvopasture can help farmers and their livestock adapt to erratic weather and increased drought. That is the climatic win-win of this solution: Silvopasture averts and sequesters emissions, while protecting against changes that are now inevitable.

6.10 Silvopasture Farming

Livestock, trees, and additional forestry products, such as nuts, fruit, and mushrooms, generate income throughout the year. Silvopasture systems are diversely productive and more resilient, allowing farmers to have less risk.

Silvopasture is the highest ranked of all of Drawdown's agricultural solutions in terms of mitigation impact. It should be a priority for scaling up wherever grasslands are humid enough to permit tree growth. This is particularly important given the need to produce climate-friendly livestock products to meet global demand for meat and dairy.

FINANCIAL COST/PAYBACK

After considering profit and operational costs, **the net gain is approximately 4 times more to farm as Silvopasture compared to conventional farming.**

Managed Grazing

There are three managed-grazing techniques that improve soil health, carbon sequestration, water retention, and food productivity:

1. Improved continuous grazing adjusts standard grazing practices and decreases the number of animals per acre.

2. Rotational grazing moves livestock to fresh paddocks or pastures, allowing those already grazed to recover.

3. Adaptive multi-paddock grazing shifts animals through smaller paddocks in quick succession, after which the land is given time to recover.

Managed grazing does not address the methane emissions generated by cattle, sheep, goats, and so on. It is my belief that there will always be the desire for large animals for many people in their diet. **Managed grazing can reduce the carbon impact of methane from animals.**

FINANCIAL COST/PAYBACK

Managed grazing can improve profits and output up to 30 percent.

Perennial Staple Crops

Perennial crop systems are clear winners at managing heavy rains. Agricultural management offers significant opportunities to buffer the damage caused by heavy rain events. The practices increase infiltration enough to absorb a heavy rain event of one inch per hour. More diverse farm systems lead to healthier soils and smarter water use. Cover crops and perennials improve the structure of the soil. Cover crops provide good cover and a dense root system to help stabilize soils and combat erosion. Clovers, annual ryegrass, Austrian winter peas, rapeseed, mustards, and cowpeas are good cover crops for erosion protection. These practices increase porosity by an average of 8 percent compared with practices that leave the soil bare for significant portions of the year.

89 percent of cultivated land, about 3 billion acres, is devoted to annuals to produce annual staple crops like maize, wheat, potatoes, and soybeans. **Lands converted from annuals to perennials sequester, on average, 1.9 tons of carbon per acre every year for decades.** What's more, perennial staple tree crops can weather and thrive under conditions that annuals cannot, which is vital in a warming world. **The right balance between annuals and perennials needs to be determined in each area of the world.** Perennial crops should be on non-degraded grassland and cropland, with no forest clearing required.

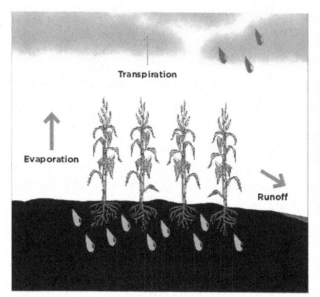 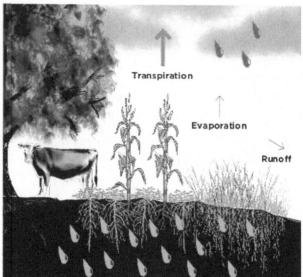

6.11 Typical Corn Belt Annual Crop System, System Incorporating Perennials, Cover Crops and Livestock

"Continuous living cover" of soil is the best strategy for improving water infiltration. This cover, which keeps living roots in the soil all year, can be achieved by introducing perennials, cover crops, or by improving grazing practices[8]. This improvement is likely related to the creation of continuous root systems in the soil, which contribute to topsoil retention, increased levels of soil carbon,

enhanced biological activity, and reduced water loss from runoff. This is a novel scientific finding that can help prioritize the practices that help reduce climate risks.

Expand incentives and strengthen up-front financial support for farmers to encourage them to adopt soil management practices that deliver flood and drought resilience.

Tree Intercropping

Tree intercropping practices vary, but all increase biomass, soil organic matter, and carbon sequestration. Like all regenerative land-use practices, tree intercropping—**intermingling trees and crops**—increases the carbon content of the soil and productivity of the land.

Common benefits include:

- Windbreaks reduce erosion and create habitat for birds and pollinators.

- Fast-growing annuals, susceptible to being flattened by wind and rain, can be protected.

- Deep-rooted plants can draw up minerals and nutrients for shallow-rooted ones.

- Light-sensitive crops can be protected from excess sunlight.

Regenerative Cropping

Regenerative annual cropping uses compost and organic production. This process reduces emissions, increases soil organic matter, and sequesters carbon. **The world cannot be fed unless the soil is fed. Regenerative agriculture enhances and sustains the health of the soil by restoring its carbon content, which in turn improves productivity.**

Regenerative agricultural practices increase carbon-rich soil. It is any annual cropping system that **includes at least 4 of the following 6 practices: compost application, cover crops, crop rotation, green manures, no-till or reduced tillage, and/or organic production.**

Drawdown has estimated that at least 50 percent of the carbon in the earth's soils has been released into the atmosphere over the past centuries. Bringing that carbon back home through regenerative agriculture is one of the greatest opportunities to address human and climate health, along with the financial well-being of farmers.

FINANCIAL COST/PAYBACK

The profit is estimated about 15–20 percent higher, and the operational costs are 60 percent less than conventional farming.

Agroforestry

Encourage "agroforestry," where food crops are mixed in with trees to improve crop varieties. Agroforestry is a collective name for land-use systems and technologies where woody perennials (trees, shrubs, palms, and bamboos) are deliberately used on the same land-management units as agricultural crops and/or animals, in some form of spatial arrangement or temporal sequence. They **can control runoff and soil erosion, thereby reducing losses of water, soil material, organic matter, and nutrients**.

By mimicking forests, agroforestry can:

- prevent erosion and flooding,

- recharge groundwater,

- restore degraded land and soils,

- support biodiversity by providing habitat and corridors between fragmented ecosystems,

- and absorb and store carbon.

Farmers gain income and resilience from multiple crops growing on unique timelines. Yet, costs to establish a complex system can be high, and tending it can be more labor intensive. Incentives can help farmers overcome financial barriers and realize the multi-layered benefits of multi-strata agroforestry.

Carbon sequestration rates of multi-strata agroforestry are very high, particularly for a food production system. The practice also offers impressive co-benefits, notably ecosystem services like habitat, erosion control, and water quality.

Conservation Agriculture

Conservation agriculture uses cover crops, crop rotation, and minimal tilling in the production of annual crops. Currently there is the education of this type of agriculture to farmers to help be more productive. In the U.S., farmers benefit from the latest equipment to allow them to manage large areas of farmland.

These ideas can be implemented in developing countries affordably. The difficulty is getting the best information out in a timely manner to help farmers everywhere. **Minimizing the tilling of the land protects soil, avoids emissions, and sequesters carbon.**

IMPROVE SOIL AND WATER EFFICIENCY

Reducing water risks from both floods and droughts by creating more absorbent, spongelike soils. This approach, which manages rainfall as it moves through soil and crops, builds holistic resilience in both wet and dry periods. Global modeling studies have found that more effective management of water in soil has significant potential both to improve crop production and to reduce the overall amount of water runoff resulting from agricultural systems.

Three core principles:

1. Minimize soil disturbance: farmers seed directly into the soil without tilling.

2. Maintain soil cover: farmers leave crop residues after harvesting or grow cover crops.

3. Manage crop rotation: farmers change what is grown and where.

Conservation agriculture makes land more resilient to climate-related events such as long droughts and heavy downpours—it is doubly valuable in a warming world. Given that many rice farming methods are long-entrenched customs, change requires helping farmers see what results are possible, cultivating necessary knowledge and skills, and implementing incentives that make new methods compelling.

6.12 Windbreaks to Protect Crops

Windbreaks are plantings of single and multiple rows of trees and shrubs that protect crops, soil, animals, homes and people from wind, snow, dust, and odors. These systems save energy and can cut home heating costs. Windbreaks help with carbon storage and improve crop yields.

Agrivoltaics: Combining solar and agriculture

The benefits are numerous, including higher crop yields, increased support of local ecosystems, improved soil, increased protection of crops, increased revenues, and water conservation.

Research has shown that the shade provided by solar arrays can potentially increase agricultural production by as much as 70 percent and reduce water use by 30 percent.

Solar panels and arrays can also reduce the stress on crops stemming from too much direct light and heat and protect them during violent storms. Evaporation of water used to irrigate plants growing under panels and the plants themselves have a cooling effect on the panels, which improves their efficiency by at least 1 percent. Panels have been shown to be effective for crops as well as when combined with animal grazing and as apiaries for bees[9].

6.13

Solar supplies an ever-growing number of benefits for agriculture businesses. The panels block the wind and limit soil erosion to maintain soil health. Farmers are able to provide additional warmth in the winter and cooler climates in the summer. **The USDA REAP Grant (Rural Energy for America Program) is for renewable energy systems and energy efficiency improvement. Essentially, the program provides guaranteed loan financing and grant funding to agricultural producers and rural small businesses. Agricultural producers may also apply for new energy-efficient equipment and new system loans for agricultural production and processing.**

The Sustainable Farming Incentive in the UK will entice 70 percent of farmers to smother 70 percent of land in the wintertime with "cover crops" such as grasses, beans, brassicas, and herbs. These crops won't be planted for harvesting; they are for improving the soil. Landholders will be incentivized for reducing the amount of fertilizer and pesticide they use. They'll be encouraged to use low-impact methods such as integrated pest management, which uses pheromones to disrupt pest mating cycles, or adopts mechanical control, such as trapping or weeding.

6.14 Combine Solar and Agriculture

	Combines trees and livestock	Three managed grazing techniques	Manage Heavy Rains	Cover crops to stabilize soli	Combines trees and crops	Compost and Annual Production	No or minimal tilling	Crop Rotation	Foof crops mixed with trees	Solar Panels with crops	Annual And Long Term Income Streams
SILVOPASTURE	▓										
MANAGED GRAZING		▓									
PERENNIAL STAPLE CROPS									▓		
TREE INTERCROPPING					▓						
REGENERATIVE CROPPING						▓					
AGROFORESTRY	▓			▓	▓				▓		▓
CONSERVATION AGRICULTURE			▓	▓		▓	▓	▓			
AGRIVOLTAICS										▓	

6.15 Characteristics of Various Farming Methods

This chart is intended to help understand the key point(s) of these various farming methods, which are developing. The new farming methods will have a significant positive impact on climate change.

KEEP SOIL COVERED

MAINTAIN LIVING ROOT YEAR ROUND

REGENERATIVE AGRICULTURE

MINIMIZE SOIL DISTURBANCE

INTEGRATE LIVESTOCK

MAXIMIZE CROP DIVERSITY

6.16

Save the Whales and Elephants

One whale is worth thousands of trees when it comes to reducing carbon globally. Great whales are the carbon-capture titans of the animal world, absorbing an average of 33 tons of CO_2 each throughout their lives before their carcasses sink to the bottom of the ocean and remain there for centuries, according to an article in the International Monetary Fund's (IMF) Finance & Development magazine. A tree, by contrast, absorbs no more than 48 pounds of the CO_2 a year. Whales accumulate carbon in their bodies during their long lives, some of which stretch to 200 years. **A tree during the same period only contributes to 3 percent of the carbon absorption of the whale**[10].

Whale populations have been decimated to 1.3 million. **Researchers argue that if the whale population were allowed to grow to around 4–5 million—the total before the era of whaling—thereby capturing 1.7 billion tons of CO_2 annually**[11].

Whales also support the production of **phytoplankton**, which contributes at least 50 percent of all oxygen to the Earth's atmosphere. **Increasing phytoplankton productivity by just 1 percent would have the same effect as the sudden appearance of 2 billion mature trees. Phytoplankton captures approximately four Amazon rainforests worth of CO_2 each year**[12].

"In a similar way, we can create financial mechanisms to promote the restoration of the world's whale populations," said the report's authors. "Incentives in the form of subsidies or other compensation could help those who incur significant costs as a result of whale protection. For example, shipping companies could be compensated for the cost of altered shipping routes to reduce the risk of collisions."

All whales dive underwater to feed and return to the surface to breath. At the surface, they release buoyant fecal plumes that are rich in nutrients that phytoplankton need to grow. Many whales migrate from nutrient-rich feeding grounds to nutrient-poor breeding grounds. On the breeding grounds, whales release nitrogen-rich urea that can stimulate phytoplankton growth.

According to Steven Lutz, director of Blue Climate Solutions, which produced a 2017 report that addresses the role of whales in carbon sequestration, "the main takeaway here is that **whales eat carbon, not fish.**"

If we can calculate their contribution to CO_2 sequestration accurately then whales could be used to reach climate objectives and may even be included by island nations when establishing their Nationally Determined Contributions (NDCs). Norway and Japan are two countries that can save many whales by stopping the hunting, which will have a significant impact on the carbon footprint of their country.

ELEPHANTS

The team has been working on a similar carbon-market-based approach for protecting elephants from poachers in the central tropical forests of Africa. If forest elephants were allowed to rebound to their former populations, their carbon-capturing value would jump to more than $150 billion.

More than 80 percent of the elephant population has been killed off in central Africa since 2002. Poachers receive pennies on the dollar for elephant tusks that, once they finally reach consumers, can fetch prices of up to $40,000 on the illegal ivory market. That pales in comparison to the **$1.75 million an elephant could be worth for its carbon sequestration services**, an amount that works out to roughly $80 a day over an elephant's 60-year average lifetime[13].

In a recent study in *Nature Geoscience* that shows how forest elephants in the Congo Basin help their rainforest homes sequester billions of tons of carbon. Elephants could become "living assets" for countries that protect them.

MAN-MADE

Man-made carbon sequestration options will clearly add costs to the consumer and should be used minimally. The oil and gas companies should be required to build and pay for their structures without any additional government subsidies.

Direct Air Capture (DAC) and Carbon Capture & Sequestration (CCS) will be a focus primarily by the fossil fuel industry to counter the amount of carbon they create. As I study all these issues related to climate change, I realize DAC and CCS will be necessary, to a certain extent, to reduce carbon. In the concrete and steel industries, it is important to use this technology only as needed. I doubt we will ever get to no need for fossil fuels, but we should be able to reduce the use significantly, then sequester the carbon. The cost of fossil fuels will go up to pay for the DAC and CCS solutions, which will drive the growth for more affordable renewable energies. **DAC, CCS with the growth of renewable energies should be able to help transition fossil fuel companies to renewable energies as they reinvent their business.**

A modest amount of fossil fuels will be necessary:

1. To tackle emissions in sectors with limited options: cement, steel and chemicals manufacturing.

2. To produce synthetic fuels for long-distance transport.

3. To provide "on-demand" to ensure the stable operation of power systems night and day.

Direct Air Capture

Direct Air Capture is a technological method that uses chemical reactions to capture carbon dioxide (CO_2) from the atmosphere. When air moves over these chemicals, they selectively react with and remove CO_2, allowing the other components of air to pass through. These chemicals can take the form of either liquid solvents or solid sorbents, which make up the two types of DAC systems in use today.

The captured CO_2 can be injected underground for permanent storage in certain geologic formations or used in various products and applications. Using the captured carbon for products such as construction material or plastics can also provide long-term storage for decades or even centuries. However, using the carbon for products like beverages would quickly rerelease carbon into the atmosphere.

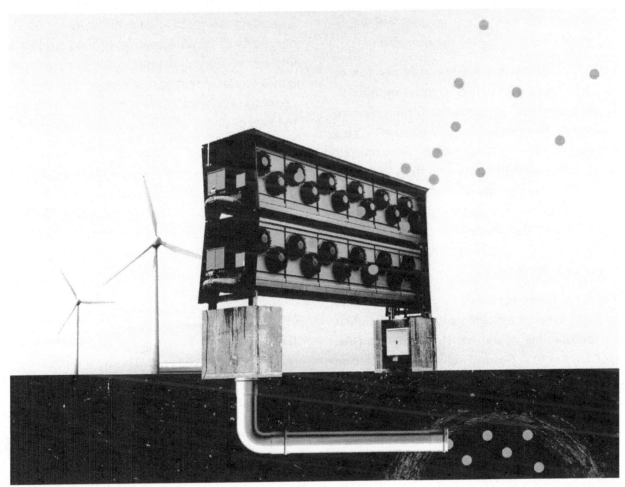

6.17

One strategy would involve converting some portion of the natural gas fleet into combined heat and power plants coupled with Carbon Capture and Storage (CCS, which captures CO_2 emissions from fuel combustion) to power DAC. The natural gas infrastructure, which otherwise would have been stranded, coupled with CCS, could provide power to the grid during times of peak demand. During non-peak hours, when excess renewable energy is produced, that renewable energy could power DAC. With this strategy, DAC would not directly compete with decarbonizing the grid and could make use of surplus renewable electricity. Over time, the use of natural gas should not be necessary as the renewable energies are able to cover the demand.

Direct Air Capture is more costly per ton of CO_2 captured compared to most mitigation approaches and most natural climate solutions. The range of costs for DAC varies between $250–$600/ton today. For context, most reforestation costs less than $50/ton. Depending on the rate of deployment, which can accelerate through supportive policies and market development, costs for DAC could fall to around $150–$200 per ton over the next 5–10 years[14].

The time taken for trees to grow to be able to absorb large amounts of carbon is similar to the timeline of the construction of a DAC or CCS facility. Natural solutions for Carbon Sequestration should be the priority and are discussed here in a few pages.

Intergovernmental Panel on Climate Change (IPCC):

"In order to keep warming below catastrophic levels, we now must also find a way to take billions of tons of the carbon dioxide we've poured into the atmosphere back out. That process is known as **carbon dioxide removal**."

Many environmental groups are deeply skeptical of carbon capture. Most of the 40 million tons in carbon gas captured today by carbon capture and storage, is from industrial smokestacks as opposed to from the plain air. It **is injected into the ground** and used to force more crude to the surface— thus further extending the life of fossil fuels. In July of 2021, hundreds of climate activist groups signed a letter encouraging the Biden administration to stay away from that sort of carbon capture. "In order to tackle the climate crisis, first we have to keep oil and coal in the ground. It is a matter of priorities." —IPCC

In the bipartisan infrastructure bill the Senate passed in August 2021, there was a record $9 billion plus for carbon capture. The bill has $3.5 billion for four regional direct air capture hubs and another $3.5 billion for transport and storage of carbon including money to build a massive pipeline network to carry captured CO_2.

DAC captures 90 percent of greenhouse gases, not 100 percent. This new technology will add costs because **power companies do not gain any energy by installing.** Founded by Climeworks, the DAC plant can remove 900 tons of CO_2 from ambient air annually.

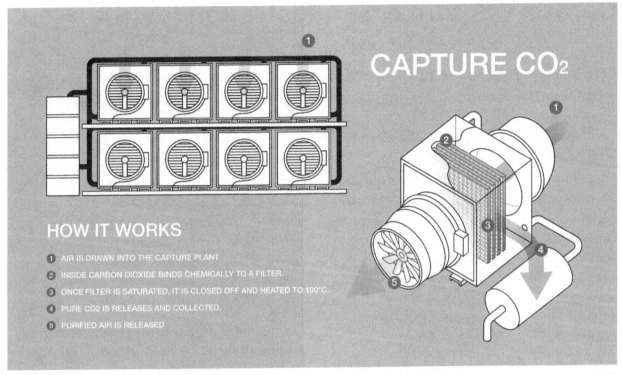

CAPTURE CO₂

HOW IT WORKS

1. AIR IS DRAWN INTO THE CAPTURE PLANT
2. INSIDE CARBON DIOXIDE BINDS CHEMICALLY TO A FILTER.
3. ONCE FILTER IS SATURATED, IT IS CLOSED OFF AND HEATED TO 100°C.
4. PURE CO2 IS RELEASES AND COLLECTED.
5. PURIFIED AIR IS RELEASED

6.18

The CO_2 is supplied as a raw material to customers in different markets, including to a nearby vegetable farm, where it is used as fertilizer. By using the filtered CO_2, Climeworks says its customers can reduce their overall emissions as well as lowering their dependence on fossil fuels.

The fans on the outside serve to suck in the ambient air. Inside each collector unit, the air goes through a process of adsorption and desorption before being blown out again with reduced CO_2 content.

The Orca plant located in Iceland is the largest in the world today and is designed to draw CO_2 out of the air and store it as rock. It can remove 4,000 tons of carbon dioxide out of the air every year, according to the company. The Orca plant was constructed by Switzerland's Climeworks and Iceland's Carbfix.

According to the US Environmental Protection Agency, that equates to the emissions from about 870 cars. The plant cost between US$10-$15million to build, Bloomberg reported. This does not account for the operational costs. **This amounts to $14,000 for each car to build the plant; then there are the yearly operational costs.**

FINANCIAL COST/PAYBACK

Under the current economic structure, the DAC will add cost that will then transfer to the consumer. The initial cost should go directly to coal, oil, and gas companies. **There is no financial payback, and this solution is basically to keep fossil fuel industries running, at a more expensive cost.**

Carbon Capture & Sequestration (CCS)

CCS is a process to capture carbon from power stations and industrials, then store it underground. It is considered a key incremental technology on the path to net-zero emissions.

According to the Global CCS Institute's 2021 Status Report, **plants in operation or under construction have the current capacity to capture 40 million metric tons of CO_2 per year (.008% for the U.S. only, which is not even close to addressing the carbon in the atmosphere).** For context, the United States emitted **over 5 billion metric tons** of CO_2 in 2019[15].

CCS deployment is in its early stages; financial returns on a CCS project are riskier than normal operations. National tax credits for carbon sequestration are created through **Section 45Q** of the Internal Revenue Code. Adding to these national tax credits, several tax credit and other crediting mechanisms exist at the state level in California, Texas, Louisiana, Montana, and North Dakota.

Consequently, investors impose higher risk premiums (the minimum amount of expected return required to attract investment), which further increases the private cost of the investment. Therefore, mitigating risk for investors is vital for incentivizing investment and development of CCS. This will be very challenging. There is much less risk in many other technologies that will reduce greenhouse gases.

There are also challenges associated with transporting CO_2 once it is captured. Significant energy is required to compress and chill CO_2 and maintain high pressure and low temperatures throughout pipelines, and the pipelines themselves are expensive to build. Existing oil and gas pipelines cannot be used[16].

To achieve a goal of net-zero emissions, more than 1,700 coal plants would have to be retrofitted with this technology. Fulfilling the potential of CCS under the Paris Agreement **would require capital investment of approximately $2.5 trillion by 2050.** $2.5 trillion can build more than enough solar panels, wind turbines and battery storage to address the country's energy needs. Again, it is recommended that coal plants be shut down and the market is driving that to happen with much more affordable options, especially renewable energies and possibly Generation IV nuclear technology.

In the U.S., there are now 12 (CCS) commercial facilities in operation of various stages of development, and two facilities that have suspended operations. **This represents about half of the total CCS projects around the globe[17].**

In its recently published report, the IEA identified four crucial ways in which CCS can contribute to a successful clean energy transition:

- CCS can be retrofitted to power industrial plants that may otherwise still be emitting 8 billion tons of CO_2 in 2050—around one-quarter of today's annual energy-sector emissions.

- CCS can tackle emissions in sectors with limited other options, such as cement, steel and chemicals manufacturing, and in the production of synthetic fuels for long-distance transport.

- CCS enables the production of low-carbon hydrogen from fossil fuels, a least-cost option in several regions around the world.

- CCS can remove CO_2 from the atmosphere by combining it with bioenergy or direct air capture to balance emissions that are unavoidable or technically difficult to avoid.

Grabbing carbon from a factory smokestack runs about $60 per ton of CO_2; removing it from ambient air can cost more than 15 times that[18].

Tesla and SpaceX CEO Elon Musk has launched the XPrize Carbon Removal competition to create devices that permanently sequester carbon dioxide to reduce the impact of climate change[19].

XPrize Carbon Removal challenges designers to develop a machine to pull large amounts of CO_2 directly from either the atmosphere or the oceans. "We want teams to build real systems that can make a measurable impact at a gigaton level," said Musk. "Whatever it takes. Time is of the essence." The four-year competition will have a prize fund of $100 million with the overall winner receiving $50 million, second place $20 million and third $10 million. According to XPrize Foundation, this makes it the largest incentive prize in history.

The overall aim of the contest is to produce a device that can remove one gigaton—one billion tons—of CO_2 from the earth per year. According to the organizer's estimates, we need to remove around six gigatons of CO_2 per year by 2030 and 10 gigatons per year by 2050 to reach the climate goals agreed in the Paris Agreement climate change treaty. "Any carbon-negative solution is eligible: nature-based, direct air capture, oceans, mineralization, or anything else that sequesters CO_2 permanently."

2021 EDITION OF THE LIVABILITY CHALLENGE:

SeaChange's technology converts dissolved CO_2 in sea water into stable solid carbonates, which can be used to make construction materials such as cement and concrete. The top prize is $735,000 in funding for their project from the backer of the contest, Temasek Foundation, the philanthropic arm of Singapore state investment firm Temasek.

The idea of having specific competitions to solve real problems should be encouraged now for ideas that may have the biggest impact on reducing the carbon. The competition entries should be shared globally. Competitions should also be focused on better storage of energy, batteries, and improving solar and wind technology. Improving these will require much less fossil fuels and the need to capture carbon.

FINANCIAL COST/PAYBACK

This solution will add cost to society.

POLICIES

Require fossil fuel companies to capture and pay for all the carbon they create and sequester that carbon.

The Internal Revenue Service (IRS) Section 45Q tax credit is given to businesses for buying and using equipment that captures and disposes of carbon dioxide from industrial emissions through a process called carbon sequestration. The tax credit should be reevaluated.

RECOMMENDATIONS

Provide significant incentives for fossil fuel companies to build and operate renewable energy facilities to accelerate the transition out of fossil fuels. Allow fossil fuel companies to build only for what they should need by 2050, and not overbuild at the cost of citizens.

Fertilizer

Nitrous Oxide (N_2O) is about 300 times as potent as CO_2 at heating the atmosphere. And like CO_2, it is long-lived, spending an average of 114 years in the sky before disintegrating. **N_2O comprises roughly 6 percent of greenhouse gas emissions**, and about three-quarters of those N_2O emissions come from agriculture. The globe's heavy use of **synthetic nitrogen fertilizer is the principal culprit.**

Most plant-available nitrogen on farms came from compost, manure and nitrogen-fixing microbes which take nitrogen gas (N2) and convert it to ammonium, a soluble nutrient that plants can take up through their roots. **This abundance of synthetic fertilizer has boosted crop yields and helped to feed people around the globe**, but **this surplus nitrate and ammonium comes with environmental costs.** Producing ammonia fertilizer accounts for about 1 percent of all global energy use and 1.4 percent of CO_2 emissions. When plant roots don't mop up the fertilizer, some of it runs off the field and pollutes waterways.

Excessive use of fertilizer is polluting waterways and lowering soil quality. Nitrogen pollution poses an invisible but dangerous threat to peatlands. Pesticides are harming wildlife including insects such as bees that pollinate many crops. **Using crop rotations, and growing more diverse crops, including** trees, and integrating them with livestock-rearing can restore biodiversity and provide more nutritious diets. Alliances between farmers and pastoralists are being formalized to allow the sharing of resources with livestock being grazed on cropland after harvest.

Switching to minimal ploughing could help reduce N_2O emissions from soils. **No-till systems also result in more carbon storage** because less ploughing means reduced conversion of organic carbon to CO_2—thereby providing an additional climate benefit.

In research on tomato farms in California's Central Valley, study plots found that reduced tillage and a drip irrigation system that slowly oozed nitrogen to plants—reducing how much of the nutrient pooled in the soil—lowered N_2O emissions by 70 percent compared with conventionally managed plots. **The farmer who implemented those changes was also compensated for his greenhouse gas reduction through the state's cap-and-trade program.**

In Missouri, farmer Andrew McCrea grows 2,000 acres of corn and soy in a no-till system. This year, he plans to trim back his fertilizer use and see if the Pivot Bio inoculant can keep his yields the same. "I think all farmers certainly care about the soil," he says. "If we can cut costs, that's great too."

FINANCIAL COST/ PAYBACK

First cost of nutrient management is $0 per hectare, as reducing the over-application of fertilizer saves farmers the cost of the extra fertilizer. The payback is immediate.

Operational cost is US$20 per hectare per year (savings in fertilizer cost), compared to the operational cost of US$23 per hectare per year for the conventional practice. (Food and Agriculture Organization Statistical Service, 2017).

RECOMMENDATION

Reducing fertilizing with nitrous oxide and using more organic fertilizer because it saves farmers money and reduces water pollution. The organic fertilizer reduces emissions of a powerful greenhouse gas.

Recycling

As Drawdown explains, "To produce new products from recovered materials requires fewer raw resources and less energy. That's how recycling household, commercial, and industrial waste can cut emissions." Sweden is recycling nearly 100 percent of their waste. All countries should set 100 percent recycling as their goal.

Recycling can reduce emissions because producing new products from recovered materials saves energy. **Forging recycled aluminum products uses 95 percent less energy than creating them from virgin materials**. It also reduces resource extraction, minimizes other pollutants, and creates jobs. Household and industrial recycling are keystone elements of a circular economy that provides industry with feedstocks to produce needed goods with fewer emissions.

FINANCIAL COST/ PAYBACK

The marginal first cost is $10 billion. When revenues from recovered materials are included in comparison to the costs of virgin materials, however, operating recycling facilities costs less than operating landfills and sourcing virgin material feedstocks for industry.

POLICIES

Encourage manufacturers to build with materials that can be recycled or reused.

Provide manufacturers incentives to used recycled materials.

POTENTIAL NEW JOBS

Ecocycle.org cites that a U.S. recycling rate of 75 percent by 2030 would create 1.1 million new jobs. Recycling and reuse create at least 9 times more jobs than landfills and incinerators, and as many as 30 times more jobs (via Ecocycle.org). According to the US Recycling Economic Information Study (REI), the U.S. Recycling Industry employed 1.25 million people whereas the U.S. Solid Waste Management industry employed only 0.25 million (recycling is more labor-intensive than landfilling or incineration, so the recycling industry creates more jobs). According to Recycling Works, union recycling firms provide starting wages of approximately $20 an hour, as well as healthcare benefits and safer work conditions.

Absorbing carbon naturally is ideal and very affordable compared to mechanical solutions. In developed countries, people are buying and preserving land where there are plenty of trees. Philanthropists should consider purchasing and preserving forest in the tropics and poorer countries. Climate change affects everywhere. We might benefit by spending money in one country that will reduce the carbon footprint more than another country with the same money. The concern is the time for trees to grow to absorb carbon. The need is now.

GOVERNMENTS

To summarize: federal, state and local governments should partner with companies and citizens with smart policies and tax incentives that drive the market to support climate change initiatives. The U.S., the European Union and China are critical decision makers to address climate change globally. All these countries need to focus on becoming more efficient and effective faster when determining their policies and helping the poorer countries.

Strategies within the U.S.

1. **Provide policies, rebates, incentives and strategies that are positive and necessary. Stay away from negative solutions like raising taxes. It is better to reduce subsidies.**

2. **Encourage behavioral changes.** Three-quarters of the carbon emissions created by behavioral changes could be directly influenced or mandated by government policies. Mitigation measures such as phasing out polluting cars from large cities and reducing wasteful energy use in homes and offices.

3. Maintain **policies that last for several years** that allow developers and businesses to invest with less risk and more confidence.

4. **Provide tax rebates to wholesale distributors and contractors**, in addition to individual customers, to accelerate change to new technology, and transition out of business as usual.

5. **"Pay As You Go"** initiatives for lower- and middle-income families to have no up-front costs but pay monthly utility bills, that are lower than their current bills because of improvements in energy efficiency.

6. **Provide a direct rebate when purchasing an EV** (cars and light duty trucks) **for all incomes**. There should be no limit to manufacturers based on how many cars you sell. Auto manufacturers will benefit by being able to sell more cars and transition easier from combustion engines to electric. This enables all people and households to benefit no matter how much they pay in federal taxes. Paperwork should be simplified to promote all electrical transportation, including used vehicles.

7. The U.S. government needs to **create very clear, easy to find, and comprehensive websites** that indicate how to qualify for tax incentives and grants. Provide simple and easy forms to fill out that also can quickly be reviewed to expedite tax breaks and grants.

Electrification is emerging as the least-cost pathway to building decarbonization, and policy should adapt accordingly. At least 30 cities have passed ordinances preferring or requiring all-electric for new construction. As building decarbonization increases in importance, all states will need to develop strategies to support these efforts[1].

Tax Incentives

BUSINESSES

Policies differ across levels of government and organization type. Tax incentives are **ways of reducing taxes for businesses and individuals in exchange for specific desirable actions or investments on** their parts. **Their purpose is to encourage those businesses and individuals to engage in behavior that is socially responsible and/or benefits the community.** Businesses receive tax incentives from the government in order to invest back in their business, make environmentally-sound choices, or to support minorities and disadvantaged business owners. **Tax incentives are exclusions, exemptions or deductions from taxes owed to the government.** Tax incentives usually are not effective for low- and moderate-income families because they do not pay enough taxes to be able to claim a tax incentive.

HOUSEHOLDS

A tax incentive (or tax break) is a tax deduction, which refers to a benefit the government offers households to reduce their total tax liability. Typically, incentives come in the form of credits and deductions. **The motivation for issuing tax breaks is commonly to stimulate the economy** by increasing the amount of money taxpayers must spend or to promote certain types of behaviors such as purchasing energy-efficient appliances or attending college. To take advantage of most tax breaks, you must claim the benefit (tax credit or deduction) on your income tax return and meet specific eligibility requirements. **Low-income households do not pay enough in taxes to benefit from most federal tax breaks. Rebates are much better to help the lower income households.**

PERSONS IN HOUSEHOLD	POVERTY LEVEL (2022)
1	$13,590
2	$18,310
3	$23,030
4	$27,750

In 2020 there was 11.4% of households; 37,200,000 people living in poverty in the U.S. This was almost a 10 percent increase from the previous year.

You will pay 10 percent on taxable income up to $10,275, 12 percent on the amount from **$10,275, to $41,775** and 22 percent above that (up to $89,075) for 2022 taxes.

Households with $41,775 income initially adds up to $5,055 in federal taxes. This equates to only 67 percent of the tax break on an electric car at $7500. **The full tax break should be automatically applied to each EV as part of the base price at purchase.**

You would need to make approximately $90,000 and higher to have to have to pay at least $7500 in federal taxes. All lower and most of the middle class do not make enough money to require paying at least $7,500 in federal taxes. It is a safe estimate to say that about **65 percent of the population makes less than $90,000 and will not be able to receive a full $7,5000 tax incentive for buying an electric car.** (Green bar below adds up to 66.5%)

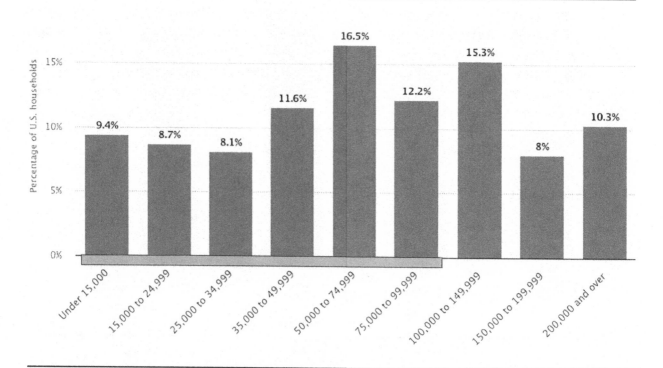

7.1 ANNUAL HOUSEHOLD INCOME IN U.S. DOLLARS

Encourgae rebates which are a partial refund from the amount of the purchase price. Items to consider for rebates include EVs, equipment to support renewable energies and education. Tax incentives should be reevaluated with rebates provided to help the low- and middle-class households.

"PAY AS YOU GO" Policies are necessary for most of the population to become much more efficient, sustainable and help reduce their carbon footprint in a faster time frame. This would encourage people of low and middle income to purchase EVs, solar panels and energy efficient solutions for their home. The up-front costs can be supported by the government and private investors.

The following is a summary of key issues to address for each of the five main categories that eliminate carbon:

1 Food, 2 Renewable Energy, 3 Transportation, 4 Cities, 5 Buildings and 6 Carbon Sequestration.

WHAT GOVERNMENTS CAN DO NOW!	PROPOSED ACTIONS
1 FOOD	Zero Food Waste
REDUCE FOOD WASTE	"Almost Perfect" food to low income and homeless/ Ban Food in Landfills
	Reduce Imports & Exports to reduce food waste
	Tax incentive for companies that contribute food to Apps like: "Too Good To Go" and "Food Rescue Hero"
PLANT RICH DIETS	Plant-based options must be available, visible, and enticing, including high-quality meat substitutes in all government buildings including public schools
	Provide grants and tax breaks for vegetarian and vegan restaurants
VERTICAL FARMING	Incentives to build and operate Vertical Farms
REFRIGERANT MANAGEMENT	Purchase HFC Refrigerants by 2030
RECYCLING	Improve Efficiency & Operations. Reduce Waste by 30%+
	Require food to be sold in compostable materials- no plastics

WHAT GOVERNMENTS CAN DO NOW!	PROPOSED ACTIONS
2 RENEWABLE ENERGY	**Tax Incentives for ALL renewables through 2030**
	Require Net Metering from Local Utility for All Renewables
	Provide tax incentives to land owners for allowing their land to include wind turbines, solar panels and battery storage installed and run by developers
	Subsidize new equipment for renewable sources.
	Subsidize education and training
ONSHORE WIND TURBINES	Construct now. Use land for solar, farming and other uses.
SOLAR FARMS	Build on landfills, water reservoirs
BATTERY STORAGE	Support Research, Development and Construction
ROOFTOP SOLAR POWER	Build Solar Panels On All New Buildings & Existing Flat Roofs
	Provide air rights from government buildings to private companies to build rooftop solar
	Require each new flat roof to have solar panels or a green roof
COMMUNITY SOLAR POWER	Support Renters and Low Income Families
	Provide tax incentives to local companies that provide community solar solutions that reduce monthly energy bills with higher tax breaks for supporting lower income families
OFFSHORE WIND TURBINES	Encourage fossil fuel companies to transition to renewables by building offshore
NUCLEAR- GENERATION IV	Research, Test, Share Technology with Other Countries
	Generation IV technology replace older models

ELECTRICITY GENERATED AND PROJECTED IN THE UNITED STATES

RENEWABLE ENERGIES	2020	2030	2050
SOLAR	2.3%	20%	37%
WIND	8.4%	15%	25%
HYDRO	7.3%	8%	9%
BIOMASS	1.4%	2%	3%
GEOTHERMAL	**0.5%**	**1%**	**1%**
	19.9%	51%	75%
NUCLEAR	**20.0%**	**20%**	**25%**
Non- Carbon	39.9%	71%	100%

BUILD BACK BETTER.

Hurricane Maria that hit Puerto Rico in 2015 set back their infrastructure by 2 decades. The new infrastructure is supposed to focus on clean energy, resiliency, and better policies. Unfortunately, the last governor pushed a very fossil dependent plan for gas, which benefits private gas companies. While people in Puerto Rico believe it is necessary to have diversity of energy source, most of the population is clearly for renewable energy. **Unfortunately making the wrong decisions makes addressing climate change at least twice as difficult.**

WHAT GOVERNMENTS CAN DO NOW!	PROPOSED ACTIONS
3 TRANSPORTATION	**All Electric**
ELECTRIC CARS/ TRUCKS/ BUSES	$7,500 tax incentive becomes subsidy for all incomes.
CARPOOLING	Encourage Carpoolong Lanes shared with Buses, Bikes & Emergency Vehicles
PUBLIC TRANSIT	Electric Vehicles
AVIATION	Mandate No Short Flights Within 200 Miles (unless on all eelctric planes)
OCEAN SHIPPING	Reduce Shipments by Boat (and Planes)
BICYCLE INFRASTRUCTURE	Provide Shared Bike & Bus Lanes (London)
WALKABLE CITIES	Advocate Sidewalks in all Planning Guidelines
HIGH SPEED RAIL	Focus on NE and West Coast to Support Major Urban Centers and to help with reduced short plane flights

4 CITIES	**Holistic Approach**
RESILIENT DESIGN	Buy flood insurance, do not allow new construction in a flood plain. Move households out of flood plains.
	Encourage Flood Insurance. Require in 100 Year Flood Plain Areas
WATER EFFICIENCY	Manage leaks, shower shorter times
DISTRICT HEATING	Look for Opportunities to Share Building Resources
PLANT TREES	Plant trees in your neighborhood, along streets, in parking lots
MIXED USE DEVELOPMENTS	Green space, community solar, shared parking, bike paths and sidewalks

WHAT GOVERNMENTS CAN DO NOW!	PROPOSED ACTIONS
5 BUILDINGS	**Rebates for Contractors to sell and buy electric energy efficient equipment**
	Require Net Zero building Codes by 2030 and be required in the International Building Code by 2030.
	Encourage renovating and reusing over demolition then new construction
	Pay for Education and Training
RENOVATE GOVERNMENT BUILDINGS	Subsidize private industry to improve energy efficiency and add renewable energy
RENOVATE LOW & MODERATE INCOME HOUSING	Subsidize private industry to improve energy efficiency and add renewable energy
PRE- ENGINEER WOOD CONSTRUCTION	Encourage for new construction
ENERGY EFFICIENCY	Contractors receive tax rebates to sell and buy electric energy efficient equipment
	Upgrade all EXISTING buildings to meet Net Zero Building Codes
	Require all NEW buildings to meet Net Zero Building Codes
INSULATION	Upgrade older buildings by 2030 to current codes or higher
SMART THERMOSTATS	Add to your home for better energy efficiency
BUILDING AUTOMATION SYSTEMS	Upgrade Older Buildings by 2030 to save on energy costs
COMMISSIONING	Have your home and work place commissioned once a year
HEAT PUMPS	Upgrade Current HVAC Equipment when it gets to old to Heat Pumps
LED LIGHTING	Always use LED lights to save energy and money
SHARING SOLUTIONS	Support District Heating & Community Solar Projects

WHAT GOVERNMENTS CAN DO NOW!	PROPOSED ACTIONS
6 CARBON SEQUESTRATION	**Preserve Existing and Grow Back to Level of 100 Years Ago**
FARMING TECHNOLOGIES	Subsidies Support Most Efficient Farming of Land
MANGROVE PROTECTION	Preserve Existing & Grow Back Destroyed Land
TROPICAL FOREST RESTORATION	Support restoration and do not allow further development
PETLAND PROTECTION	High Tax on Peat Moss/ Ban Altogether
PLANT TREES	Thoughtful, Strategic Long Term Planning for Success
INDIGENOUS PEOPLES TENURE	Support
ORGANIC FERTILIZER	Advocate with Planning Guidelines
DIRECT AIR CAPTURE	Have Fossil Fuel Companies bear the majority of the cost
CARBON SEQUESTRATION	Have Fossil Fuel Companies bear the majority of the cost

* INCLUDES SILVOPASTURE, MANAGED GRAZING, PERENNIAL STAPLE CROPS, TREE INTERCROPPING, CONSERVATIVE AGRICULTURE AND ABANDONED FARMLAND RESTORATION.

7.2

Research & Development

Government Research is critical to support innovation

Many teams now work globally with labs in multiple locations and countries. The research receiving government funding should be more specific to address climate change. The Tesla electric car came from government funding by the Department of Energy in 2010 and has transformed the automobile industry in just 10 years by having no carbon emissions. **The following is a short list of very significant discoveries that were funded by the U.S. Government: supercomputers, LED lights, autonomous robots, bar codes, and the Human Genome project.**

"An independent study of the Human Genome project found that every **$1 invested by the federal government in the project generated $141 in returns to the U.S. economy.**"[2] Also life expectancy has tripled in the past 200 years primarily driven by research discoveries. Investing in research and innovative ideas is critical. **The U.S. Federal government funded research has averaged at least one major discover every two years.**

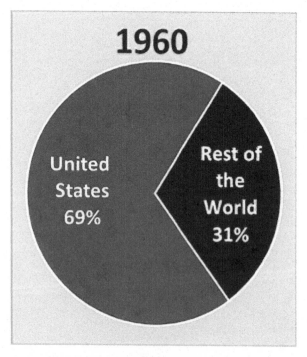
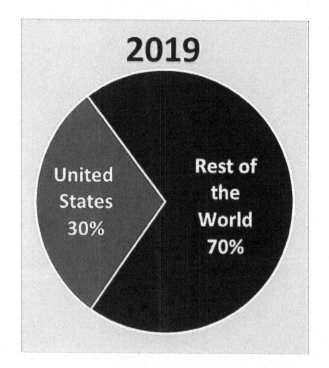

7.3 U.S. Share of Global R&D

U.S. Federal Research & Development spending as a percentage of the gross domestic product (GDP) peaked at above 2 percent in the 1970s and has declined since, from a little over 1 percent in 2001 to 0.7 percent in 2018. In 1960, the U.S. invested in 69 percent of the research done globally. In 2019, that amount is only 30 percent with China showing the most significant growth and may pass the U.S. by 2030 in investing in research. Germany and South Korea have also committed to more research over this period[3].

A recent success story is SunShot Initiative by the U.S. Department of Energy in 2011. Collaboration was emphasized to encourage private companies, universities and government laboratories to concentrate on efforts like lowering the cost of solar power systems, removing bureaucratic barriers, and making it cheaper to finance a solar power system. The goals were met in 2017, three years ahead of schedule.

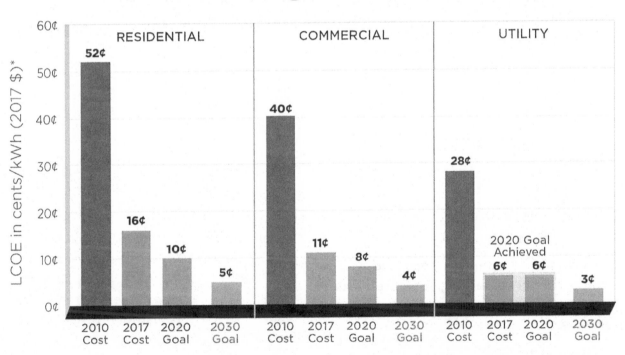

SunShot Progress and Goals

7.4

Solar Energy Technologies Office set goals for 2030. The goals cut the **Levelized Cost Of Energy** (LCOE) of photovoltaic solar by an additional 50 percent to $0.03 per kWh for utility-scale and cut the LCOE of concentrating solar power to $0.05 per kWh for baseload power plants, while also addressing grid integration challenges.

In March 2021, DOE announced an update to the targets and around $128 million in additional funding to "lower costs, improve performance, and speed the deployment of solar energy technologies." The new targets include cutting the costs of solar from its current price of $0.046/kWh to $0.03/kWh by 2025 and reaching $0.02/kWh by 2030.

The Department of Energy's Office of Energy Efficiency and Renewable Energy today announced a commitment for its SunShot Initiative to cut the cost of solar-generated electricity by **50 percent between 2020 and 2030**. The goals also address market barriers that limit solar adoption, including streamlining processes to reduce project time cycles, expanding access to solar, and accurately representing the value of solar in a more integrated energy system.

Combining very low-cost storage (capital costs at $100/kWh for an 8-hour battery by 2040) with low-cost PV will enable solar energy to supply a large share of U.S. electricity by 2050.

Fund more research specifically for better solutions to address climate change. **Improve and develop more cost-effective solutions for DAC and CCS technology.**

Encourage more design competitions now.

Jobs

Every politician is focused on creating jobs. There are plenty of opportunities.

Every $1 million spent on solar and wind creates 7.5 full-time jobs, compared with just 2.7 jobs for every $1 million spent on fossil fuels.

On-the-job training for renewable energy solutions usually lasts between 1 month and 1 year. The Department of Energy is creating **30,000** new solar jobs due to increased demand because of the affordability of the new permit process.

Mark Jacobson, researcher at Stanford University, projects 2,238,188 construction jobs and 3,020,594 operational jobs produced for a total of 5,258,782 jobs to support the renewable energies. The number of jobs **transitioning from** fossil fuel companies is estimated at 2,203,722. **Consequently, the renewable movement will add a total of 3,055,510 to the energy sector.** It is paramount to remain aware that not every worker in the fossil fuel industry can ease into a clean energy job, so governments need to promote training and devote resources to facilitating new opportunities. **Support a just transition** for fossil fuel workers and communities by covering income, training, and optional relocation for workers facing job loss. Transition programs to help diversify economic activity in communities currently reliant on fossil fuels.

A $1 million investment in energy efficiency, improving buildings and operations, creates around eight full-time jobs, nearly three times as many as an investment in fossil fuels[4]. There must be a sufficient and well-trained workforce ready to sell and install these devices. Over 100,000 new HVAC contractors and workers will be needed by 2022. Supporting contractors to specialize and become skilled at electrification and heat pump projects is crucial for success. **The work can also save small businesses 10 percent–30 percent in utility costs**—something that could help those businesses survive.

Transition Federal Subsidies for Oil, Gas, and Coal to Renewable Energies

UNITED STATES

Subsidies are much different than tax incentives; rather than reducing how much a firm owes, **subsidies directly give money to the firm. Fossil fuel companies have been heavily subsidized for many decades.**

A 2020 report by IRENA tracked some $634 billion in energy sector subsidies in 2020 and found that around 70 percent went to fossil fuels. **Public monies no longer should be used to fund fossil fuels. It is impractical to stop all subsidies at one time, but they should be phased out over a period.** Fossil fuel subsidies undermine efforts to mitigate climate change by artificially lowering the price of fossil fuels.

Recommend fossil fuel subsidies be reduced by 10 percent annually for the next 10 years. This money is transitioned to green technology initiatives while providing fossil fuel companies a clear plan and time to adjust to improve their business.

One way to overcome political hesitancy to remove energy subsidies is to maintain support but simply make it contingent on a move to greener energy. Some fossil fuel support should be retained to support carbon capture and storage for industrial processes for cement and steel production.

GLOBAL

Fossil fuel subsidies are one of the biggest financial barriers hampering the world's shift to renewable energy sources. Each year, governments around the world pour around half a trillion dollars into artificially lowering the price of fossil fuels—more than triple what renewables receive.

The G20 agreed in 2009 to phase out "inefficient" fossil fuel subsidies but did not define inefficient and little progress had been made. The U.S. increased subsidies for fossil fuels by 37 percent from 2015 to 2019. The report, by Bloomberg NEF and Bloomberg Philanthropies, found that **60 percent of the fossil fuel subsidies went to the companies producing fossil fuels and 40 percent to cutting prices for energy consumers. Even with the subsidies, recently oil companies have made record profits due to the increase in gasoline prices driven by the Russian war against Ukraine.**

Setting fossil fuel prices that reflect their true cost would cut global CO$_2$ emissions by over a third, the IMF analysts said. The comprehensive IMF report found that prices were at least 50 percent below their true costs for 99 percent of coal, 52 percent of diesel, and 47 percent of natural gas in 2020. Five countries were responsible for two-thirds of the subsidies: China, the U.S., Russia, India and Japan. Without action, subsidies will rise to $6.4 trillion 2025, the IMF said.

The right price is the socially-efficient price that reflects the full societal costs of fuel use—not just the supply costs (labor, capital, and raw materials) but also the environmental costs, including carbon dioxide (CO$_2$) emissions, local air pollution, and broader externalities associated with fuel use (road congestion), as well as general taxes applied to household products. These are called external costs.[5] Some analysts argue that the hidden costs of fossil fuels—such as their impacts on air pollution and global warming—are, in effect, **a kind of subsidy, because polluters are not paying for the damage they cause**.

All levels of the government should reduce, then minimize subsidies to fossil fuel companies, while at the same time transitioning to support green initiatives. The government and society have been paying for the health problems from pollution created over decades by the fossil fuel companies. Accelerate manufacturing and implementation of renewables: wind, solar, and storage.

Global Strategies

1. **Share technology**

   U.S. government should support other countries interested in new technology. For example, Terracon was close to building six new Generation IV nuclear plants in China until the previous government decided against this. Sharing technology to reduce carbon should be encouraged and used to collaborate with countries. The Generation IV nuclear projects are now moving forward with several countries collaborating on this new technology.

2. **Reduce imports & exports**

   Countries become more self-sufficient by creating less waste and requiring less fossil fuels for transportation.

3. **Ban the purchase and use of peat moss.**

   Use organic materials for fertilizer.

4. **Implement net-zero building codes into the international building codes.**

5. **"Pay as you go" financial support in local areas to accelerate change to save money.**

6. **Fossil fuel subsidies reduced 10 percent annually for the next 10 years.**

   Shift the money to renewable energy construction.

7. **Share and implement the best strategies from all countries.**

8

BUSINESSES

Businesses include companies that provide services, energy, transportation, food, education, manufacturing, farming and develop new technologies. Much of private industry needs to drive research with financial incentives and support from the government. It is critical that business leaders stay focused on climate change solutions regardless of who is in political office. Hopefully politicians will be supportive.

Strategies for Businesses

1. Renovate and Reuse More Efficiently

Reduce embodied carbon by updating existing structures the first choice over new construction. Add the latest technology and best practices to make renovated buildings work as good as newly constructed buildings.

2. New Creative Financing Models

Support the development and use of renewable energy sources.

3. Partner with Government and other Businesses

Support low- and middle-income families.

4. Drive Research and Innovation

Improve efficiencies that will support growth.

5. All-electric

Focus on building electric homes, renewable energy sources and electric transportation.

6. Improve Supply Chain

Improve efficiency, lower cost, and support growth.

Good business is an opportunity for brands to have a positive environmental and social impact that drive growth and profit. Building thriving economies within the boundaries and limits of planetary resources requires a collaborative effort from governments, individuals, Non-governmental Organizations (NGOs), and businesses alike. But the scale, reach, and impact of businesses, combined with their financial clout and political influence, means contributions from businesses is critical.

Switching to sustainable resources, materials or processes can cost less, and makes good financial sense in the short-term. Now, business leaders are showing that over the long-term, it's worth it. What might once have been about "doing the right thing" is now "a huge business opportunity," according to Simon Caspersen, co-founder and communications director of innovation lab Space10. Building sustainable goals into business strategy is an opportunity to innovate, drive efficiency and productivity, drive profit, and to build loyal and lasting relationships with customers. Sustainability is now a business imperative and model.

Green Tax Incentives

"It's no secret in the building community that federal tax incentives for energy-efficient homes and buildings have been weak, inconsistent, and outdated for quite some time. So much so that many had given up on them," U.S. Green Building Council (USGBC).

Biden's Build Back Better agenda aims to allocate $320 billion for clean energy tax credits and incentives. The money would go to all sorts of tax breaks that property owners could use, such as a boost to solar energy incentives and EV charging. But the leading candidates for major updates are for residential homes and commercial buildings. Any building portfolio with long-term growth goals must think about getting cleaner and greener sooner rather than later. Currently, property owners can get a deduction of up to $1.80 per square foot for building floor areas with the new systems installed to prove energy savings of at least 50 percent. If you don't meet the 50% energy savings mark, you can still get a partial deduction of $0.60 per square foot if you show more than 16 percent energy reduction certification.

The tax incentive will use the most recent Standard 90.1 published by ASHRAE (American Society of Heating, Refrigerating and Air-Conditioning Engineers)as the benchmark to test energy efficiency. Introduced legislation that would boost 179D's deduction to a new sliding scale system with deductions from $2.50 to $5 per square foot for new buildings based on how well they perform against the ASHRAE standard[1].

Case Study of a Large Company—Amazon—Stepping Up to Meet the Challenge

I have taken Amazon as an example of what large companies can do to help climate change. Amazon benefitted significantly during the pandemic, but most people do not know during this time they were also focused on reducing their carbon footprint. They have developed meaningful carbon reduction strategies to reach net-zero carbon emissions across their business by 2040. The following is a long list of actions with many saving Amazon and the consumer money while reducing the carbon footprint:

FOOD

"Compact by Design," is a new certification for products designed to reduce carbon emissions through increased efficiency and better packaging enabling more to be transported in the same space. My family buys and enjoys many of these products partly because they take up less space in our home. It is necessary to create devices with more recycled materials and more sustainable packaging.

Many of Amazon-branded products qualify for "Climate Pledge Friendly" certification to help customers understand the products better. You can find this information out on the Amazon App while you are shopping. The Alexa energy dashboard works with compatible smart lights, plugs, switches, water heaters, thermostats, televisions, and Echo devices, allowing customers to easily estimate the energy used. Customers can also enable Alexa to help them conserve energy with Hunches. For example, if Alexa has a Hunch that a customer is away and forgot to turn off a light, Alexa can automatically turn it off, helping customers save energy and reduce carbon emissions.

Free & (k of 1)

☆☆☆☆☆ 321

$12⁹⁹ ($0.20/load)

✓prime FREE Delivery Sat, Sep 19

🦅 Climate Pledge Friendly
See 1 certification

8.1

RENEWABLE ENERGY

Amazon is on a path to **powering their operations with 100 percent renewable energy by 2025**—five years ahead of their original target of 2030. In 2020, Amazon became the world's largest corporate purchaser of renewable energy, reaching 65 percent renewable energy across their business.

On December 10, 2020, Amazon became the world's largest corporate purchaser of renewable energy. The Amazon-Shell HKN Offshore Wind Project is Amazon's largest single-site renewable energy project to date. It is scheduled for operation by 2024 and will have an overall capacity of 759 MW that will supply the electrical grid powering the Netherlands without government subsidies. Amazon is purchasing over 50 percent of that capacity, a total of 380 MW, to power their operations in Europe. They have developed several unique innovations for the wind farm. These include a floating solar park, short-term battery storage, optimally tuned turbines, and 'green hydrogen.' Amazon operates 187 solar and wind projects worldwide, 62 utility-scale wind and solar projects. In addition, 125 solar rooftops on fulfillment centers and sort centers around the globe fitted with 11,500 module solar panels, which generate enough electricity to power 700 homes for one year. This averages out to 16 panels per home. The company has approximately 10 GW of electrical production capacity.

Amazon's approach employs several strategies to meet their renewable energy goals:

- **Energy Efficiency:** Innovate to continuously increase the energy efficiency of their operations and devices.

- **Off-Site Renewable Projects:** Invest in new, utility-scale renewable energy projects.

- **On-Site Solar:** Deploy rooftop solar systems on buildings we operate.

- **Site Energy Contracts:** Participate in green tariff programs with utilities and pursue new renewable projects through competitive site energy contracts.

- **Policy Engagement**: Support public policy that advances access to and the expansion of clean energy for Amazon and their customers.

Amazon may choose to partner with their electricity supplier to source renewable energy through electricity contracts. These commitments result in adding new renewable energy to the grid, beyond business as usual for the utility or energy supplier. Amazon uses environmental attributes, such as Renewable Energy Certificates (RECs), to track and record the environmental benefits of our renewable energy projects.

TRANSPORTATION

Amazon will buy 100,000 Rivian electric delivery vehicles. My wife has her Rivian truck on order now. They plan to have 10,000 vehicles on the road as early as 2022 and 100,000 vehicles deployed by 2030. Amazon was one of 18 companies to sign the Buyer's Principles, demonstrating their commitment to accelerate the transition to low-carbon commercial transportation solutions.

In more than 100 cities across India, Amazon orders ship in their original packaging and are transported in protective containers that delivery drivers can reuse. This should become a global practice. Amazon uses data and algorithms to consolidate as many shipments as possible onto a single vehicle or plane, and they analyze which items are ordered most frequently by location to minimize long-distance deliveries. By boosting efficiency across their network, they can put fewer vehicles and planes into service, reducing the carbon intensity of each package.

Amazon is investing in sustainable aviation fuels, which are derived from renewable resources and generate fewer carbon emissions than standard aviation fuel does. This fuel has been used to power the Amazon Air network in the U.S., reducing their carbon emissions in flight up to 20 percent over standard aviation fuel.

BUILDINGS & CITIES

The stores use steel byproducts (waste) in the concrete floor to reduce the embodied carbon—the carbon associated with the manufacturing and installation of the flooring—by nearly 40% compared to a standard concrete floor.

Amazon Web Services incorporates direct evaporative technology to cool their data centers, reducing energy and water consumption. During cooler months, outside air is supplied directly to the data center without using any water. During the hottest months of the year, outside air is cooled through an evaporative process using water before being pushed into the server rooms.

Focusing on Net-Zero Building Codes, Amazon is constructing highly efficient buildings that use no on-site fossil fuels, and produces on-site, or procures, enough carbon-free renewable energy to meet building operations energy consumption annually.

CORPORATE

Amazon formed a $1 billion sustainability bond to finance sustainability projects that fall under five categories: renewable energy, clean transportation, sustainable buildings, affordable housing and socio-economic advancement and empowerment.

Amazon is in it for the long haul, and it has the deep pockets and scale to push for change on all levels—corporate, governmental, and individual. The Amazon Web Services original four-part Climate Next documentary series features stories about people and communities around the world driving innovation and creating scalable solutions to address climate change.

Buying consciously is now a mainstream mindset. 87 percent of people surveyed would prefer to buy from brands which demonstrate a commitment to sustainability, while more than two-thirds (70 percent) claim to be willing to pay more for products and services with these credentials. Through innovation, companies can help consumers turn their aspirations into habits, making the sustainable choice the obvious choice[2].

WHAT BUSINESSES CAN DO NOW!	In 1 Year	Up To 7 years	PROPOSED ACTIONS
1 FOOD			**Support Low and Moderate Income Families**
REDUCE FOOD WASTE	■		Provide "Almost Perfect Food" to low income and homeless
	■		Enlist well-known chefs to inspire less wasteful kitchen habits at restaurants, writing books and mentoring on TV shows
PLANT RICH DIETS	■		Develop Meat Alternatives, Vegan and Vegetarian Restaurants
VERTICAL FARMING		■	Build and operate Vertical Farms especially in major cities
		■	Food Hubs and Culinary Incubators
		■	Improve soil quality and reducing the need for water
REFRIGERANT MANAGEMENT		■	Find more cost effective ways to address the old refrigerant
RECYCLING	■	■	Food should only be sold in compostable materials- no plastics
	■		Support Apps to Reduce Waste and Help Lower Income Households

2 RENEWABLE ENERGY			**Advance, Build and Scale Up New Techologies**
ONSHORE WIND TURBINES		■	Construct now. Use land for solar panels, farming and other uses.
SOLAR FARMS	■	■	Partner with Governments to build on landfills and reservoirs
BATTERY STORAGE	■	■	Key Focus Area for Research and Development
		■	Scale Up Solar Panels with Battery Storage Projects
ROOFTOP SOLAR POWER	■	■	Create companies that focus on the installation
COMMUNITY SOLAR POWER	■	■	Build On All New Buildings & Existing Flat Roofs
		■	Support Low and Moderate Income Neighborhoods
OFFSHORE WIND TURBINES		■	Construct soon and tie into major cities near the water
GEOTHERMAL		■	Build where possible including under existing buildings
WASTE TO ENERGY	■	■	Keep waste as low as possible, ideally no waste
NUCLEAR- GENERATION IV		■	Research, Test, Share Technology with Other Countries

WHAT BUSINESSES CAN DO NOW!	In 1 Year	Up To 7 years	PROPOSED ACTIONS
3 TRANSPORTATION			**All Electric**
ELECTRIC CARS/ TRUCKS/ BUSES	■	■	Provide EV chargers in parking- Type 1, 2 and 3
CARPOOLING	■		Incentivize Carpooling by Employees/ Public
PUBLIC TRANSIT(Subway)	■		Encourage Employees to take Public Transportation
AVIATION		■	No Short Flights Within 200 Miles. Look for more green fuels
OCEAN SHIPPING		■	Reduce Imports and Exports
BICYCLE INFRASTRUCTURE	■	■	Provide Shared Bike/ Bus Lanes/ and Emergency Vehicle Lanes
3D PRINTING		■	Build and manufacture many products locally
RESEARCH & DEVELOPMENT		■	ENERGY made with solar panels on roofs, collect electric from friction on roads and tracks
		■	Autonomous Technology Reduce Number of Cars & Parking Spaces

4 CITIES			**Share Resources**
RESILIENT DESIGN	■		Buy flood insurance, do not build in a flood plain
	■		Construct Resilient Micro-Grids
WATER EFFICIENCY	■	■	Manage Leaks
DISTRICT HEATING		■	Look for Opportunities to Share Building Resources
PLANT TREES		■	Plant trees in neighborhoods, along streets, in parking lots
	■		Reduce Heat Island Effect
INTERNET OF THINGS	■		Improve Efficiencies with latest technologies

WHAT BUSINESSES CAN DO NOW!	In 1 Year	Up To 7 years	PROPOSED ACTIONS
5 BUILDINGS			
PRE- ENGINEER WOOD CONSTR.		■	New Construction. Reduce need for Concrete and Steel
		■	Flexible, Adapatable Buildings for the Long Term
ENERGY EFFICIENCY	■		Renovate Existing Buildings. Model from Netherlands
INSULATION	■	■	Insulate Roofs, Add Solar Panels
SMART THERMOSTATS	■		Add to your home for better energy efficiency
BUILDING AUTOMATION SYSTEMS		■	Upgrade Older Buildings by 2030 to save on energy costs
COMMISSIONING	■		Have your home and work place commissioned once a year
HEAT PUMPS		■	Upgrade Current HVAC Equipment when it gets to old
LED LIGHTING	■		always use LED lights to save energy and money
RENOVATE & REUSE BUILDINGS	■	■	Upgrade to Net Zero Building Codes
6 CARBON SEQUESTRATION			
FARMING TECHNOLOGIES*	■	■	Use Subsidies to support more efficient farming
MANGROVE PROTECTION			Do not purchase products from disturbed mangroves. Address in your supply chain.
TROPICAL FOREST RESTORATION			
PETLAND PROTECTION			Do not buy or sell peat
PLANT TREES		■	Thoughtful, Strategic Long Term Planning for Success
INDIGENOUS PEOPLES TENURE			Support
ORGANIC FERTILIZER	■	■	Advocate with Planning Guidelines
DIRECT AIR CAPTURE	■	■	Fossil fuel companies to pay for the construction and operation
CARBON SEQUESTRATION	■	■	Fossil fuel companies to pay for the construction and operation

* INCLUDES SILVOPASTURE, MANAGED GRAZING, PERENNIAL STAPLE CROPS, TREE INTERCROPPING, CONSERVATIVE AGRICULTURE AND ABANDONED FARMLAND RESTORATION.

8.2

Research & Innovate

Academic institutions performed around **60 percent of federally funded basic research, 27 percent of federally funded applied research, and 6 percent of federally funded experimental development**. Research & Development (R&D) conducted by higher education institutions is a key component of the overall R&D system of the United States. The federal share has declined, and academic institutions are playing a more important funding role than in the past[3].

Private funding for research comes from **philanthropists, crowdfunding, private companies, non-profit foundations,**

and professional organizations. In 2020, the United States is estimated to have spent **$708 billion** on R&D. Most of those investments—$532 billion—came from the private sector.

New technology like the smartphone and the electric car have changed the world for the better and have helped to combat carbon in our environment. The energy and material benefits of accessing services via a mobile phone is a diary, personal assistant, MP3 player, video player, word processor, and games console. Its one device but with many functions which you do not need to buy separately[4].

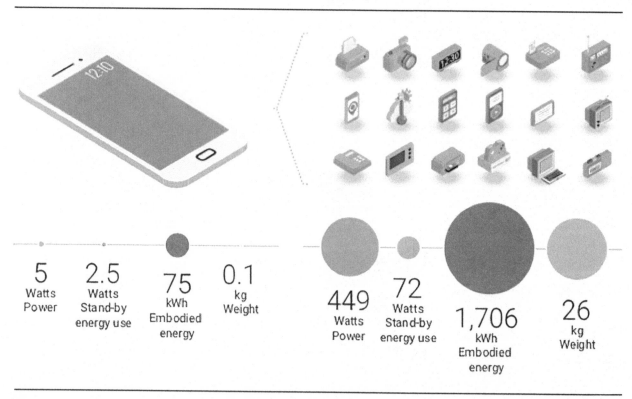

| 5 Watts Power | 2.5 Watts Stand-by energy use | 75 kWh Embodied energy | 0.1 kg Weight | | 449 Watts Power | 72 Watts Stand-by energy use | 1,706 kWh Embodied energy | 26 kg Weight |

8.3

Private companies need to continue to innovate for social good with support from the government. Collaboration between various groups, and various countries should be encouraged to accelerate discoveries. Major competitions should be held now and supported by the wealthiest such as battery storage, more efficient renewable energies, and improvements to meat alternatives.

Over the next 10 years, the growth and development of the EVs will provide many more benefits than the combustion engine vehicles:

- Less parts to maintain.
- Last longer.
- Battery can be used at home during outages.
- Autonomous vehicles with ownership not required, less parking spaces needed, and managed remotely.

Private companies working with university research teams are focused on improving most technologies especially with solar, wind, and battery storage. There is the opportunity to improve solar panels from 21 percent efficiency to 33 percent, which will continue to drive the cost down and make solar a very sound investment. Wind turbines will be constructed by large companies. The U.S. continues to improve the technology and manufacturing to improve efficiency and drive the cost down. This will be critical to enable developing countries to afford renewables sooner.

Fossil fuel companies will continue to develop new technologies to support their products by absorbing carbon such as Direct Air Capture (DAC) and Carbon Sequestration. There are also the new nuclear plant designs to consider. **These technologies cost a large sum of money and will take time to get online.** The carbon capture and sequestration will keep fossil fuels in business longer but will add cost to the consumer and take much more time to get running compared to solar, wind, and storage.

Change driven by improvements in technology and new breakthroughs happen faster than ever. Discoveries by the private sector since 2010 include iPads, Google, apps, landing on Mars, ReWalk exoskeleton, smartwatches, fitness trackers, true wireless earphones, electric cars, and 3D printers, to name a few. Significant improvements in solar and wind technology have occurred during the past 10 years. Improvements will continue over the next 10 years in renewable energy, development of battery storage in the marketplace, and potential success with carbon capture solutions and Generation IV nuclear projects.

Financing

GREEN BANKS

Institutional investors are also increasingly concerned about Environmental, Social Governance (ESG), prompting building owners to report on what they're doing to reduce carbon footprints. Investors are increasingly applying these non-financial factors as part of their analysis process to identify material risks and growth opportunities. Green Banks are public financial institutions that use innovative financing methods to accelerate and fund clean energy technologies. In 2020, nearly $2 billion of Green Bank funds generated $7 billion of investment in projects around the country, without federal investment. There are 18 Green Banks in the U.S. and 27 worldwide. Green Banks make it **easier to finance projects in new markets**, geographies, and technologies that otherwise couldn't be built. This means cheaper and cleaner energy for customers and more investment for private capital providers. The result is more clean energy being deployed at lower cost. Green Banks also use on-bill financing that enables building owners and consumers to repay energy upgrade loans through their utility bills, which offers security to lenders in a developing market.

Green banks, quasi-public entities are meant to sway investment into sustainability initiatives, and can lead to new solar panels, energy efficiency solutions, and other sustainable infrastructure initiatives[5].

8.4 Green Banks support financing sustainable projects.

GREEN LOANS

The ESG movement has grown from an initiative launched by the United Nations into a massive global phenomenon accounting for about $30 trillion in worldwide assets under management. Green loans are a form of financing similar to green bonds in that they raise capital for environmentally friendly projects. The World Bank's International Finance Corporation defines green loans as an exclusive type of financing that enables borrowers, such as property owners, to fund projects that significantly contribute to helping the environment. Unlike green bonds, a green loan is typically smaller and done in a private operation. The Green Loan Principles (GLP) were issued in 2018 to promote consistency for financial markets. The World Bank reports there's currently an estimated $33 billion in outstanding green loans worldwide, and the demand is outpacing the growth of the green bond market. The incentive of lowering borrowing terms for green performance is like health insurance companies that penalize smokers. The loan to Phillips extends until 2022, and if the company's ESG rating goes up, the interest rate goes down and vice-a-versa[6].

COMMERCIAL PROPERTY-ASSESSED CLEAN ENERGY (C-PACE)

Another way that buildings are getting financing for sustainability upgrades are from **Commercial Property-Assessed Clean Energy (C-PACE)** financing. C-PACE financing is a structure in which building owners borrow money for energy efficiency, renewable energy, or other types of retrofits and make payments through an assessment on their property taxes. One of the most significant benefits of C-PACE financing is it can cover 100 percent of the project cost over a typical 10 to 20-year term, resulting in lower annual payments that are usually less than the energy savings. C-PACE offers favorable financial terms that enable owners to cover up-front costs and keep positive cash flows.

To be eligible for C-PACE financing, a project must be in a county or municipality that has approved C-PACE programs within a state that has passed PACE-enabling legislation. For more details on where C-PACE is available, use the tools provided by PACENation. Note that Residential PACE (R-PACE) is also available in some jurisdictions.

The parties involved in a C-PACE deal usually include:

- A PACE administrator that manages the project and ensures adherence to program requirements.

- A local government collects the property tax assessment and cancels payment to the capital provider(s) if necessary.

- A contractor or energy services company (ESCO) installs the equipment.

- The building owner (customer) receiving the upgrade or tenants working in concert with their landlord.

- Private investors, bondholders, or a government to provide the capital.

C-PACE assessments are linked to the property and automatically transfer to a new owner upon the sale of the property. C-PACE provides strong security for investors because the financing is repaid on the property tax bill. This allows lenders the ability to offer better interest rates and longer repayment terms than are otherwise available.

Global Company Initiatives

The 450 firms that make up the Glasgow Financial Alliance for Net Zero (GFANZ) and its subsector initiatives committed more than $100 trillion to transition the global economy to net-zero emissions by 2050. This group includes 95 banks representing 40 percent of global banking assets, shepherded by the Net-Zero Banking Alliance (NZBA). 40 countries signed up to the Glasgow Breakthroughs, which calls for "near-zero emission steel production established and growing in every region by 2030."[7]

The International Energy Agency's call to end fossil fuel investments and triple clean energy funding to US$4 trillion by 2030, or ideally sooner, will help in "creating momentum for the change we need."

Investors with $41 Trillion Ask G-7 to Stop Subsidizing Fossil Fuels

A coalition of 457 investors overseeing a combined $41 trillion of assets have called on world leaders to set more ambitious greenhouse gas emissions targets and end support for fossil fuels. The money managers requested all governments commit to net-zero emissions by mid-century, increase their 2030 emissions reductions targets in line with limiting global warming to 1.5°C, remove fossil fuel subsidies and phase out thermal coal-based electricity generation. The coalition argues that **countries that move swiftly to decarbonize and prepare for a future less dependent on fossil fuels are also likely to attract more capital.** Those who set ambitious targets in line with achieving net-zero emissions and implement consistent national climate policies in the short-to-medium term, will become increasingly attractive investment destinations.

There are many large companies that can have a very positive impact to address climate change. The largest companies are bigger than most countries! There are only 7 countries in the world with a higher GDP than Apple's $2.3 trillion—meaning the tech giant is richer than a whopping **96 percent of the world**. Microsoft's $1.8 trillion market cap puts it as the third largest company in the list (after Apple and Saudi Aramco, the petroleum and gas company). Online retailer Amazon is without a doubt one of the biggest tech giants worldwide and has only seen its sales soar over the COVID-19 pandemic. Its market capitalization of $1.6 trillion makes the company richer than **92 percent of countries**.

BILLIONS U.S. DOLLARS (2020)

#		
1.	U.S.	$21,433.2
2.	China	$14,342.9
3.	Japan	$5,081.8
4.	Germany	$3,861.1
5.	India	$2,868.9
6.	United Kingdom	$2,829.1
7.	France	$2,715.5
8.	**APPLE**	**$2,296.0**
9.	Italy	$2,003.6
10.	**Saudi Aramco**	**$1,990.0**
11.	Brazil	$1,839.8
12.	**MICROSOFT**	**$1,827.0**
13.	Canada	$1,736.4
14.	Russia	$1,699.9
15.	**AMAZON**	**$1,688.0**
16.	South Korea	$1,646.7
17.	**ALPHABET (GOOGLE)**	**$1,411.0**

Ultimately, 5 companies make their way into the top 17 wealthiest countries and companies in the world, all with a lion's share of the world's total GDP. The United Nations lists 195 countries in the world.

The ten largest U.S. companies make approximately half of what the entire country makes! These companies are (rankings vary throughout the year):

1. Apple,

2. Microsoft,

3. Amazon,

4. Alphabet,

5. Facebook,

6. Tesla,

7. Berkshire Hathaway,

8. Visa,

9. JP Morgan Chase and

10. Johnson & Johnson.

In 1990, half of the top 12 companies were oil companies. Over 30 years later, no U.S. oil company is in the top 12.

If each of these top companies could invest in one significant climate change idea with research, funding competitions, and supply chain improvements, then positive change should happen sooner and support the growth of the U.S. economy.

HOW TO PAY FOR THESE IMPROVEMENTS

Performance Contracting. Make no initial capital investment, decrease energy costs, and simultaneously reserve available capital for other projects by using an Energy Service Company.

Public/Private Partnerships. Private sector companies can bring capital and expertise to help your city optimize operations and save money[8].

Incentives can lower the costs or increase the benefits of action. Grants and rebates as well as tax incentives help pay down some of the up-front cost of investing in energy efficiency.

Non-financial incentives, such as granting developers priority processing of permits or higher density, may be attractive to the private market while requiring little or no investment by local governments. Higher density by increasing the number of floors and building height, as well as allowing larger floor plans are some examples of easily increasing the density, which makes projects more financially viable.

Financing products can spread the initial cost of efficiency investment over many years, allowing financial benefits to be received sooner. Revolving loan funds, trust funds, and tax-lien financing are mechanisms to expand the pool of available funds for efficiency investments.

GREEN MORTGAGES

An innovative approach that allows homeowners to borrow money for energy-efficient features and repay them gradually on a monthly basis.

Partnerships between the private sector and local governments are essential to achieve widespread success. Cities can help overcome "split incentives" between building owners and occupants by guiding the real estate market with **green lease contract** clauses, which align the interests of owners and tenants. A collaborative green leasing process can create a win-win, helping tenants to lower operating costs, and helping owners by improving building value and marketability. If the owner does not see a financial benefit, then they are less likely to improve the building, which leaves tenant with the high utility bills and the carbon footprint not improved.

Behavior change among private-sector companies can be motivated by workplace engagement programs, competitions, challenges, awareness campaigns, and other incentives that reward the best performers.

Energy Performance Contracts (EPCs) are financing mechanisms that allow energy efficiency investments to be repaid through realized energy savings over time. Energy-inefficient equipment and systems are replaced with energy-efficient technologies, and the capital investment, installation, commissioning, and ongoing management are paid for by an Energy Service Company (ESCO) or third-party financier. The building owner pays the ESCO from the operational energy savings created over a set period of time up to 20 years. ESCO payments are directly linked to the amount of energy saved, with no need for up-front capital investment by the building owner[9].

The Retrofit Chicago Energy Challenge supports voluntary energy efficiency steps by commercial, institutional and private buildings. It aims to help participants reduce energy consumption by 20 percent over five years.

In Boston, a public-private partnership called the Renew Boston Trust directs private investor funds into energy projects in commercial properties.

Lawsuits

So far, (June 2021) around 1,500 climate-related lawsuits have been brought before the courts around the world. A recent case against Shell was decided by a civil court in the Netherlands. The judge ruled that, by 2030, the company must cut its CO_2 emissions by 45 percent compared to 2019 levels. The verdict also indicated that the Shell group is responsible for its own CO_2 emissions and those of its suppliers. Researchers have been able to show that climate change linked to human activities made the European summer heatwave in 2019 both more likely and more intense. A recent paper on Hurricane Sandy—the deadly storm that wreaked havoc from the Caribbean to New York in 2012—showed that climate change was responsible for about 13 percent of the $62 billion in losses caused by the event. As this science improves, the boards of individual fossil fuel companies should be preparing for their day in court, to respond to charges that they are to blame for increased natural disasters and disruptions to the planet's climate stability[10].

In April 2021, Germany's highest court paid due respect to the now. In response to a complaint by young environmental activists, the court ordered the federal government to enforce "more urgent and shorter-term measures" to reach emissions targets for 2030. The judges declared that young people's "fundamental rights to a human future" would be jeopardized if global warming went much past 1.5 degrees Celsius[11].

The Intergovernmental Panel on Climate Change (IPCC) is a group of scientists whose findings are endorsed by the world's governments. **The IPCC's document says, "it is unequivocal that human influence has warmed the atmosphere, oceans and land."** With this more detailed research opens the probability for more lawsuits against fossil fuel companies that will be won by citizens.

9

CITIZENS

"Be the change that you want to see in this world."
Mahatma Gandhi

People who focus on reducing their food waste now, improve their diet, purchase green power and EVs, continuously learn about the best solutions, and advocate to reduce greenhouse gases will help with beating climate change.

Citizens can make decisions that can reduce at least 30 percent of the greenhouse gas problem created by the U.S., and cost less than the status quo. A substantial body of research shows that small changes to **everyday behaviors can significantly reduce energy demand**. This may be the biggest way individuals and families can contribute to lowering fossil fuel consumption and reducing carbon emissions[1].

Strategies for Citizens

1. **Reevaluate the food you eat.** Eat healthier, eat less red meat, and have less waste.

2. **All-electric energy and transportation.** Transition to using renewable energy and use EVs as much as possible.

3. **All-electric homes** by purchasing water heaters, heating and air conditioning units, stoves, heat pumps that run off electric.

4. **Reduce the time you need for travel.** Less travel, lower carbon footprint.

5. **Use EVs when traveling**—cars, buses, trains.

6. **Renovate and improve energy efficiency with new technology installed in your home.** Electric mechanical systems, heat pumps, Energy Star appliances and add solar panels if possible.

7. **Plant trees to reduce the local heat island effect and absorb carbon.** Trees are a natural way of absorbing carbon. Focus on natural solutions are affordable and a long-term solution.

Citizen participation and action has proved effective at getting decision-makers to act. According to the Sierra Club, through citizen-driven action, over 180 cities, more than 10 counties and eight U.S. states have made commitments to transitioning to 100 percent renewable energy. Consequently, over 100 million U.S residents already live in a community with a 100 percent renewable energy target. New York's measure mandates that the state shift to 100 percent renewable energy by 2040 and that its emissions from all sources drop 40 percent by 2040 and 85 percent by 2050.

How and where people spend their money can also influence corporate behavior. Some of the world's biggest brands have responded to this pressure with claims of already being powered by 100 percent renewable energy, including Google and Apple.

COMPONENTS OF REAL GDP (2019)

Component	Percentage of U.S. GDP
Consumer spending	**70%**
Government spending	17%
Business investment	16%
Net exports	-5%
TOTAL GDP	100%

The Size of an Individual's Carbon Footprint

The US is among the worst offenders. Each person emits 19 tons of greenhouse gases per year on average. **The International Energy Agency estimate that around 55 percent of the cumulative emissions reductions are linked to consumer choices such as purchasing** an EV, changing what we eat, retrofitting a house with energy-efficient technologies, replacing car trips with walking, cycling or public transport, or foregoing a plane flight, installing a heat pump and minimizing waste.

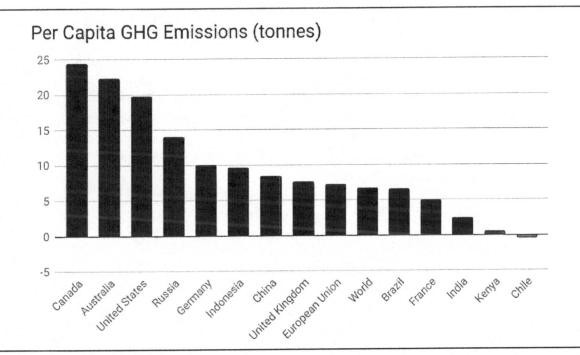

Per Capita GHG Emissions (tonnes)

9.1

The U.S. citizen, per capita, has a higher rate of GHGs than people living in 99 percent of the countries. There is plenty of room for improvement with many items being easy to do. The list that follows is a good start.

The behavioral choices will help reduce your carbon that each person decides:

1. You can reduce your calories from red meat with fish, eggs and poultry. Like most Americans, you get close to 30 percent of your calories from meat, dairy and poultry. Your diet contributes to over 3,274 pounds of food. Vegetarian diets contribute half that (1,600 pounds of food saved). **Less calories, less carbon, better health, and longer life.**

2. **Reduce CO_2 annually for every degree you lower your thermostat below 70 in winter.**

3. **Reduce CO_2 annually in the summer for every degree above 72 you raise your thermostat.** Ceiling fans can help keep spaces cool without air conditioning and use much less energy. An average house with central air uses 3,500 watts of electricity each day compared to a ceiling fan that uses 30–50 watts per day. If you need seven ceiling fans to manage your entire home, that is 350 watts, which is 10 percent of what central air requires.

4. Take 2 minutes off your shower; it can reduce CO_2 annually.

5. Pre-2001 fridges are much less energy-efficient than today's Energy Star models. Clean your refrigerator's coils, defrost regularly and keep the top clear of clutter.

6. Wash clothes in cold water. A clothes washer reduces 240 pounds of CO_2 annually if you wash just 75 percent of your loads in cold water instead of hot water. Most clothes can be washed in cold water. Ninety percent of the electricity a washing machine consumes goes to heat the water.

7. Use line- or rack-drying for half your loads will reduce CO_2 annually.

These are things all families, no matter their income, can do to help reduce greenhouse gases.[2]

Total direct spending on energy is estimated to hold steady at around 8% to 2030 (like the average over the last five years), but then decline to 6% by 2050. The decline will evolve from renewable resources providing more cost-effective energy, and improvements to buildings and transportation leading to more energy efficiency. The transition to all-electric technology can save money today and will be a long-term investment to continually reduce energy bills for everyone.

Philanthropy

Philanthropists, in 2017, contributed support for **44 percent of basic science research** at universities and non-profit research institutes. **The Bill & Melinda Gates Foundation** just announced their intent in the summer of 2022 to increase their donations by 50 percent over pre-pandemic levels, from nearly $6 billion to $9 billion annually by 2026.

Gates Foundation spending

Historical and projected through 2026.

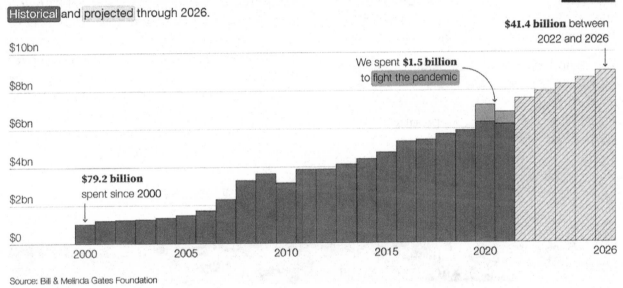

$41.4 billion between 2022 and 2026

We spent **$1.5 billion** to fight the pandemic

$79.2 billion spent since 2000

Source: Bill & Melinda Gates Foundation

9.2

This increase is the result of two decades of generous contributions from Bill Gates, Melinda French Gates, and Warren Buffett. **Bill announced that he is transferring $20 billion** to the foundation's endowment and reiterated his intention to give nearly all his wealth to the foundation. This gift meets and exceeds Bill and Melinda's commitment last year. It also builds on Warren Buffett's immense generosity, including **his annual $3.1 billion gift in June**, 2022. This brings Mr. Buffett's contributions to more than $36 billion since 2006. **Since 2000, the three have donated over $115 million dollars to try to solve global issues and help others!**

Yvon Chouinard, founder and majority owner of Patagonia, dominated the headlines in early September for doing something that no other billionaire has: **donating almost all his wealth at once**. He gave his apparel company and its millions in annual profits to an environmental nonprofit and placed its voting stock into a trust. Chouinard, 83, transferred 98% of Patagonia shares to Holdfast Collective, a nonprofit that will deploy its roughly $100 million in annual profits to fighting the environmental crisis and defending nature.

Kristine Tompkins—the founder and CEO of Tompkins Conservation—signed the largest national park donation (public or private) in history. The designation protects 10 million acres of new land in Patagonia, Chile.

The Giving Pledge is a campaign encouraged by extremely wealthy people to contribute most of their wealth to philanthropic causes. As of August 2020, the pledge had 211 signatories from 23 countries. Most of the signatories on the pledge are billionaires. The combined wealth of the 62 living U.S.

pledgers, who were billionaires in 2010, has increased by 95 percent, from $376 billion in 2010 to $734 billion as of July 18, 2020, according to "Gilded Giving 2020." **There are many wealthy individuals who can make a difference. If these people collectively decided to contribute more of their wealth now and over the next 10 years, that can help accelerate solutions to reduce greenhouse gases.**

One option is each year money from the Giving Pledge be donated based on the amount of the increased value. If that amount from the Giving Pledge increased on average 10 percent each year, that will provide approximately $75 billion dollars annually to invest in green solutions. The recently passed Inflation Reduction Act has $369 billion over 10 years for addressing climate change. My proposed trust fund from philanthropists can provide twice as much funding over the same period of time! Donating later may be too late. The donations from non-U.S. citizens should be invested in their home countries and countries of their choice.

WHAT CITIZENS CAN DO NOW!	Within 1 Year	Within 7 years	PROPOSED ACTIONS
1 FOOD			Biggest Opportunity for a person to reduce their carbon
REDUCE FOOD WASTE	■		Buy Local and Seasonal Food
	■		Eat "Almost Perfect" Food
	■		Stock Up on Non-Perishables
PLANT RICH DIETS	■		Eat less meat each week- at least 10–20% less
	■		Eat at Vegatarian annd Vegan restaurants
VERTICAL FARMING		■	Buy food from vertical farms- Encourage Facility in neighborhood
REFRIGERANT UPDATE		■	Purchase HFC Refrigerants by 2030
RECYCLING		■	Reduce waste, donate, buy less new products, buy used
LOCAL FARMING		■	Buy local, purchase less that travels more

WHAT CITIZENS CAN DO NOW!	Within 1 Year	Within 7 years	PROPOSED ACTIONS
2 RENEWABLE ENERGY			**Buy and Use Renewable Energy as much as possible**
SOLAR FARMS		■	Buy green energy
BATTERY STORAGE		■	Buy storage wiith rooftop solar
ROOFTOP SOLAR		■	Install panels as much as possible
COMMUNITY SOLAR		■	Purchase Energy as Main Utility from Community Solar Projects

WHAT CITIZENS CAN DO NOW!	Within 1 Year	Within 7 years	PROPOSED ACTIONS
3 TRANSPORTATION			**Short Commutes, Use Electric Vehicles**
ELECTRIC VEHICLES		■	Purchase/Benefit from Tax Break and lower maintenance costs
		■	Install Type 2 charger at home/ garage
CARPOOLING	■		Carpool as much as possible
PUBLIC TRANSIT		■	Support and ride as much as possible
AVIATION		■	Fly less each year, take the train
OCEAN SHIPPING		■	Purchase less that has to travel more
BICYCLE INFRASTRUCTURE	■		Ride bikes for health and savings
	■		Consider an Electric Bike
WALKABLE CITIES	■		Buy local products, Enjoy local Parks and Sidewalks
HIGH SPEED RAIL		■	Train instead of plane flight

WHAT CITIZENS CAN DO NOW!	Within 1 Year	Within 7 years	PROPOSED ACTIONS
4 CITIES			**Urban Cities are More Energy Efficient**
RESILIENT DESIGN	■		Buy flood insurance, do not live or rent in a flood plain
WATER EFFICIENCY		■	Manage leaks, shower shorter times
TRAVEL TOGETHER	■		Carpool, Ride Bikes and Walk Together
PLANT TREES		■	Plant trees in your neighborhood, along streets, in parking lots
			Healthy approach to sequester carbon

WHAT CITIZENS CAN DO NOW!	Within 1 Year	Within 7 years	PROPOSED ACTIONS
5 BUILDINGS			**Renovate, Improve Energy Efficiency, Buy New Technology**
ENERGY EFFICIENCY	■		Upgrade your home, business
INSULATION	■	■	Upgrade older buildings by 2030 to current codes or higher
SMART THERMOSTATS	■		Add to your home for better energy efficiency
BUILDING AUTOMATION SYSTEMS		■	Upgrade Older Buildings by 2030 to save on energy costs
COMMISSIONING	■		Have your home and work place commissioned once a year
HEAT PUMPS		■	Upgrade Current HVAC Equipment when it gets to old
LED LIGHTING		■	Use LED lights to save energy and money

2023 TAX INCENTIVES TO CONSIDER:

Battery Storage Installation	30%
Geothermal Heating Installation	30%
Electric Panel	$600
Electric Vehicle Charger	$1,000
New Electric Vehicle	$7,500
Used Electric Vehicle	$4,000
Heat Pump Air Conditioner/ Heater	$2,000
Heat Pump Water Heater	$2,000
Rooftop Solar Installation	30%
Weatherization	$1,200

	Within 1 Year	Within 7 years	
6 CARBON SEQUESTRATION			**Go Back and Support the Land– Farm, Reforest**
FARMING TECHNOLOGIES	■	■	Be aware and receptive to improving your farming processes
ORGANIC FERTILIZER			Do Not Use Fertilizer Unless It Is Organic
			Do Not Use Peat Moss

* INCLUDES SILVOPASTURE, MANAGED GRAZING, PERENNIAL STAPLE CROPS, TREE INTERCROPPING, CONSERVATIVE AGRICULTURE AND ABANDONED FARMLAND RESTORATION.

9.3

GLOBALLY

77 percent of the population eats leftovers,

77 percent recycle,

65 percent do not get a plastic bag when shopping,

63 percent avoid single use items like straws, water bottles and plastic cutlery,

and 62 percent limit water use in their home.

The U.S. percentages are much lower than the global statistics listed, meaning there is plenty of room for improvements in behavior.

These changes will also cost less than the status quo. Much of it is simply going back to more sustainable habits we had 100 years ago.

Get involved in your community as a volunteer, mentor, politician, and advocate. It is very important that citizens stay focused on reducing your carbon footprint. The government may or may not be as supportive as needed all the time to address climate change due to changes during elections. Businesses and citizens need maintain leadership, stay focused and hopefully get very good support from politicians.

The Circular Economy

The circular economy aims to transform the current financial model by fighting against all forms of waste. The circular economic model extends the life of products and gives them a second, third, and maybe fourth life.

Redesign products to consider environmental impacts.

Reduce your consumption, pollution, waste, and optimize resources.

Reuse giving a second use to products.

Repair lengthening the useful life of a product.

Renovate reusing products for other things which may also be useful.

Recover the circular economy favors sharing things.

Recycle by giving a second life to our waste to increase the life cycle of a product.

Examples of the circular economy:

Gomi: A company that makes hand-made portable speakers from plastic bags and powered by used e-bike batteries.

Goods for Good: A charity that donates new and unwanted overproduced goods and items to vulnerable communities.

Young Planet: An app for parents looking to give or receive children's items—toys, clothes, and more[3].

GREEN ECONOMY

The United Nations Environment Program (UNEP) defines the green economy as "an economy which leads to greater human well-being and social equity, significantly reducing environmental risks and ecological scarcity."

Financing

Third-party financing has emerged in the solar industry as one of the most popular methods for consumers to realize the benefits of solar energy. Third-party financing of solar energy primarily occurs through two models:

LEASE

Under a lease, the solar provider installs and owns the system, and the customer makes monthly payments to the solar provider.

POWER PURCHASE AGREEMENTS (PPA)

For PPAs, the customer pays an agreed-upon rate over an extended period for the electricity generated by the system. The solar company installs a solar system, often with no up- front costs, and is responsible for system upkeep.

Other financing opportunities include applying for government and bank loans at low rates to purchase an EV, solar panels, and make your home more energy efficient. **For renters and homeowners, who cannot build their solar panels, then advocate for and lease from community solar projects. Lease your air rights to developers, who will install solar energy systems.**

PURCHASING GREEN ENERGY

Homeowners and renters who purchase green energy through any of the financial options should sign contracts where your new utility bill with renewable sources will be lower than your existing with fossil fuels. You should expect solar panels to be at least 20% efficient and last for at least 20–25 years. If energy storage is a part of the green energy package, one still should expect the utility bill to be lower. The company will simply have a longer period of time before they see the financial payback and the government may need to subsidize or incentivize the project more to be financially viable for all parties involved.

Training

Educate contractors. Today, there are cold-climate heat pumps designed to address concerns of low capacity and efficiency in cold temperatures, best practice design guidelines, and case studies proving the value added of cold-climate heat pumps. Promote contractor readiness as all-electric building codes come online. **Policymakers, regulatory agencies, and businesses should establish contractor training, fund them, and provide rebates on purchasing new electric equipment. The technology is available and affordable today. Implementing the new technology in a timely manner is the challenge.** Anything purchased and installed using fossil fuels today is 20-25 years of more greenhouse gases. Pay contractors for their time to attend training and have their certification be a requirement for bidding projects. Educate consumers and developers.

A people-centered world moving collectively and consistently toward net-zero emissions by mid-century is necessary to be a key part of solving the climate crisis.

There are many individuals who have made a big difference in the world. Jose Andres is one of those wonderful people who started the World Central Kitchen (WCK). World Central Kitchen is a not-for-profit NGO devoted to providing meals in the wake of natural disasters. Founded in 2010 by celebrity chef José Andrés, the organization provided food in Haiti after the 7.2 magnitude earthquake.

9.4 Jose Andres

SUPPORTING COMMUNITIES IN TIMES OF CRISIS

WCK responds to natural disasters, man-made crises, and humanitarian emergencies around the world. They're a team of food first responders, mobilizing with the urgency of now to get meals to the people who need them most, deploying quick action, leveraging local resources, and adapting in real time. A nourishing meal in a time of crisis is so much more than a plate of food—it's hope, it's dignity, and it's a sign that someone cares.

Recent work includes helping people in Ukraine, meals for Afghan refugees, helping with Covid-19 response, Venezuelan refuge crisis, serving refugees at the U.S./Mexican border and helping residents when the volcano erupted in Tonga. These are major global events just in the last four years that Jose Andres and his organization have stepped up to immediately provide help. This is a great organization.

Elected officials and companies got to where they are today because of individuals. We decide whom to support by giving them our votes and our money. Citizens are the ones with the power if enough people are on the same page to activate this power. **Using our voices, money, and votes, we collectively determine the various officials and companies that serve us**[4].

"I alone cannot change the world, but I can cast a stone across the waters to create many ripples." – Mother Theresa

10

COUNTRIES

The focus of this book has been the U.S. reducing its carbon footprint, but the U.S. is only 4 percent of the entire global population. Another book can be written for each of these areas around the world. This chapter provides some insight, data, and success stories from various places around the world that I was able to document while doing my research over the 3+ years. Many of the ideas from each country should be considered for most or all countries.

PROJECTED POPULATION GROWTH BY CONTINENT 2020 TO 2100

	2020	% Global	2100	% Global	% Increase
Asia	4,641,054,775	59.5%	4,719,420,000	43.5%	+1.7%
Africa	1,340,598,147	17.2%	4,280,130,000	39.5%	+319.3%
Europe	747,636,026	9.6%	629,560,000	5.8%	-16.2%
North America	592,072,212	7.6%	702,740,000	6.5%	+18.6%
South America	430,759,766	5.5%	429,300,000	4.0%	-1.0%
Australia/Oceania	43,111,704	0.6%	74,920,000	0.7%	+173.8%
Antarctica	0	0			
TOTAL	7,952,326,630	99.5%	10,836,070,000	100%	+136.3%

Africa is poised to lead the world's cleanest economic revolution by using renewable energy sources to power a massive spread of urbanization, says an IEA report. The report forecasts that Africa's appetite for energy will grow at double the rate of the global average in the coming decades as the continent overtakes China and India as the most populated region in the world. Africa's population is expected to grow to more than 2 billion people by 2040, a rise of 800 million from today or the population equivalent of the US and Europe combined.

Energy Needed

17.7 Terawatts of power globally is needed on an annual basis from all sources of energy. A total of **173,000 terawatts** (trillions of watts) of solar energy strikes the Earth continuously. That's more than 10,000 times the world's total energy use and that energy is completely renewable.

Cost

$5 trillion is necessary by 2030 to put the world on the pathway to being climate-safe[1]. The International Monetary Fund calculated total fossil fuel subsidies in 2020 at $5.9 trillion, or almost 7 percent of global gross domestic product (GDP), largely as a result of these external costs including air pollution and climate change.

The G20 countries emit almost 80 percent of global greenhouse gases. More than 600 global companies in the We Mean Business coalition, including Unilever, Ikea, Aviva, Siemens and Volvo Cars, recently urged G20 leaders to end fossil fuel subsidies by 2025.

Subsidies

Fossil fuel subsidies are one of and possibly the biggest financial barriers hampering the world's shift to renewable energy sources. Each year, governments around the world pour around half a trillion dollars into artificially lowering the price of fossil fuels—more than triple the amount that renewables receive.

G20 states subsidized fossil fuels by $3.3 trillion since 2015 and the Paris Agreement. **The $3.3** trillion **could have built solar plants equivalent to three times the US electricity grid, the report says**[2].

The G20 countries account for nearly three-quarters of the global carbon emissions that drive global heating. Australia increased its fossil fuel subsidies by 48 percent over the period, Canada's support rose by 40 percent and that from the US by 37 percent. The biggest subsidies came from China, Saudi Arabia,

Russia and India, which together accounted for about half of all the subsidies.

G-20 Government fossil fuel subsidy supports by type– 2019:

45 percent State-owned businesses

21 percent Consumer lower energy prices

14 percent Tax breaks

12 percent Concessional loans/grants

8 percent Direct budgetary transfers

Complete removal of consumption Fossil Fuel Subsidies (FFSs) reduces GHG emissions by an average of 6.09 percent across these 32 countries. **In total, these countries account for 77 percent of global CO$_2$ emissions, 72 percent of global GDP, and 72 percent of the global population.** The 32 countries modeled in the research are Algeria, Argentina, Australia,

Bangladesh, Brazil, Canada, China, Egypt, Ethiopia, Germany, Ghana, India, Indonesia, Iran, Iraq, Japan, Mexico, Morocco, Myanmar, Nigeria, Pakistan, Russia, Saudi Arabia, South Africa, Sri Lanka, Tunisia, United Arab Emirates (UAE), the United States, Venezuela, Vietnam, the Netherlands, and Zambia.

Cumulative fiscal savings from Fossil Fuel Subsidies versus Renewables (FFSR) alone by 2030 total $2.96 trillion across the countries analyzed.

Fossil fuel subsidies generally take two forms. Production subsidies are tax breaks or direct payments that reduce the cost of producing coal, oil, or gas. A report found that 60 percent of the fossil fuel subsidies went to the companies producing fossil fuels and 40 percent to cutting prices for energy consumers. Reforming fossil fuel subsidies aimed at consumers in 32 countries could reduce CO_2 emissions by 5.5 billion tons by 2030, equivalent to the annual emissions of about 1,000 coal-fired power plants.

There are two main concerns to removing production subsidies. First, fossil-fuel companies are powerful political groups. Second, there are potential job losses in communities that have few alternative employment options. With more energy-efficient buildings, all-electric transportation, with affordable solar and wind solutions, there should be less risk of rising energy prices.

Money not given to fossil-fuel firms can be redistributed for renewable projects that reduce energy prices because the renewables are bringing the more cost-effective electricity to the consumer. One way to overcome political hesitancy to remove energy subsidies is to maintain support but simply make it contingent on a move to greener energy.

According to the GSI Environmental, the Philippines, Indonesia, Ghana, and Morocco each introduced cash transfers and social support, such as education funds and health insurance for poor families, to compensate for the removal of subsidies[3].

Region or Country

ASIA

From 1998 to present, I have worked on the design and construction of seven major projects research campuses in China and four very large medical school campuses in Saudi Arabia. These countries have the capabilities, and finances to build very large projects quickly. Hopefully they will be able to focus on net-zero solutions moving forward.

China

China has repeatedly broken annual wind or solar addition records in the past few years as costs drop and developers rush to meet national subsidy deadlines to build the world's largest renewable generation fleet and may decide to set an even more ambitious national goal. The country installed more than 100 gigawatts of solar and wind power in 2020. A massive renewable build-out in the country's desert areas and a national push to install solar panels on rooftops are set to continue driving that stellar pace. China could hit its 2030 renewables target at least 5 years early if local governments meet the ambitious goals they've laid out.

Development plans from 22 of China's 34 regional governments are aiming for more than 600 gigawatts of renewable capacity combined to be added from 2021 through 2025. That would more than double the 535 gigawatts of wind and solar capacity in place at the end of 2020 and approach President Xi Jinping's target of having 1,200 gigawatts of renewables in place by the end of the decade[4]. Chinese firm, MingYang, recently announced plans for an even more powerful device clocking in at 16MW, for example. Just four years ago, the maximum capacity of an offshore turbine was 8MW.

China will start selling only "new energy" cars in 2035. As a reminder, China is the world's largest car market, with **over 20 million cars sold in 2020 alone**.

China and developing countries need to rethink the cement they use for construction. China adds 20–25 percent more concrete each year than the U.S. Getting the growing countries to understand the problems with cement and the opportunities to improve the cement mixtures while reducing carbon is critical. The new cement mix should not compromise the strength or cost any more. It simply is a new and smarter solution.

China is planting new forests covering an area roughly the size of Ireland this year (2018/19) as it aimed to increase forest coverage to 23 percent of its total landmass by the end of 2020. The government is currently promoting an "ecological red line" program, which will force provinces and regions to restrict "irrational development" and **curb construction near rivers, forests, and national parks.**

Singapore

The Government of Singapore has devised a strict system of vehicle registration fees and road taxes in a bid to improve the city state's air quality and reduce carbon emissions. A nationwide ban on the import of cars over three years old and increased rates of road tax for vehicles over ten years old have all been introduced to try and encourage a shift towards a more modern, efficient vehicles by both consumers and taxi fleets[5].

10.1 Singapore is known for vegetation growing on outside of buildings.

This is one way of introducing nature-based solutions, such as green roofs and living walls. Green infrastructure increases biodiversity has a cooling effect from the evaporation of vegetation, and it can absorb some particulate pollution in the air. Vegetation growing on walls and roofs of buildings in Singapore is very common.

Bangladesh is a striking example of the power of effective adaptation against natural disasters. Starting with early warning systems, scaled-up disaster response has included cyclone shelters, building civic awareness, strengthening buildings, and improving post-disaster recovery.

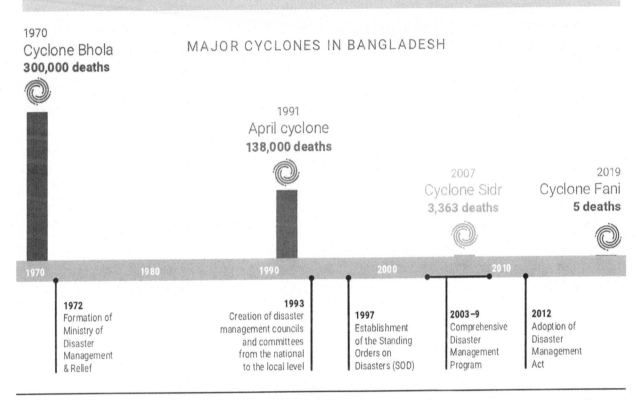

BANGLADESH IS A STRIKING EXAMPLE OF THE POWER OF EFFECTIVE ADAPTATION:
Starting with **early warning systems**, scaled-up disaster response has included **cyclone shelters**, **building civic awareness, strengthening buildings**, and improving **post-disaster recovery**

MAJOR CYCLONES IN BANGLADESH

1970
Cyclone Bhola
300,000 deaths

1991
April cyclone
138,000 deaths

2007
Cyclone Sidr
3,363 deaths

2019
Cyclone Fani
5 deaths

1972
Formation of Ministry of Disaster Management & Relief

1993
Creation of disaster management councils and committees from the national to the local level

1997
Establishment of the Standing Orders on Disasters (SOD)

2003–9
Comprehensive Disaster Management Program

2012
Adoption of Disaster Management Act

10.2 Key Policy Interventions in Bangladesh Contributed to Reduced Deaths from Climate Disasters[6].

United Arab Emirates

UAE is looking beyond its fossil fuel history and has just started up the first of four nuclear reactors, which by the middle of this decade will supply 25 percent of its electricity.

Saudi Arabia

A country going in the wrong direction is the state-owned oil giant Saudi Aramco, which plans to sharply increase the amount it invests in energy production, after it reported

a doubling of profits in 2021. The firm aims to boost output significantly over the next five years. Saudi Aramco said it planned to increase its capital expenditure to $45–$50bn this year with further increases until the middle of the decade. The oil company more than doubled its net profit to $110 billion in 2021, up from $49 billion in 2020. The war in Ukraine and a reluctance to rely on Russia for energy has added to the pressure to find additional sources of energy. **In 2019, Saudi Arabia provided $28.7 billion of subsidies for fossil** fuels, second to China in total amount but first per capita by far.

Saudi Arabia and all other countries in the Middle East have the sun as an even better natural resource than fossil fuels. Solar farms should be built now to replace fossil fuels in these countries to benefit their next generation, and all generations.

EUROPE

Europe is closer to net zero with 64.1 percent of electricity generated by non-carbon sources—renewables and nuclear—with the U.S. at only 40 percent at the end of 2020. Expect to see growth in nuclear power in several countries in Europe. An international task force is sharing Research & Development for six Generation IV nuclear reactor technologies. All six systems represent advances in sustainability, economics, safety, reliability, and proliferation-resistance. Europe is pushing ahead with three of the fast reactor designs.

Power Mix
Europe gets about a fifth of its electricity from gas

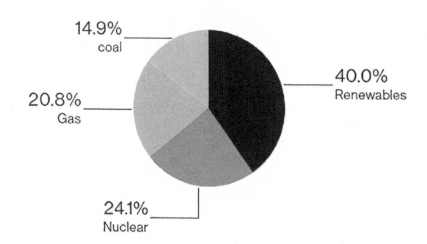

10.3 Europe has almost 65% of electricity from non-carbon sources (Renewables & Nuclear)

RECENT GLOBAL DEVELOPMENTS have had countries scrambling to reduce their reliance on Russia's oil and gas in the wake of its invasion of Ukraine. The European Union (EU) gets roughly 40 percent of its gas from Russia. The EU has laid out a strategy that could cut reliance on this fuel source by two-thirds within a year.

The REPowerEU plan aims to make Europe independent of Russian fossil fuels by 2030, but the initial efforts focus solely on gas. The roadmap essentially proposes finding alternative supplies of gas, boosting energy efficiency, while doubling down on greener sources of power for the long term. **The EU is implementing a massive ramping up of renewables, biogas, and hydrogen.** The Commission also believes the reliance on Russia will be eased as there are new renewable energy projects coming online. The construction of most wind and solar projects should take up to one year, which helps.

The Commission document also says that renewable energy projects must be fast-tracked and says there is huge potential in domestic rooftop solar power. Up to a quarter of the bloc's electricity consumption could be generated from panels on homes, farms and commercial building, the Commission says. This crisis has brought it to a head, and you're probably going to get decisions made in the 2020s to bring it all forward at least 10 years. Wind turbines can be built and installed in approximately one year. Large solar projects take three months or longer to install.

In Europe, roughly 15,000 existing houses need to transform for energy efficiency every day for the next 30 years.

There are currently **21,387 existing hydropower plants in Europe, with 8,785 additional plants planned or under construction**. Almost half of these are in the Balkans and Eastern Mediterranean, where many plants are financed by the EU. Over 90 percent of all the existing and planned hydropower plants in Europe are small, meaning that **each plant generates at most 10 MW of electricity**.

WWF advocates for there to be no more new hydropower development in Europe, and for investments to move into the refurbishment of existing plants to lessen their impact on biodiversity. WWF recommended switching to low-cost solar and wind power. WWF is also advocating **ending subsidies and public financing for new hydropower development in Europe**[7]. Solar and wind are more affordable and faster to build than hydropower projects.

France

The French have a ban on plastic packaging for fruit and vegetables[8]. President Emmanuel Macron showed the country's commitment to phase out single use plastics by 2040. More than a third of fruit and vegetable products in France are thought to be sold in plastic wrapping, and government officials believe that the ban could prevent a billion items of single use plastics being used every year.

From 2021, the country banned plastic straws, cups, and cutlery, as well as polystyrene takeaway boxes. And later in 2022 public spaces will be forced to provide water fountains to reduce the use of plastic bottles. Publications will have to be shipped without plastic wrapping, and fast-food restaurants will no longer be able to offer free plastic toys.

France receives 70 percent of its electricity from nuclear power plants. Nuclear generates nearly 800 billion kilowatt hours of electricity each year. This avoids <u>more than 470 million metric tons</u> of carbon each year, which is the equivalent of removing 100 million cars off of the road.

Paris

In Paris, the mayor is using the Rue de Rivoli as a prototype for a future metropolis in which no Parisian should need to travel more than 15 minutes on foot or by bike to work, shop, or work with a government agency.

Paris officials plan to ban private vehicles from the historic heart of the city by early 2024 in a move designed to decrease congestion and improve air quality in the French capital. The plan does not allow through traffic in four central districts, giving priority instead to cyclists, pedestrians, and public transportation. The low-traffic zone will result in a "less polluted, greener, more peaceful and safer city," the council says. During the pandemic, Paris has added hundreds of kilometers of cycle lanes. Mayor Anne Hidalgo was reelected last year on a platform of creating the "**15-minute city**," making it easier for residents to access shops, schools, and services within a quarter of an hour from home, either on foot or bicycle. Residents and businesses will still be allowed to drive in the central area, but through traffic would be banned.

Germany

Germany announced that it would ban Internal Combustible Engines (ICE) vehicles by 2030.

In Ulm, southern Germany, the Energon building uses a process called passive heating, drawing on natural energy sources to regulate the building's temperature. Underground canals around the building sneak in and heat incoming air in winter and cool the system in summer with the help of probes extending 330 feet (100 meters) underground, where the earth's natural temperature can be used to cool or heat the air above. This allows the building to use 75 percent less energy for heating and cooling than a standard office building[9].

Across Germany many barn roofs have installed solar panels by the government to provide electricity to the local farmer and reduce carbon in the country.

United Kingdom

Plans to ban sales of peat compost to gardeners in England by 2024.

England's homes produce more carbon emissions every year than all the country's cars[10].

Key points of the new energy strategy

Nuclear - building as many as eight new nuclear reactors, including two at Sizewell in Suffolk. Building Generation IV, the newest design model for nuclear power.

Wind - Reform planning laws to speed up approvals for new offshore wind farms. **For onshore wind farms, it wants to develop partnerships with "supportive communities"**

who want to host turbines in exchange for guaranteed cheaper energy bills.

Hydrogen - Targets for hydrogen production are being doubled to help provide cleaner energy for industry as well as for power, transport, and potentially heating.

Solar - Reforming rules for installing solar panels on homes and commercial buildings to help increase the current solar capacity by up to five times by 2035.

Heat pumps - There will be a £30 million "heat pump investment accelerator competition" to make British heat pumps, which reduce the demand for gas.

Italy

Enel, one of the world's largest power companies, has developed a second-generation smart meter that allows the collection of more than 7,000 billion data points per year, including almost real-time use and electrical parameters to enable big-data analytics for the grid. In Italy alone, the Open Meter will reach more than 35 million customers by 2025, improving customers' awareness of their electricity consumption habits and favoring more efficient and sustainable consumption models. The Open Meter is designed and manufactured using regenerated plastics, emitting 6 percent less carbon dioxide and producing 122g less waste for each Open Meter compared to a conventionally produced meter.

Netherlands

Energiesprong is coordinating a system of mass retrofits of existing residential properties that will make the units very energy-efficient, lower utility bills, and enable the occupants to live in their home or apartment during the retrofit.

The Netherlands is aiming for its constructed environment to be circular by 2050. A Finnish study from 2020 estimated that, if 80 percent of Europe's construction switched to wood as its primary material, the amount of carbon sequestered would be equivalent to 47 percent of the emissions from the continent's concrete industry.

Danish wind turbine manufacturer Vestas will put up a 15MW wind turbine that will be powerful enough to provide electricity to roughly 13,000 British homes.

Copenhagen aims to build 360 wind turbines by 2025 to supply most of the electricity demand in the city.

Norway

It took Norway only 10 years to move from 1 percent of car sales being EVs to 65 percent. The number in May 2022 was 85.1 percent when you include plug-in hybrids. Some believe strong demand-side policies kept in place for a long time supported the quick growth of the EVs. The government therefore taxes the sales of new polluting cars but does not tax EVs at all. The Norwegian parliament has also decided that all sales of new cars and vans shall be zero emission by 2025. The key is to start taxing new sales of at least the most polluting car models. This is a fair way to implement climate policies as it is aimed at people buying a new car, not an indiscriminate tax at the gas pump for all internal combustion cars, used and new. Consumers are given an option when buying a new car. **Norway took 2.5 years to move from 2 percent to 10 percent EV market share, UK took 1.5 years and Germany only one.**

CENTRAL AMERICA

Mexico

In 2014, the government imposed a tax on sugary drinks. **The tax contributed to a 6 percent drop in soda drinking in its first year**, according to government research, while milk and water consumption climbed.

Last year, the Caribbean had a record-breaking 30 tropical storms—including six major hurricanes. The World Meteorological Organization says the region is still recovering. On islands like Antigua and Barbuda, experts say that many buildings have been unable to withstand the intense winds these storms have brought. "We used to see category four hurricanes, so that's what we have prepared for with our adaptation plans, but now we are being hit by category five hurricanes," says Diann Black Layner, chief climate negotiator for the Alliance of Small Island States. "Category five hurricanes bring winds as strong as 180 miles per hour, which the roofs cannot withstand because it creates stronger pressure inside our houses," she said[12].

SOUTH AMERICA

Brazil

91% of the Amazon rainforest destruction is a result of animal agriculture. Brazil impacts the survival of our planet in many ways, particularly since it produces around 6 percent of the globe's oxygen. Restoring forest ecosystems involves returning trees to former forest land and improving the condition of degraded forests. Land cleared for farming that falls into disuse is ideal for forest restoration[13].

Between 2001 and 2015, almost a third of the world's deforestation was due to commodity production—including cattle, soy, palm oil, and paper. In Brazil, where deforestation has reached a 12-year high, the chief reason is beef. Two-thirds of cleared land in the Amazon and the Cerrado Savannah have been converted to cattle pastures. Deforestation could not happen on this scale without vast financial investment. Loans totaling $249 billion were extended to companies linked to deforestation between 2013 and April 2020. Meanwhile, **three of the world's largest asset managers, BlackRock, Vanguard, and State Street, had $12.1 billion invested in producers and traders, whose activities are claimed to be directly driving deforestation, according to one analysis by the environmental campaign group Friends of the Earth in September 2020. Citizens must hold banks and investors accountable.**

10.4 Rainforests being destroyed for agriculture.

Brazil, home of much of the Amazon rainforest, is also the world's largest exporter of beef.

Colombia has planted 30 green corridors along 18 roads and 12 waterways, with 8,300 trees and 350,000 bushes. This has reduced the local temperature by more than 2°C[14].

AUSTRALIA

Wind sources from the country's onshore production have 7.4 gigawatts of capacity and supplied 10 percent of Australia's power in 2020; the 10 offshore projects the country is planning will produce three times as much electricity, totaling up to 40 percent of the electricity.

AFRICA

Africa has a "unique opportunity" to leapfrog the fossil fuel dependency of other industrialized regions and be the first economic transformation that did not contribute to the climate crisis. Africa's total contribution to cumulative global emissions from energy over the last 100 years is only 2 percent, which is half the emissions of Germany today.

Some 600 million people in Africa don't have access to energy—limiting their ability to start and run businesses. Businesses must deal with rolling power blackouts. So, the country is using microgrids—independent energy systems serving specific areas—to provide low-cost, clean energy, powered by solar and wind power to isolated communities. By the end of this decade, 65 million new jobs around the world are expected to be created in the so-called low-carbon industries, and firms offering training for jobs in solar are springing up across Africa. It is a welcome intervention—as in some African countries, unemployment has risen to 33 percent[15].

M-KOPA Solar in Kenya, **'pay-as-you-go' energy** is provided for off-grid customers by supplying solar products that are affordable to low-income households on a pay-per-use instalment plan[16].

Mobile money is being used by innovators in off-grid solar power, targeting Africa's mobile industry. Instead of costly energy contracts, customers can pay small pay-as-you-go instalments using their mobile phones. Usually these payments are like, or less than, their usual weekly expenditure on kerosene. **In practice, solar kits are paid off after 18 months and subsequent electricity is free to the new owner**[17].

In Africa the Microloans "Social Impact Investing" Program is commercial lending to get water to people who make less than $6/day. **There is a market to be served** and an investment opportunity. There is an estimated $18 billion demand for water for 800 million people in poverty.

Our World In Data estimates about 790 million people worldwide did not have access to electricity in 2020, most of them living in sub-Saharan Africa and developing Asia. Around 2.6 billion people did not have access to clean cooking options: 35 percent of them were in sub-Saharan Africa, 25 percent in India, and 15 percent in China. **More than 80 percent of people gaining access to electricity by 2030 will be supplied by renewable power and just over half via off-grid systems**.

A GLOBAL SYMBOL

The Great Green Wall isn't just for the Sahel. It is a global symbol for humanity overcoming its biggest threat – our rapidly degrading environment.

It shows that if we can work with nature, even in challenging places like the Sahel, we can overcome adversity, and build a better world for generations to come.

10.5 Inspiring project started in 2007 and is scheduled to be complete by 2030.

Africa's Great Green Wall initiative is an ambitious project, which aims to transform lives by **planting a vast 8,000 km stretch of trees and grasslands on the edge of the Sahara**, providing jobs and land suitable for growing crops for border communities. The project, which is backed by multiple nations as well as footwear giant Timberland, Danish fashion brand Vero Moda, and tree-planting search engine Ecosia, **received a $14.3 billion dollar boost in funding in January 2021. This has the potential of being a great project and important landmark for Africa. Development along this area can be very sustainable with the very latest and best technologies. The project started in 2007 and is expected to be completed by 2030. Tourism can be a key added value of this project.**

Kenya installed the first solar plant that transforms ocean water into drinking water. Kiunga is the name of the fishing town, where the project is operating successfully. It was funded by the non-profit Givepower and the organization is already planning to replicate the project in other countries, such as Colombia and Haiti, thanks to its achievements.

Global Issues in Developing Countries

FOOD

Vegetarian facts for 2022:

Twenty two percent of the global population is vegetarian but only 5 percent of U.S. citizens are vegetarian. **There are an estimated 1.5 billion vegetarians globally**[18]. A global shift to a vegetarian diet could save $1 trillion annually.

Thirty nine percent of the total population in India is vegetarian[19]. India is the country with the highest number of vegetarians. Additionally, 81 percent restrict meat in their diet in some form. For example, they refrain from eating certain meat or avoid eating meat on certain days. With 74.90 percent, Rajasthan has the highest vegetarian percentage by state, followed by Haryana (70 percent) and Punjab (66.75 percent).

In a year, the vegetarian population in Nigeria grew to 1.4 million people[20]. The most recent data shows that vegetarianism is becoming popular in many developing regions, especially among the young, middle and high-income population. In fact, Nigeria is the leading country in increasing the vegetarian population.

Furthermore, stats on vegetarianism suggest that Pakistan and Indonesia saw a significant increase and now have 1.19 million and 270,600 vegetarians, respectively. Germany, Brazil, and Italy are also on the list of countries with the most significant growth of vegetarian population in one year.

TRANSPORTATION

The world is getting there. Multiple countries across the world have been releasing their plans for phasing out internal combustion engines. **Norway** aims for 2025. **India**, with a population of 1.4 billion people, by 2040. **The United Kingdom** will be done with internal combustion engine cars also by 2040.

FORESTS

Forests still cover about 30 percent of the world's land area, but they are disappearing at an alarming rate. Since 1990, the world has lost 420 million hectares or **about a billion acres** of forest mainly in Africa and South America, according to the Food and Agriculture Organization of the United Nations. Especially beneficial are reforestation efforts in the tropics and subtropics, where land is relatively cheap, and trees grow fast.

The restored forests have the potential to soak up the equivalent of 5.9 gigatons (Gt) of carbon dioxide—more than the annual emissions of the U.S. William Baldwin-Cantello of WWF said **natural forest regeneration is often "cheaper, richer in absorbing carbon, and better for biodiversity than actively planted forests."** To avoid dangerous climate change, we must both halt deforestation and restore natural forests . . . Deforestation still claims millions of hectares every year globally, vastly more than is regenerated. Forests are extremely important to food security, water security and livelihoods—200 million people live in forests and 1.6 billion depend on them for their livelihoods.

Tropical Forest Restoration

Tropical forests have suffered extensive clearing, fragmentation, degradation, and depletion of biodiversity. Restoring these forests also restores their function as carbon sinks. This is similar for abandoned farmland restoration and tree plantations. **Bringing them back to their original use will help absorb carbon.** Natural regeneration of tropical forests offers benefits including biodiversity conservation, watershed protection, soil protection, and resilience to pests and disease.

Ninety five percent of global deforestation occurs in **the tropics**. Tropical deforestation claimed **roughly 13 million hectares (32,123,700 acres) of forest per year** during the first half of this decade. Brazil and Indonesia alone account for almost half. After long periods of forest clearance in the past, most of today's richest countries are increasing tree cover through afforestation.

The simplest scenario is to let a young forest rise on its own. Other techniques are more intensive, such as cultivating and planting native seedlings and removing invasive plants to accelerate natural ecological processes.

10.6 Chaco forest destroyed for soybeans.

Deforestation solutions:

Improve governance to curb illegal conversion and degradation of forests and reduce mismanagement of resources.

Use full-cost accounting to incorporate the real costs of externalities and perverse subsidies that drive environmental degradation, while aligning economic incentives with forest-friendly practices and policies.

Strengthen transparency around land use and commodity sources to improve accountability.

Engage stakeholders in and around forest areas to determine how conservation efforts can support local livelihoods and help make land use more sustainable.

Recognize the land rights of forest-dependent peoples to ensure the forests they traditionally use aren't taken away from them.

Educate the public on the importance of forest ecosystems, including the services they afford.

Take personal responsibility for how you use resources. The decisions we as consumers make have a direct impact on the fate of forests. As such, you have a powerful voice in asking companies what actions they are taking to eliminate deforestation from their supply chains.

Vote for representatives who support thoughtful, forest-friendly policies[21].

The international community has pledged to restore 350 million hectares (865 million acres) of degraded forest land by 2030. Tropical forest regrowth is often rapid, and results in impressive rates of carbon sequestration. Right Now Climate Fund, a $100 million pot of money Amazon set aside in 2020 in partnership with the Nature Conservancy, to back projects that protect or restore forests, wetlands, and peatlands.

Areas of our planet that absorb more carbon from the atmosphere and store the carbon are known as sinks. Since the 1960s, these sinks have taken in around 25 percent of carbon emissions from the use of fossil fuels.

Significant parts of the world's largest tropical forest have started to emit more CO_2 than they absorb. Earlier this year, a study showed that the rainforest in Brazil released about 20 percent more CO_2 into the atmosphere than it took in over the period from 2010–2019. They found a very clear division between the eastern and western parts of the rainforest. In the eastern part of the Amazon, which is around 30 percent deforested, this region emitted 10 times more carbon than in the west, which is around 11 percent deforested.

The biggest problem of deforestation is occurring in the following countries:

Nigeria, Indonesia, North Korea, Bolivia, DR Congo, Nicaragua, Brazil, and Cambodia.

China and the U.S.—the world's first and second largest producers of carbon emissions, respectively—ranked in the bottom five (low risk) on the Deforestation Index. In both countries, heavy investments in reforestation projects have aided the return of forest cover since the 1990s.

TEMPERATE FORESTS

Almost all temperate forests have been altered in some way— timbered, converted to agriculture, disrupted by development. Restoring them sequesters carbon in biomass and soil.

Brazilian wood is purchased in U.S. preserving land in Brazil. The process is called **Reduced-Impact Logging (RIL) techniques**, reduces residual damage to vegetation and soils and enhances the long-term economic viability of timber operations. Additionally, the economic value of selectively logged forests prevents them from being converted into agricultural plantations, which results in a tremendous loss of biodiversity. Loggers harvest dead, dying, and mature trees and replant new trees, as mandated by law. The trees to be harvested are chosen individually, under government supervision, based on the number of trees in each area. Replacing these trees with new healthy seedlings provides the necessary sun exposure for the healthy new growth. Government sourcing regulation and regrowth requirements drastically enhances the sustainability of forests around the world.

Most Latin American countries, including Brazil, have banned the clear-cut sourcing of Ipe and adopted forms of RIL. Clear cutting is not only unnecessary, time-consuming, costly, and illegal, it also cuts directly against the motivations and longevity of the groups that harvest them.

Tree Plantations/Afforestation

Tree plantations create a carbon sink, drawing in and holding on to carbon and distributing it into the soil. Tree plantations are the cultivation of trees for timber or other biomass uses on degraded land, providing an alternative source of timber. This practice replaces annual cropping.

FINANCIAL COST/PAYBACK:

- Net profit per hectare (2.41 acres) is calculated at $594 per year for the solution compared to $38 per year for the conventional practice.

- Annual operational cost per hectare is calculated at $123 for the solution compared to $81 for the conventional practice.

- The payback is **10 times more** to change to tree plantations than business as usual.

Peatland Protection

Peatland is a wetland **ecosystem** that is found across the world. Year-round wet conditions slow the process of plant decomposition so that that partially decomposed organic matter accumulates to form what is called 'peat.' Peat acts as a carbon store, is a great habitat for wildlife, has a role in water management, and preserves things well for archaeology.

Though peat covers only 3 percent of the world's land, it stores one-third of all soil carbon. Peatlands store nearly 550 billion tons of carbon—as much carbon as is contained in all terrestrial biomass (**grasses, trees and shrubs)** and twice as much as in all the world's forests. **Peatland ecosystems are second only to oceans in the amount of carbon they store—***twice* **that held by the world's forests, at an estimated 500–600 gigatons.** Protecting them through land preservation and fire prevention is a prime opportunity to manage global greenhouse gases. Considering this, **peatlands are one of the greatest allies and potentially one of the quickest wins in the fight against climate change.** By conserving and restoring peatlands globally, we can reduce emissions and revive an essential natural carbon sink. The carbon it contains is highly vulnerable to loss through deforestation, drainage, drying, burning, conversion to agriculture, and industrial extraction. Conversely, the restoration of peat domes, mires and fens offers further great potential for carbon withdrawal.

The sale and use of peat should be banned globally by 2025. Replace the lost income in those countries with financing or trading sustainable solutions. The other option is to fund the replacing of lost peat. Use organic compost instead of peat. **The sale of peat will be banned in many countries. The UK plans to ban sales of peat compost to gardeners in England by 2024** and provide funding to restore 35,000 hectares (86,000 acres) of degraded peatlands in the next four years, about 1 percent of the UK's total.

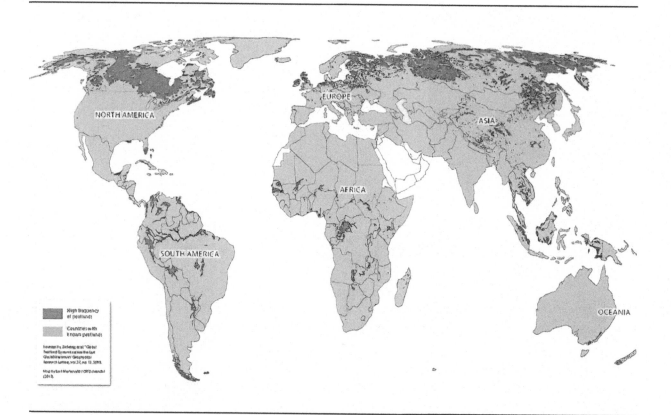

10.7 Peatland Regions

Peatlands are vital, super-powered, carbon-rich ecosystems. Peatlands protection and restoration can be a low-cost, low-tech, and high impact nature-based solution for both climate action and biodiversity.

Grassland Protection

Grasslands hold large amounts of carbon, largely underground. Protecting them shields their carbon and avoids emissions. Grasslands preserve important global carbon stocks and provide important ecosystem services. They are highly at risk of conversion to grazing, cropland, and biomass/bioenergy crops. Protection of grassland is an important strategy to limit emissions from land use change.

Most costs for grassland protection are at the cost of a government or NGO.

Negative Impacts of Global Warming

The parts of the world suitable for growing coffee, cashews, and avocados will change dramatically as the world heats up, according to a new study. Key coffee regions in Brazil, Indonesia, Vietnam and Colombia will all "drastically decrease" by around 50 percent by 2050. Coffee is the crop that is most susceptible to high temperatures. In the lowest temperature scenario, there would be a reduction of 76 percent in Brazil's most suitable areas for coffee. In Colombia, it would shrink by 63 percent. **Brazil's deforestation is hurting its coffee industry.**

Some regions at the northern and southern ends of today's growing areas will become more suitable, including Argentina, South Africa, China and New Zealand among others[22].

There are too many climate-related threats—most specifically wildfires. "Unprecedented wildfires," notably in Siberia, the US and Australia, have generated tens of millions of tons of CO_2. World Heritage sites that were net carbon contributors from 2001-2020:

1. The tropical rainforest in Sumatra, Indonesia

2. The Río Plátano Biosphere Reserve, Honduras

3. Yosemite National Park, US

4. Waterton Glacier International Peace Park, Canada and US

5. The Barberton Makhonjwa Mountains, South Africa

6. Kinabalu Park, Malaysia

7. The Uvs Nuur Basin, Russia and Mongolia

8. Grand Canyon National Park, US

9. The Greater Blue Mountains area, Australia

10. Morne Trois Pitons National Park, Dominica

"Even the best and most protected forest areas in the world are threatened by the global climate crisis."[23]

Water

Approximately 2.2 billion people worldwide do not have access to safe drinking water facilities. 7 Ways Technology Will Provide Water for the World:

- Smart water metering
- More efficient desalination
- Wastewater
- Rainwater harvesting
- Condensation and fog harvesting
- Sustainable water filtration
- Laser cloud seeding

DESALINATION OF WATER

For off-grid communities around the globe, access to water can be very complex, and access to clean water can be even more difficult. WaterKiosk is a company that can deliver high quality hygiene drinking, irrigation, fish farm and sanitation water from any kind of high saline and polluted water resources.

The main characteristic of this solution is that it is powered fully by solar, the simplicity of its design and its affordability. Systems offered by Boreal Light are ideal island solutions with no need of battery, diesel, or grid, just powered by solar! It requires low maintenance, as over 80 percent of the maintenance needs just a wrench and a screwdriver!

This solution reduces the cost of clean drinking water from $4 to $0.10 for 20 liters (5 gallons).

Other innovations in water technology are documented by SOLARIMPULSE:

SOLARIMPULSE Foundation has been collecting 1,000 energy-efficient solutions to share globally to try and help innovators to develop their technology to market. Many of these ideas can be very beneficial to people in developing countries. The following pages have some examples of innovative solutions, but I encourage people to review their website for more ideas.

| Exploring Efficient Solutions

Q

⊙

⚲

ⓘ

Towards a portfolio of 1000 labelled solutions

**Our Solar Impulse Label awards efficient, clean and profitable
solutions with a positive impact on environment and quality of life.**
Here are the Efficient Solutions which have been already selected and
labelled to be included in our 1000 Solutions Portfolio. Let's explore the
ingenuity and the creativity of our World Alliance Members.

→   ABOUT THE LABEL

10.8

COLLABORATION

The World Alliance has entered in close
and impactful collaboration with several
international institutions, states, and cities
around the world to facilitate the selection,
funding and implementation of the
#1000solutions.

About a billion people do not have access to
reliable electricity today—many in sub-Sahara
Africa. Make energy available to the poor.
Income and energy use go hand in hand. The
countries and people with more money use
more energy than poorer countries[24].

BOREAL- WATER KIOSK
DESALINATION SOLUTION

This solution offers an affordable and simple
battery-free solar water desalination system
that can deliver different water qualities for
different applications, such as irrigation and
drinking.

KEY FEATURES:

Saves 925 tons of CO_2 per year from every
WaterKiosk.

Minimizes travels to fetch water and food.

Eliminates the need of cutting firewood to boil and disinfect water.

Eliminates the need of burning fossil fuel to run desalination systems in rural off-grid villages[25].

Hydro-panel that makes drinking water from sunlight and air. **Zero Mass Water** is dedicated to transforming drinking water for every person every place. At Zero Mass Water, they have a vision to perfect water for every person in every place. Their technology and product, SOURCE Hydro-panels, deliver optimized water almost anywhere on Earth, off-grid and infrastructure-free. Today, SOURCE is installed across 5 continents in over 23 countries. Installations include farms, offices, government buildings, orphanages, schools, homes, eco resorts, restaurants, fire stations,

public gardens and many others. Hydro-panels make water an unlimited resource with arrays sized to meet the consumption needs of any application. Drinking water stress is experienced by almost every human and on every continent yet is a fundamental human right that requires potable government supply and infrastructure or purchased bottled water to secure.

Another innovative idea is "solar water farms," made of solar panels producing 50 kilowatts of energy. There are high-performance Tesla batteries to store it, and 2 water pumps operating 24 hours a day that provide 35,000 citizens with drinking water each day. The NGO is GIVEPOWER.

10.9 Innovative solutions from developing countries.

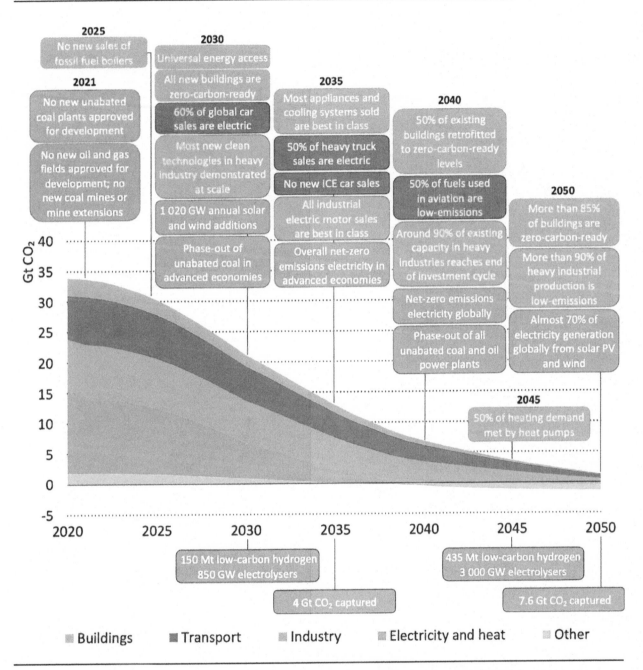

10.10 Selected Global Milestones for policies, infrastructure, and technology deployment in the Net–zero Economy

11

SUMMARY
KEEP IT SIMPLE & SUSTAINABLE

Once people can connect with an issue, a grassroots demand for change can gather momentum. The documentary *Blue Planet* by David Attenborough in 2001 drove an outpouring of concern over marine pollution on social media and prompted many to call for a ban on single-use plastics. **Nine out of ten people say they would be more likely to adopt sustainable behaviors if they could see the impact of climate change themselves. 88 percent say, if a sustainable lifestyle could save them money, they would adopt one[1].**

The data and research explained throughout this book shows that All-electric Solutions do Save Money!

Holistic Study Transitioning to an All-Electric Lifestyle

Most of the numbers presented in this study are based on real data using personal utility bills, the purchasing of equipment and my experiences from implementing these changes in my household. In sharing my story, I hope to clarify many misperceptions, add believers supporting renewable energy, and help people make better financial investments. The information in this document has been peer reviewed by experts from the National Renewable Energy Lab (NREL). There are many different scenarios depending on more specific information. I am sharing my story.

Sustainable practices are included in Chapter 2– Renewable Energy for solar panels and battery storage. Chapter 3– Transportation has more information on EVs. Chapter 5 has solutions for electric homes.

1. All-Electric Homes

Newly constructed homes should require less electric than homes 20 years or older because of improved efficiency in equipment (all-electric heating and cooling, energy efficiency electrical appliances) and technology (better insulation, more efficient glazing, air-tight homes, SMART homes).

The average-size new home constructed in U.S. in 2020 was 2,491 square feet. The size of the home in square feet is for heated spaces only. **The U.S. has the highest average size home of any country in the world, but smaller is more sustainable.**

I have chosen data from my **home in Duluth, Georgia, from 1996 to 2014, which was 2,500 gross square feet (gsf) and had annual electric and natural gas bills totaling $3,493.** This house was built in 1967.

TYPICAL NATURAL GAS + ELECTRIC HOME ENERGY BILLS (home in Duluth, Ga.)

	MONTH	ANNUAL
Electric Utility Bill (55%)	$159	$1,913
Natural Gas/ Propane/Oil (45%)	$132	$1,580
TOTAL	**$291**	**$3,493**

I will use $3,493 as my estimate for all electric costs for my new home in this study based on what I used from my previous home. The difference is that the cost is all electric, combining my previous costs for natural gas and electric.

2. Add Solar Panels

A kilowatt-hour is the energy, while a kilowatt is simply the rate energy is used in any given moment. Your energy provider bills you based on your overall usage in kilowatt-hours per month. **The average 2,500 square foot home uses 12,271 kWh annually. I purchased solar panels that are designed to produce 12.45kW of energy to my home[2].**

To estimate the energy production of photovoltaic (PV) solar panels in your location, use NREL's PVWatts Calculator[3]. To estimate the carbon emissions reduction in your location use the EPA eGRID Power Profiler[4].

SOLAR PANELS

For the average 2,500 square foot home cost with a 12.45–kw system is $25,620 after the federal tax break.

Divide $25,620 by annual utility bill of the Duluth home at $3,493 for a payback of 7.3 years. A financial payback within seven years is considered favorable by most investors. This will work if your local utility provider offers net metering. Most states and local utilities offer net metering, but not all. Where I am in Tennessee, today Sequatchie Valley and TVA do not offer me net metering. To then be more effective with the solar panels, I have installed battery storage to maintain my electricity on site and can use all the electricity generated by the solar panels.

3. Add Battery Storage

COST OF BATTERY BACKUP

To support a 12.45 kw system, a 13kw battery is needed. A Tesla or Enphase battery is approximately $11,634 after the federal tax credit. The battery storage supplies on-site electricity 24/7 and does not go down during power outages. Also, the electricity is used as efficiently as possible with most of the technology located on site.

The total installed cost of the solar panels and battery is $37,254. Divide by the annual utility bill of the Duluth home at $3,493 for a payback of 10.7 years. Net metering will reduce the need for battery storage for most homeowners. In 2023 you can receive a 30 percent tax break for solar and battery storage. In 2021 and 2022 I received 26%, a cost difference of $1,490.

4. Add Electric Vehicle(s)

When you include EVs for your mode of transportation, you will use more electricity at your home, but not have to pay for gasoline.

15,000 annual miles/350 miles per charge = **43 charges annually x $15 = $645 electric cost.** The cost to be fully charged will vary but the $15/ charge is a good conservative average based on multiple sources.

ELECTRIC UTILITY BILL $3,493 (house) **+ $645** (one car) = **$4,138**

ELECTRIC UTILITY BILL $3,493 (house) **+ $1,290** (two cars) = **$4,783**

For this study assume gasoline on average of $4 per gallon. Currently, gasoline prices are higher in most areas of the country but over time, the price may come down. I have tried to take a conservative estimate with all the calculations to reinforce the point that electric is more cost-effective than gasoline and other fossil fuels.

A new Tesla 3 will average approximately 131 miles compared to one gallon of gasoline. This information is based on buying a new Tesla 3 purchased in June 2022. Actual results will vary but the average new combustion engine vehicle gets 27 mpg based on government data[5]. Cost estimates for electric are based on 15,000 miles per year at 0.13 kW-hr. Use the government website www.fueleconomy.gov to better understand the comparison of cost of electric versus gasoline based on miles driven.

Assume 15,000 miles annually to align with how the EPA estimates for electric cars. 27 miles per gallon the vehicle traveling uses 556 gallons annually. **Assume $4 per gallon of gasoline totaling $2,224.**

	MONTHLY	ANNUAL
Gasoline (Car)	$185	$2,224 (556 gallons x $4)
Electric (Tesla 3)	$54	$645 (becomes part of electric bill)
Electric Car Savings	**$131**	**$1,579**

Annual maintenance savings for EVs over gasoline vehicles is approximately $600.

Another way to calculate the difference in cost between gasoline and electric over 15,000 miles is to use the study:

Gasoline 15,000 miles x .33cents/ mile	= $4,950
Electricity 15,000 miles x .22cents/ mile	= $3,300
Difference	= $1,650 annual savings with EV

The two studies are within 5%. Moving forward, I will use the lower annual savings at $1,579.

The current Tesla 3 information states saving $4,000 in fuel costs over five years. This was based on gasoline costing $2.33/ gallon. The savings today with the higher gas prices is twice as much! If you purchase a Tesla 3 today based on recent gasoline costs over 5 years is **$7,895 savings ($1,579 x 5) over 5 years.** The savings is better than advertised at almost twice the benefit. The 353 miles on the Tesla Long Range 3 All Wheel Drive costs $15 to fully charge at home with a Type 2 charger. Using the Tesla Supercharger is approximately twice the cost[6].

Fuel: <u>Electric savings over Gas</u>	**$1,579**
Savings on Maintenance	**$600**
Added Cost for Outlet to Charge	**-$200**
	$1,979 annually ($165 monthly)

Saves $165 on your monthly bills over the 7 years, and each year after that! On average, there are **1.88 vehicles per U.S. household** according to the U.S. Department of Transportation. **For two-car families with two EVs, the savings would almost double to $3,758 annually**, assuming the same type of car and mileage traveled. I assumed the two cars would share one electric charger.

	ONE CAR FAMILY	TWO CAR
Electric Annual Bill including EV additional electric	$4,138	$4,783
ELECTRIC CAR(savings over gasoline & maintenance)	$1,979	$3,758
Annual	$6,117	$8,541

These numbers reflect the savings compared to a traditional home with a gasoline vehicle. The top line is the cost of electricity that the solar panels are paying for at the home and electric vehicle(s). The second line item is the savings the solar panels provide for charging the electric cars instead of paying for gasoline. Added together is the cost benefit to run the home and car(s) off the solar panels. The Cost Benefit divided into the Cost of the Investments will provide you with the payback in years.

INVESTMENTS	Initial Purchase with 30% Tax Incentive
2. Cost of Solar Panels	$25,620 (home) + $2,000 (electric cars)
3. Cost of Battery Storage	$11,634 (home)
4. Additional Battery	$ 2,600 (electric cars)
5. Additional Solar Panels	$ 2,000 (electric cars)
	$41,854

Add an additional small battery ($2,600) and three solar panels ($2,000) to be able to support charging the electric car(s).

1. Solar Panels Only

For an average 2,500 square foot home, cost is $25,620 in 2022 after 30% Federal Incentive.

Divide $25,620, by annual utility bill at $3,493 for a payback of 7.3 years for solar panels. This assumes net metering is available to allow for the full use of the electricity generated by the solar panels. After 7.3 years your electric is free for the life of the panels!

2. Solar Panels + Battery Storage

The total installed cost of the solar panels and battery for the house is $37,254 ($25,620 + $11,634). Divide by the annual utility bill of the Duluth home at $3,493 for a **payback of 10.7 years**.

3. Solar Panels + Battery Storage (Home + EV) + One Electric Car

Investments ($41,854) divide Savings ($6,117) = **6.8 years for the payback one car family.** The savings in the EV pays for the cost of the battery storage.

4. Solar Panels + Battery Storage (Home + EVs) + Two Electric Cars

Investments ($41,854) divide Savings ($8,541) = **4.9 year payback for two cars.** All my electric is then free for decades!

5. Electric Car only Annual Savings is $1,979 compared to Gasoline Vehicle

The payback will be faster if calculating including inflation. (The two-electric car scenario is what my wife and I have created building a net-zero home with 30 solar panels at 12.45kw and battery storage backup. Each year we will collect data to verify and update to share with others.)

BUY ELECTRIC CARS

The life of the electric car is 2–5 times longer and will clearly offset the additional initial cost—if there is an additional cost over the gasoline vehicles.

My example may be considered the more ideal scenario, but this study also shows many of the cost benefits of buying an electric car, solar panels, battery storage and building an all-electric home. Each solution can save you money and reduce the carbon footprint. My scenario is not as common today but should be much more common in 5 to 10 years.

Remaining Key Points for All-Electric

1. Generate and store electricity locally, which is the most energy-efficient way.

2. Replace natural gas and propane with electric to reduce greenhouse gases.

3. Other models need to be developed to include low income, renters and other scenarios. Building and buying green energy should support many families who cannot afford the solar and battery storage on their site. Building at a larger scale will be more cost-effective.

4. Properties with all-electric solutions will become more resilient to weather and more cost- effective to operate.

5. Energy will cost less, be more stable and be able to manage energy peaks much better.

6. Battery storage will work during power outages.

The more detail and study one does for all-electric solutions, the clearer the choice and direction is to go to renewables and an all-electric lifestyle. Building, creating your own electricity, and driving with all-electric is simply an investment in our future now and for the long term.

Inflation Reduction Act of 2022

The following is a summary specific to energy security and climate change. The U.S. federal government has put the country on a path to roughly 40 percent emissions reduction by 2030 and represents the single biggest climate investment in U.S. history.

It is important for continued support at the federal level and to see all state and local governments step up and do their share. Businesses and private citizens need to continue to do their part and lead as much as possible. The responsibility and opportunity to address climate change is here now for all of us. The U.S. can lead globally, which will help U.S. businesses and citizens.

1. Lower Consumer Energy Costs

This bill will provide a range of incentives to consumers to relieve the high costs of energy and decrease utility bills. This includes direct consumer incentives to buy energy efficient and electric appliances, clean vehicles, and rooftop-solar, and invest in home energy efficiency, with a significant portion of the funding going to lower income households and disadvantaged communities.

- $9 billion in **consumer home energy rebate programs,** focused on low-income consumers, to electrify home appliances and for energy-efficient retrofits.

- 10 years of **consumer tax credits to make homes energy-efficient and run-on clean energy**, making heat pumps, rooftop solar, electric HVAC, and water heaters more affordable.

- $4,000 consumer tax credit for lower/middle income individuals to buy used clean vehicles, and up to $7,500 tax credit to buy new clean vehicles.

- $1 billion grant program to make affordable housing more energy efficient.

2. American Energy Security and Domestic Manufacturing

- This bill will support energy reliability and cleaner energy production coupled with historic investments in American clean energy manufacturing. It includes over $60 billion to onshore clean energy manufacturing in the U.S. across the full supply chain of clean energy and transportation technologies. These manufacturing incentives will help alleviate inflation and reduce the risk of future price shocks by bringing down the cost of clean energy and clean vehicles and relieving supply chain bottlenecks.

- Production tax credits to accelerate U.S. manufacturing of solar panels, wind turbines, batteries, and critical minerals processing, estimated to invest $30 billion.

- $10 billion **investment tax credit to build clean technology manufacturing facilities,** like facilities that make EVs, wind turbines, and solar panels.

- $500 million in the Defense Production Act for heat pumps and critical minerals processing.

- $2 billion in **grants to retool existing auto manufacturing facilities to manufacture clean vehicles**, ensuring that auto manufacturing jobs stay in the communities that depend on them.

- Up to $20 billion in loans to build new clean vehicle manufacturing facilities across the country.

- $2 billion for National Labs to accelerate breakthrough energy research.

3. Decarbonize the Economy

The investments in this bill will reduce emissions in every sector of the economy, substantially reducing emissions from electricity production, transportation, industrial manufacturing, buildings, and agriculture.

- Tax credits for clean sources of electricity and energy storage and roughly $30 billion in targeted grant and loan programs for states and electric utilities to accelerate the transition to clean electricity.

- Tax credits and grants for clean fuels and clean commercial vehicles to reduce emissions from all parts of the transportation sector.

- Grants and tax credits to reduce emissions from industrial manufacturing processes, including almost $6 billion for a new Advanced Industrial Facilities Deployment Program to reduce emissions from the largest industrial emitters like chemical, steel and cement plants.

- Over $9 billion for Federal procurement of American-made clean technologies to create a stable market for clean products, including $3 billion for the U.S. Postal Service to purchase zero-emission vehicles.

- $27 billion **clean energy technology accelerator** to support deployment of technologies to reduce emissions, especially in disadvantaged communities.

- A **Methane Emissions Reduction Program** to reduce the leaks from the production and distribution of natural gas.

4. Invest in Communities and Environmental Justice

Building on regular engagement with EJ (Environmental Justice) leaders from across the country, this package includes over $60 billion in environmental justice priorities to drive investments into disadvantaged communities. Some of the highlights include:

- The **Environmental and Climate Justice Block Grants**, funded at $3 billion, invest in community-led projects in disadvantaged communities and community capacity building centers to address disproportionate environmental and public health harms related to pollution and climate change.

- The **Neighborhood Access and Equity Grants**, funded at $3 billion, support neighborhood equity, safety, and affordable transportation access with competitive grants to reconnect communities divided by existing infrastructure barriers, mitigate negative impacts of transportation facilities or construction projects on disadvantaged or underserved communities, and support equitable transportation planning and community engagement activities.

- **Grants to Reduce Air Pollution at Ports**, funded at $3 billion, support the purchase and installation of zero-emission equipment and technology at ports.

- **$1 billion for clean heavy-duty vehicles,** like school and transit buses and garbage trucks.

- Some of the previously mentioned programs that focus on disadvantaged and low-income communities are also important to environmental justice, like the **technology accelerator and consumer home energy rebate programs.** In addition, the many of the **clean energy tax credits** include either a bonus or set-aside structure to drive investments and economic development in disadvantaged communities.

5. Farmers, Forestland Owners, and Resilient Rural Communities

This bill will make historic investments to ensure that rural communities are at the forefront of climate solutions. The investments affirm the central role of agricultural producers and forest landowners in our climate solutions by investing in climate- smart agriculture, forest restoration and land conservation. It also makes significant investments in clean energy development in rural communities.

- More than $20 billion to support **climate-smart agriculture practices.**

- $5 billion in grants to support healthy, fire resilient forests, forest conservation, and urban tree planting.

- Tax credits and grants to support the domestic production of biofuels, and to **build the infrastructure needed for sustainable aviation fuel and other biofuels.**

- $2.6 billion in **grants to conserve and restore coastal habitats** and protect communities that depend on those habitats.

Additional Hope!

The pillar of regeneration lies in understanding the business impact on natural capital. In the context of regeneration, it means acknowledging and tackling environmental harms. But it's also about going further, restoring and enriching ecosystems, replenishing natural resources, and ensuring that natural systems can thrive for future generations. **Thinking regeneratively means thinking for nature by thinking as nature.**

THE NEW SUSTAINABILITY: REGEN*ERATION*

INNOVATION GROUP J. WALTER THOMPSON INTELLIGENCE

11.1

Governments must improve polices to support climate change initiatives now and for the long term. Business must lead the way by showing leadership on societal challenges and innovations with technology. Those that advocate and elevate expectations will build resilience, for society and themselves. Individuals make decisions every day that add up to have an impact in fighting climate change. Make behavioral changes to reduce your carbon footprint. If all decision makers make the right decisions, with today's technology and future improvements, WE CAN AND SHOULD LIVE IN A REGENERATIVE WORLD THAT IS MORE COST-EFFECTIVE AND HEALTHIER THAN WHAT WE HAVE TODAY.

Acknowledgements

Thank you to the governments that are aggressively enacting policies that address many of the problems created by climate change. The politicians working together will make the future brighter for everyone.

Thank you to the businesses, who are stepping up to provide innovative solutions, funding for green projects, and leading to solve problems created by climate change. These groups are creating lasting changes while also benefiting from the financial opportunities of environmental action.

Thank you to citizens who are stepping up each day with sustainable habits that will quickly add up to reduce climate change. The individuals who are able to donate significant portions of their savings to combat the effects of climate change are critical in meeting today's challenges.

Solutions require everyone to not only be informed, but also to enact.

I am grateful for the collaboration and sharing of information for decades with Architecture 2030 and Ed Mazria, National Renewable Lab (NREL) and Otto Van Geet, United States Green Building Council (USGBC), and Rocky Mountain Institute (RMI) with Victor Olgyay.

I thank Perkins & Will for the opportunity to collaborate with many great people on several outstanding projects that have benefitted society. I had the good fortune to work there for over 25 years on very large projects in nine countries, each focused on sustainable solutions. Perkins & Will continues to lead in sustainable designs with thoughtful research that is shared to help elevate the architectural profession. The firm is in excellent hands with the leadership of Phil Harrison, Peter Busby and Kathy Wardle.

I want to thank my wife for always being there as well as for sharing some information to add value to this book. As always, thanks to my four daughters Megan, Kalie, Quinn, and Lucie. I especially want to thank Lucie, who edited several chapters of this book and Kalie for helping with the design of the book cover.

Bibliography

Bernheimer, Andrew. *Timber In The City*, ORO, 2014

Cary, John. *Design For Good*, Island Press, 2017

Doerr, John. *Speed & Scale:Am Action Plan For Solving Our Climate Crisis Now* , Penquin Random House LLC, 2021

Gates, Bill. *How to Avoid a Climate Disaster; The Solutions We Have And The Breakthroughs We Need*, New York: Knopf, 2021

Goodall, Chris. *What We Need To Do Now: For A Zero Carbon Society*, Profile Books, 2020

Green, Jared. *Good Energy*, Princeton Architectural Press, 2021

Hawken, Paul. *Drawdown; The Most Comprehensive Plan Ever Proposed to Reverse Global Warming*, Penquin Random House LLC, 2017

Hawken, Paul. *Regeneration: Ending the Climate Crisis In One Generation*, Penquin Random House LLC, 2021

Hampshire- Waugh, Matthew. *Climate Change and The Road To Net-Zero*, Crowstone Publishing, 2021

Jacobson, Mark Z. *100% Clean, Renewable Energy and Storage For Everything*, Cambridge University Press, 2021

Lovins, Amory B. *Reinventing Fire*, Green Press Initiative, 2011

McLaren, Duncan and Agyeman, Julian. *Sharing Cities*, MIT Press, 2015

Maas, Winy. Haikola, Pirjo. Hackauf, Ulf. *Green Dreams: How Future Cities Can Outsmart Nature*, Nai publishers, 2018

Olgyay, Victor. *Design With Climate*, Princeton University Press, 2015

Thunberg, Greta. *No One Is Too Small to Make a Difference*, New York: Penquin, 2018

DOCUMENTARIES

An Inconvenient Truth, Davis Guggenheim, performance by Al Gore and more, 2006. https://www.imdb.com/title/tt0497116/

Chasing Coral, Directed by Jeff Orlowski, performance by Zachery Rago, Trevor Mendelow, Mark Eakin, Andrew Ackerman, Joanie Kleypas, Pim Bongaerts, Phil Dunstan, and more. Netflix, 2017.

Climate Next: Technologies For Sustainability, Dr. Werner Vogels, Amazon, 2022.

David Attenborough- A life On Our Planet (2020)

Follow The Food, director David Cicconi, BBC TV series, 2020 to 2022.

Forks Over Knives, directed by Lee Fulkerson, performances by T. Colin Campbell, PhD; Neal D. Barnard, MD; Caldwell Esselstyn, MD; Rip Esselstyn; and more , Virgil Films, 2011.

Kiss the Ground, directed by Josh Tickell, Rebecca Harrell Tickell, performance Ian Someerhader, Woody Harrelson, Tom Brady, and more, Netflix, 2020.

Life in Color with David Attenborough, directed by Adam Geiger, performance by David Attenborough, Netflix, 2021.

Our Planet, directed by Sophie Lanfear, performances by David Attenborough, Penelope Cruz and Salma Hayek, Netflix, 2019.

Rotten,directed by Lucy Kennedy, Ted Gesing, Bill Kerr and more, performances by Latif Nasser, Jonathan Walker, Sonny Nguyen, 2019.

The Game Changers, directed by Louie Psihoyos, perfomances by Patrik Baboumian, Rob Bailey and more, ReFuel Productions, Oceanic Preservation Society, Diamond Docs, 2018.

Veganlife, directed by Carolyn Wagner, performances by Samantha Jane Faircloth, Teagan Berger, Shannon Brierley and more, Pegasus Entertainment, 2017.

What the Health, directed by Kip Andersen, Keegan Kuhn, performers Kip Andersen, Larry Baldwin, Neal Barnard and more, Amazon Prime, 2017.

WEB SITES

Architecture 2030.org

Bloomberg New Energy Finance, bnef.com

Breakthrough Energy Innovation, breakthrougenergy.org

Department of Energy.gov

Environmental Defense Fund, https:www.edf.org

FEMA.gov

IEA.org, International Energy Agency Report, iea.org/reports/net-zero-by-2050

IPCC Report from the Intergovernmental Panel on Climate Change, https://www.ipcc.ch

Nature Conservatory, https://www.nature.org

NREL.gov

Patrick at Urbanvine.co

Perkins&Will, perkinswill.com

RMI.org

SolarImpulse.com

World Wildlife Fund, https://worldwildlife.org

Footnotes

INTRODUCTION

1. Eia.gov, What are greenhouse gases and how do they affect the climate?, https://www.eia.gov/tools/faqs/faq.php?id=81&t=11

2. EPA.gov, Sources of Greenhouse Gas Emissions, https://www.epa.gov/ghgemissions/sources-greenhouse-gas-emissions

3. What is your Carbon Footprint? The Nature Conservatory, https://www.nature.org/en-us/get-involved/how-to-help/carbon-footprint-calculator/

4. Rebecca Hersher, Eliminating fossil fuel air pollution would save about 50,000 lives, study finds, https://www.npr.org/2022/05/17/1099482986/eliminating-fossil-fuel-air-pollution-would-save-about-50-000-lives-study-finds

5. Nicholas A. Mailloux, David W. Abel, Tracey Holloway, Jonathan A. Patz, GeoHealth Nationwide and Regional PM2.5-Related Air Quality Health Benefits From the Removal of Energy-Related Emissions in the United States, May 16 2022, https://doi.org/10.1029/2022GH000603

1. FOOD

1. The energy loss/ Too good to go.pdf, Where Do We Get This Energy From and What's The Issue With These Energy Sources?, https://toogoodtogo.com/en-us/movement/knowledge/the-energy-loss

2. The energy loss/ Too good to go.pdf, How is Food Waste Contributing to This Problem, https://toogoodtogo.com/en-us/movement/knowledge/the-energy-loss

3. The energy loss/ Too good to go.pdf, Methane Emissions, https://toogoodtogo.com/en-us/movement/knowledge/the-energy-loss

4. The energy loss/ Too good to go.pdf, Methane Emissions, https://toogoodtogo.com/en-us/movement/knowledge/the-energy-loss

5. H.Claire Brown, The Counter, The top five meat and dairy companies emit more carbon than the gasoline giants, https:///www.fao.org/3/az775e/az775e.pdf

6. The energy loss/ Too good to go.pdf, By Throwing Away Food, We Are Not Only Wasting The Actual Produce But Also The Resources and Energy Within It, https://toogoodtogo.com/en-us/movement/knowledge/the-energy-loss

7. USDA, Food Loss, https://www.ers.usda.gov/data-products/food-availability-per-capita-data-system/food-loss/

8. Food and Agriculture Organization of the United Nations, Food Wastage: Key facts and figures, https://www.fao.org/news/story/en/item/196402/icode/

9. restaurantbusiness.com, Starbucks expands its food donation program.pdf, Starbucks expands its food donation program.pdf, https://www.restaurantbusinessonline.com/marketing/starbucks-expands-its-food-donation-program

10. The-New-Sustainability-Regeneration-25.09.2018, Cooking Up Change, p.63, https://www.are.na/block/2775642

11. ers.usda.gov, Local Food Sales Continue to Grow Through a Variety of Marketing Channels, by Stephen Martinez, October 4 2021, https://www.ers.usda.gov/amber-waves/2021/october/local-food-sales-continue-to-grow-through-a-variety-of-marketing-channels/

12. USDA ERS- Food Prices and Spending.pdf, https://www.ers.usda.gov/data-products/ag-and-food-statistics-charting-the-essentials/food-prices-and-spending/

13. Science, Veganism is 'Single Biggest Way' to Reduce Our Environmental Impact, Olivia Petter, https://www.independent.co.uk/life-style/health-and-families/veganism-environmental-impact-planet-reduced-plant-based-diet-humans-study-a8378631.html

14. Plant Based News, https://plantbasednews.org/lifestyle/food/mostly-vegetarian-industry-report/

15. Medical News Today, EurekAlert, https://www.medicalnewstoday.com/articles/321992#Plant-based-diets-and-heart-health

16. National Center for Biotechnology Information, https://www.ncbi.nlm.nih.gov/pmc/articles/PMC3048091/

17. Nutrition, Metabolism, and Cardiovascular Diseases Journal, https://www.ncbi.nlm.nih.gov/pmc/articles/PMC6153574/

18. Livestock and climate change/ impact of livestock on climate and mitigation strategies | Animal Fron.pdf, https://www.theguardian.com/world/2016/jun/20/chinas-meat-consumption-climate-change

19. Vegansociety.com; September 2019, https://www.vegansociety.com/news/market-insights/plant-milk-market

20. Can Urban Food Incubators Accelerate Adoption of Plant-Based Diets?.pdf, https://www.greenbiz.com/article/can-urban-food-incubators-accelerate-adoption-plant-based-diets

21. Rethinking Food and Agriculture 2020–2030: The Second Domestication of Plants and Animals, the Disruption of the Cow, and the Collapse of Industrial Livestock Farming, Catherine Tubb and Tony Seba, https://www.liebertpub.com/doi/10.1089/ind.2021.29240.ctu

22. Plant-based diet can fight climate change-BBC by Roger Harrabin, https://www.bbc.com/news/science-environment-49238749

23. Burger King to sell vegan nuggets in bid to go 50% meat-free- BBC news.pdf-1-7-22, https://www.bbc.com/news/business-59865780

24. California Will Start Paying Restaurants To Deliver Food to Seniors in Need.pdf, May 9, 2020, https://www.goodnewsnetwork.org/california-will-start-paying-restaurants-to-deliver-food-to-seniors-in-need/

25. goodnewsnetwork.com, The Largest Urban Rooftop Farm in the World is Now Bearing Fruit (and More) in Paris.pdf, https://www.goodnewsnetwork.org/the-largest-urban-rooftop-farm-in-the-world-is-now-bearing-fruit-and-more-in-paris/

26. VERTICAL FARMING USING INFORMATION AND COMMUNICATION TECHNOLOGIES Manoj Kumar Gupta and Sreedhar Ganapura, https://www.infosys.com/industries/agriculture/insights/documents/vertical-farming-information-communication.pdf

27. The energy loss/ Too good to go.pdf, Hydrofluorcarbons Emissions, https://toogoodtogo.com/en-us/movement/knowledge/the-energy-loss

28. The Role of Refrigeration in Worldwide Nutrition, https://iifiir.org/en/fridoc/the-role-of-refrigeration-in-worldwide-nutrition-2020-142029

29. Dan Gibson, The salmon you buy in the future may be farmed on land, April 2021 BBC, https://www.bbc.com/news/business-56829129

30. Martha Henriques and Zaria Gorvett, The climate benefits of veganism and vegetarianism - BBC Future.pdf 1/5/2022, https://www.bbc.com/future/article/20220429-the-climate-benefits-of-veganism-and-vegetarianism

31. Victoria Gill, Mine e-waste, not the Earth, say scientists - BBC News.pdf, https://www.bbc.com/news/science-environment-61350996

2. RENEWABLE ENERGY

1. NREL 6/6/2022, https://www.nrel.gov/news/features/2022/re-futures.html

2. United Nations Climate Change, Renewable Power Remains Cost-Competitive amid Fossil Fuel Crisis, July 14 2022, https://unfccc.int/news/renewable-power-remains-cost-competitive-amid-fossil-fuel-crisis

3. How to store excess wind power underwater - BBC News.pdf, https://www.bbc.com/news/business-60066690

4. 1000 SOLUTIONS - MAY 01, 2019 Tristan Lebleu, https://solarimpulse.com/news/sabella-sustainable-and-reliable-electricity-from-the-power-of-tides

5. U.S. Department of Energy, Office of Energy Efficiency & Renewable Energy, Solar Futures Study Fact Sheet, https://www.energy.gov/sites/default/files/2021-09/Solar_Futures_Study_Fact_Sheet.pdf

6. seia.org, https://www.seia.org/initiatives/net-metering

7. Solar Canal Solution Extending the Lifecycle of Water. 1-14-22, https://sustainablewater.com/the-solar-canal-solution/

8. First Solar Canal Project is a Win for Water, Energy, Air and Climate in California- Propmoda, 2/23/2022 by Roger Bales, https://theconversation.com/first-solar-canal-project-is-a-win-for-water-energy-air-and-climate-in-california-177433

9. 'Solar For All' Brings Clean Energy to Low- and Middle-Income DC Residents (5/14/2021), https://nextcity.org/urbanist-news/solar-for-all-brings-clean-energy-to-low-and-middle-income-dc-residents

10. Solar Manufacturing | Department of Energy.pdf, https://www.energy.gov/eere/solar/solar-manufacturing

11. SolarApp-webinar, May 23 2019, https://solarapp.nrel.gov/

12. https://www.nrel.gov/docs/fy22osti/81603.pdf

13. National Energy Renewable Laboratory (NREL), Solar Futures Study, https://www.energy.gov/eere/solar/solar-futures-study

14. Bloomberg NEF L.P. 2020. Developed in partnership with the Business Council for Sustainable Energy, The Sustainable Energy in America 2022 Factbook, https://bcse.org/market-trends/

15. Ameresco adding 6-MWh Battery Storage to Solar installation at Army's Fort Detrick | EnergyTech.pdf 3/9/2022 Rod Walton author, https://www.energytech.com/energy-storage/article/21237527/ameresco-adding-6mwh-battery-storage-to-solar-installation-at-armys-fort-detrick

16. Storage Futures Study Key Learnings for the Coming Decades, https://www.nrel.gov/docs/fy22osti/81779.pdf

17. 2022-Sustainable-Energy-in-America-Factbook-Executive-Summary, bcse.org, https://bcse.org/market-trends/

18. Newatlas, Bill Gates's next-gen nuclear plant packs in grid-scale energy storage, https://newatlas.com/energy/natrium-molten-salt-nuclear-reactor-storage/

19. Solar Futures Fact Sheet, https://www.energy.gov/sites/default/files/2021-09/Solar_Futures_Study_Fact_Sheet.pdf

20. Solar battery price drops NREL. pdf, https://www.nrel.gov/docs/fy21osti/77324.pdf

21. The Engineering and Construction of Offshore Oil Platforms.pdf, https://interestingengineering.com/science/the-engineering-and-construction-of-offshore-oil-platforms

22. generation180.org, The absurd truth about fossil fuel subsidies 10/13/21, https://generation180.org/the-absurd-truth-about-fossil-fuel-subsidies/

3. TRANSPORTATION

1. insideevs.com, https://insideevs.com/news/559261/tesla-models-p85-1500000-kilometers/

2. Electrek1/5/2022, https://electrek.co/2022/01/05/tesla-model-s-752-miles-range-one-energy-dense-battery-pack/

3. Keith Naughton and Kyle Stock, Bloomberg News 4-9-22, https://www.bloomberg.com/news/articles/2022-04-09/how-ford-s-electric-f-150-pickup-truck-will-cut-carbon-pollution

4. Keith Naughton and Kyle Stock, Bloomberg News 4-9-22, https://www.bloomberg.com/news/articles/2022-04-09/how-ford-s-electric-f-150-pickup-truck-will-cut-carbon-pollution

5. Keith Naughton and Kyle Stock, Bloomberg News 4-9-22, https://www.bloomberg.com/news/articles/2022-04-09/how-ford-s-electric-f-150-pickup-truck-will-cut-carbon-pollution

6. How Much do Solar Panels Save? Solar Savings by State | EnergySage.pdf, https://news.energysage.com/much-solar-panels-save/

7. Project Drawdown.org, https://drawdown.org/solutions/electric-cars

8. KPMG survey shows published Tue, Nov 30 2021, https://www.cnbc.com/2021/11/30/auto-executives-say-more-than-half-of-us-car-sales-will-be-evs-by-2030-kpmg-survey-shows.html

9. General Motors, PG&E pilot EVs as backup power sources for homes – TechCrunch.pdf, 3/8/2022 by Rebecca Bellan, https://techcrunch.com/2022/03/08/general-motors-pge-pilot-evs-as-backup-power-sources-for-homes/

10. https://www.cleanenergyreviews.info/blog/bidirectional-ev-charging-v2g-v2h-v2l 6/3/22

11. Ford launches its bi-directional home charging station at a surprisingly good price - Electrek.pdf, https://electrek.co/2022/03/01/ford-launches-bi-directional-home-charging-station-surprisingly-good-price/

12. Electric Vehicle Myths | US EPA.pdf, https://www.epa.gov/greenvehicles/electric-vehicle-myths

13. Electric cars 'will not solve transport problem,' report warns - BBC News, https://www.bbc.com/news/uk-48875361

14. newsroom.aaa.com, https://newsroom.aaa.com/wp-content/uploads/2020/12/Your-Driving-Costs-2020-Fact-Sheet-FINAL-12-9-20-2.pdf

15. http://www.urb-i.com/before-after

16. ATLANTIC CITYLAB More Before-&-After Photos of the World's Best Street Designs Feargus O'Sullivan March 30,2016, http://www.urb-i.com/before-after

17. http://www.urb-i.com/before-after

18. The Hill, Sidewalks, bike lanes and trails are essential transportation infrastructure, 05/24/21, https://thehill.com/blogs/congress-blog/politics/555087-sidewalks-bike-lanes-and-trails-are-essential-transportation/

19. Passenger Air Vehicle (PAV).pdf, https://www.boeingfutureofflight.com/pav

20. Mongabay; How much does air travel warm the planet? New study gives a figure; Liz Kimbrough on 6 April 2022, https://news.mongabay.com/2022/04/how-much-does-air-travel-warm-the-planet-new-study-gives-a-figure/

21. World Economic Forum; If shipping were a country, it would be the world's sixth biggest greenhouse emitter; 4/18/18, https://www.weforum.org/agenda/2018/04/if-shipping-were-a-country-it-would-be-the-world-s-sixth-biggest-greenhouse-gas-emitter

22. 3D printingindustry.com, https://3dprintingindustry.com/news/michelins-uptis-airless-tire-takes-to-the-road-with-3d-printing-197629/

4. CITIES

1. How can we make cities more sustainable? | World Economic Forum.pdf 9/4/2020, https://www.weforum.org/agenda/2020/09/cities-sustainability-innovation-global-goals/

2. Five ways to make cities healthier and more sustainable | FAO Stories | Food and Agriculture Organi.pdf 9/16/2020, https://www.fao.org/fao-stories/article/en/c/1260457/

3. UN forum spotlights cities, where struggle for sustainability 'will be won or lost' - United Nations.pdf, https://www.un.org/sustainabledevelopment/blog/2018/07/un-forum-spotlights-cities-where-struggle-for-sustainability-will-be-won-or-lost-2/

4. How is Curitiba Sustainable.pdf, https://www.greenmatters.com/p/curitiba-sustainable

5. LIVING CITIES: Transforming APEC Cities into Models of Sustainability by 2030.pdf, https://www.scholars.northwestern.edu

6. Climate emergency: how our cities can inspire change| World Economic Forum.pdf, https://www.weforum.org/agenda/2020/01/smart-and-the-city-working-title/

7. Keep Liberty Beautiful.org, http://keeplibertybeautiful.org/the-benefit-of-trees.html

8. Public_Health_Benefits_Urban_Trees_FINAL.pdf, https://www.nature.org/content/dam/tnc/nature/en/documents/Public_Health_Benefits_Urban_Trees_FINAL.pdf

9. Climate Next: Using data to address tree cover and climate change, March 17 2022, https://www.aboutamazon.com/news/aws/climate-next-using-data-to-address-tree-cover-and-climate

10. Bringing Back Trees To 'Forest City's' Redlined Areas Helps Residents And The Climate June 23, 2021, https://www.npr.org/2021/06/23/1006223328/bringing-back-trees-to-forest-citys-redlined-areas-helps-residents-and-the-climate

11. How green spaces could stop cities from overheating/ Geography/The Guardian.pdf, https://www.theguardian.com/news/datablog/2014/may/22/how-green-spaces-could-stop-cities-from-overheating

12. NREL energy efficient city planning.pdf, https://www.nrel.gov/docs/fy02osti/30389.pdf

13. Rooftop Gardens: Benefits for Energy Consumption.pdf, https://www.epa.gov/heatislands/using-green-roofs-reduce-heat-islands

14. Boston underwater: How the rising sea levels will affect the city.pdf, http://archive.boston.com/yourtown/specials/boston_under_water/

15. Delivering climate resilient infrastructure through the private sector.pdf, https://blogs.worldbank.org/ppps/delivering-climate-resilient-infrastructure-through-private-sector

16. openknowledge.worldbank.org, Investing in Climate Adaption Delivers High Returns, GCA 2019, page 7, https://openknowledge.worldbank.org/bitstream/handle/10986/35203/Enabling-%20%20Private-Investment-in-Climate-Adaptation-and-Resilience-Current-Status-Barriers-to-Investment-and-Blueprint-for-Action.pdf?sequence=5

17. Greenresilience.com, https://www.greenresilience.com/smart-growth

18. http://www.urb-i.com/before-after, created by Yuval Fogelson

5. BUILDINGS

1. iea.org, https://www.iea.org/reports/global-status-report-for-buildings-and-construction-2019

2. buildinggreen.com, https://www.buildinggreen.com/feature/whole-building-life-cycle-assessment-taking-measure-green-building

3. Carbon Smart Materials Palette- Actions for Reducing Embodied Carbon at Your Fingertips.pdf, https://materialspalette.org

4. BuildingGreen, Rethinking the All-Glass Building, https://www.buildinggreen. com/feature/rethinking-all-glass-building

5. The Scandinavian way to zero-carbon construction - BBC Future, https://www. bbc.com/future/article/20210622-the-scandinavian-way-to-zero-carbon-construction

6. https://architecture2030.org/why-the-building-sector/

7. Zero-Codes_Paybacks-of-Powering-Buildings-with-Clean-Energy.pdf, http://zero-code.org/wp-content/uploads/2021/07/Zero-Codes_Paybacks-of-Powering-Buildings-with-Clean-Energy.pdf

8. Washington State Could Lead the Nation on Building Electrification Codes - RMI. pdf, https://rmi.org/washington-state-could-lead-the-nation-on-building-electrification-codes/

9. Climate change/ Satellites map huge methane plumes from oil and gas - BBC News.pdf, https://www.bbc.com/news/science-environment-60203683

10. Climate change: Curbing methane emissions will 'buy us time' By Matt McGrath 8-11-21, https://www.bbc.com/news/science-environment-58174111

11. edf.org, https://www.edf.org/climate/methane-crucial-opportunity-climate-fight

12. 2020 Sustainable Energy in America Factbook Executive Summary, https://www.eesi.org/briefings/view/022020factbook

13. Grid-Interactive Buildings Key in Fight Against Climate Change - Propmodo. pdf, https://www.propmodo.com/grid-interactive-buildings-are-key-in-fight-against-climate-change/

14. https://hub.jhu.edu/2022/02/22/gas-stoves-environment-warning/

15. Climate change: Can the Russian energy crisis help to curb global heating? 11 March, 2022, https://www.theguardian.com/environment/2022/mar/03/turn-down-heating-reduce-need-russian-imports-europeans-told

16. Scientists look for the Holy Grail/ The whitest paint ever | Grist.pdf, https://grist.org/buildings/scientists-look-for-the-holy-grail-the-whitest-paint-ever/

17. This Dutch construction innovation shows how to retrofit buildings quickly.pdf, 1-14-2022, https://www.fastcompany.com/90712613/this-dutch-construction-innovation-shows-its-possible-to-quickly-retrofit-every-building

18. Building Electrification zLab Write-up. pdf, Oct 9, 2019, page 3, https://rmi.org/wp-content/uploads/2020/02/Electrification-zLab-Writeup-Final.pdf

6. CARBON SEQUESTRATION

1. The world's first virtual fence for grazing animals.pdf, https://www.theexplorer.no/solutions/the-worlds-first-virtual-fence-for-grazing-animals/?gclid=EAlaIQobChMIw8K6O_ff-gIVYhTUAR2SjQxcEAAYASAAEgIEcvD_BwE

2. fs.usda.gov, https://www.fs.usda.gov/science-technology/energy-forest-products/wood-innovation

3. Carbon Capture and Storage 101.pdf, https://www.usda.gov/media/blog/2019/04/22/state-forest

4. Forest Facts- Forest Laandowners.pdf, https://www.forestlandowners.com, https://www.forestlandowners.com/forest-facts/

5. decadeonrestoration.org, Tree planting and ecosystem restoration: a crash course, https://www.decadeonrestoration.org/Interactive/tree-planting-and-ecosystem-restoration-crash-course

6. Precision agriculture's role in the new era of farmland sector.pdf, https://www.manulifeim.com/institutional/us/en/viewpoints/private-markets/precision-agriculture-s-role-in-the-farmland-sector-s-new-era?

7. nrdc.org, Regenerative Agriculture 101, https://www.nrdc.org/stories/regenerative-agriculture-101

8. GreenLands BlueWaters, Continuous Living Cover, https://greenlandsbluewaters.org/continuous-living-cover/

9. USDA, Five Ways Agroforestry Can Grow Forest Products and Benefit Your Land, Your Pockets & Wildlife, February 21 2017, https://www.usda.gov/media/blog/2016/10/19/five-ways-agroforestry-can-grow-forest-products-and-benefit-your-land-your

10. UN environment programme, Protecting Whales to protect the planet, October 14, 2019, https://www.unep.org/news-and-stories/story/protecting-whales-protect-planet

11. Time, One Whale Is Worth Thousands of Trees in Climate Fight, New Report Says, https://www.google.com/search?client=safari&rls=en&q=Report%3A1+1+Whale+is+Worth+Thousands+of+Trees+in+Climate+Fight&ie=UTF-8&oe=UTF-8

12. How whales help cool the earth- BBC Future, Sophie Yeo, 1/19/21, https://www.bbc.com/future/article/20210119-why-saving-whales-can-help-fight-climate-change

13. African forest elephant helps increase biomass and carbon storage; EurekaAlert! Science News, https://www.eurekalert.org/news-releases/729132

14. 6 Things to Know About Direct Air Capture.pdf, https://www.wri.org/insights/direct-air-capture-resource-considerations-and-costs-carbon-removal

15. Global Status Report- Global CCS Institute.pdf, https://www.globalccsinstitute.com/resources/global-status-report/download/

16. dspace.lib.cranfield.ac.uk, https://dspace.lib.cranfield.ac.uk/bitstream/handle/1826/12443/A_systematic_review_of_key_challenges_of_CO2_transport_via_pipelines-2017.pdf;jsessionid=7F0DBFCA993168D5CA18ADBD2A61DED0?sequence=1

17. spglobal, Record 51 US carbon capture projects announced in 2021, but finance, policy lag, https://www.spglobal.com/marketintelligence/en/news-insights/latest-news-headlines/record-51-us-carbon-capture-projects-announced-in-2021-but-finance-policy-lag-69026384

18. Elon Musk, Alphabet Invest in Carbon Removal Technology - Bloomberg.pdf 5/3/2022, https://www.bloomberg.com/news/articles/2022-05-03/elon-musk-alphabet-invest-in-carbon-removal-technology?leadSource=uverify%20wall

19. Elon Musk, Alphabet Invest in Carbon Removal Technology - Bloomberg.pdf 5/3/2022, https://www.bloomberg.com/news/articles/2022-05-03/elon-musk-alphabet-invest-in-carbon-removal-technology?leadSource=uverify%20wall

7. GOVERNMENT

1. Regulatory-Solutions-Framework-Report-070820.pdf

2. web.ornl.gov, https://web.ornl.gov/sci/techresources/Human_Genome/project/economics.shtml

3. Global Research and Development Expenditures: Fact Sheet, September 14, 2022, https://sgp.fas.org/crs/misc/R44283.pdf

4. Green Building Tax Breaks Primed for a Big Boost from Uncle Sam, https://www.propmodo.com/green-building-tax-breaks-primed-for-a-big-boost-from-uncle-sam/

5. Union of Concerned Scientists, https://www.ucsusa.org/resources/hidden-costs-fossil-fuels

8. BUSINESSES

1. Green Building Tax Breaks Primed for a Big Boost from Uncle Sam, https://www.propmodo.com/green-building-tax-breaks-primed-for-a-big-boost-from-uncle-sam/

2. The-New-Sustainability-Regeneration-25.09.2018.pdf, https://www.scribd.com/document/408014677/The-New-Sustainability-Regeneration-25-09-2018-pdf

3. ncses.nsf.gov, National Scientific Board/ Science & Engineering Indicators, https://ncses.nsf.gov/pubs/nsb20202/academic-r-d-in-the-united-states

4. The Multi-purpose Mobile Phone, by Colin Campbell, https://www.streetdirectory.com/travel_guide/156383/cell_phones/the_multi_purpose_mobile_phone.html

5. The Lean, Green Banks Behind Building Energy Upgrades- Propmodo.pdf, https://www.propmodo.com/the-lean-green-banks-behind-building-energy-upgrades/

6. Europe Leads on Green Loans, but the Rest of the World is Catching Up – Propmodo.pdf, https://www.propmodo.com/europe-leads-on-green-loans-but-the-rest-of-world-is-catching-up/

7. Glasgow Financial Alliance for Net Zero (GFANZ), https://assets.bbhub.io/company/sites/63/2021/11/GFANZ-Progress-Report.pdf

8. A smarter way to think about public-private partnerships, by Frank Beckers and Uwe Stegemann, https://www.mckinsey.com/capabilities/risk-and-resilience/our-insights/a-smarter-way-to-think-about-public-private-partnerships

9. Accelerating Building Efficiency, https://publications.wri.org/buildingefficiency/#sec2

10. Climate change: Courts set for rise in Top Stories compensation cases By Matt McGrath, https://www.bbc.com/news/science-environment-57641167

11. energypost.eu, https://energypost.eu/germanys-highest-court-rules-climate-laws-are-insufficient-violate-rights-unfairly-burden-future-generations/

9. CITIZENS

1. The Conversation November 22, 2021; The average person's daily choices can still make a big difference in fighting climate change – and getting governments and utilities to tackle it, too, https://theconversation.com/the-average-persons-daily-choices-can-still-make-a-big-difference-in-fighting-climate-change-and-getting-governments-and-utilities-to-tackle-it-too-170442

2. nps.gov, How you can help reduce greenhouse gas emissions at home, https://www.nps.gov/pore/learn/nature/climatechange_action_home.htm

3. Circular economy/ definition, examples and principles.pdf, https://climate.selectra.com/en/environment/circular-economy

4. Climate Change/ Can One Person Really Make a Difference? | Crowdsourcing Sustainability.pdf, https://crowdsourcingsustainability.org/climate-change-can-one-person-really-make-a-difference/

10. GLOBAL

1. Fossil Fuel Industry Subsidies of 11m dollars a minute IMF finds.pdf, https://www.theguardian.com/environment/2021/oct/06/fossil-fuel-industry-subsidies-of-11m-dollars-a-minute-imf-finds

2. The Guardian, https://www.theguardian.com/environment/2021/jul/20/g20-states-subsidised-fossil-fuels-2015-coal-oil-gas-cliamte-crisis

3. NATURE 20 October 2021, https://www.nature.com/articles/d41586-021-02847-2

4. https://www.carbonbrief.org/analysis-what-do-chinas-gigantic-wind-and-solar-bases-mean-for-its-climate-goals/

5. https://www.nea.gov.sg/our-services/pollution-control/air-pollution/air-pollution-regulations

6. Asian Disaster Reduction Center (ADRC), https://blogs.worldbank.org/endpovertyinsouthasia/bangladeshs-50-years-journey-climate-resilience

7. WWF (World Wildlife Federation) Hydropower website, https://www.wwf.eu/what_we_do/water/hydropower/

8. French Ban on Plastics for Packaging Fruits and Vegetables BBC 12-31-21, https://www.bbc.com/news/world-europe-59843697

9. 20211115-how-cities-are-going-carbon-neutral.pdf, https://www.bbc.com/future/article/20211115-how-cities-are-going-carbon-neutral

10. Climate change/ Consumer 'confusion' threatens net zero homes plan - BBC News, August 25, 2021, https://www.bbc.com/news/science-environment-58320578

11. Energy strategy/ UK plans eight new nuclear reactors to boost production - BBC News.pdf 4/7/2022 Roger Harrabin, https://www.bbc.com/news/business-61010605

12. Climate change/ Low-income countries 'can't keep up' with impacts - BBC News 8/1/22, https://www.bbc.com/news/world-58080083

13. The Global Partnership on Forest and Landscape Restoration- Forests, https://rainforests.mongabay.com/amazon/amazon_destruction.html

14. 20211115-how-cities-are-going-carbon-neutral.pdf, https://www.bbc.com/future/article/20211115-how-cities-are-going-carbon-neutral

15. Can green energy power Africa's future? - BBC News.pdf, https://www.bbc.com/news/business-58652848

16. http://www.m-kopa.com/

17. Mobile Money in Africa, https://www.weforum.org/agenda/2021/09/mobile-money-africa-prevalence-economics-technology/

18. Deals On Health, Darko Jacimovic, January 18, 2022, https://dealsonhealth.net/vegetarian-statistics/

19. Pew Research, The Indian Blog, Darko Jacimovic, January 18, 2022, https://dealsonhealth.net/vegetarian-statistics/

20. Statista, Pew Research, The Indian Blog, Darko Jacimovic, January 18, 2022, https://dealsonhealth.net/vegetarian-statistics/

21. https://www.forestcarbondataviz.org, SOURCES: Forest Storage and Sequestration: FIA, FIA/RPA 48 States Emissions: EPA, US DoT, SOCCR2, NCASI, Urban Forest: Nowak et al, Wood Products Storage: EPA

22. Climate change/ Key crops face major shifts as world warms - BBC News.pdf, https://www.bbc.com/news/science-environment-60141387

23. Earth Org, Olivia Lai, October 28, 2021, https://earth.org/10-unesco-forests-are-now-sources-of-carbon-due-to-human-activity/

24. gatesnotes.com, https://www.gatesnotes.com/energy/two-videos-illuminate-energy-poverty-bjorn-lomborg

25. solarimpulse.com, https://solarimpulse.com/solutions-explorer/waterkiosk

11. SUMMARY

1. Forbes November 21, 2018; 88% Of Consumers Want You To Help Them Make A Difference, https://www.forbes.com/sites/solitairetownsend/2018/11/21/consumers-want-you-to-help-them-make-a-difference/?sh=2d7a6f4e6954

2. How Much Energy Does a House Use? | Constellation.pdf, https://blog.constellation.com/2021/02/25/average-home-power-usage/

3. https://pvwatts.nrel.gov/

4. https://www.epa.gov/egrid/power-profiler#/

5. ScienceDirect, https://www.sciencedirect.com/topics/engineering/fuel-economy

6. How much does it cost to Charge a Tesla? Energy Sage.pdf, https://news.energysage.com/tesla-charging-cost-vs-gas/

Credits

1. FOOD

1.1 Food Systems Dashboard What is it? & What is it good for?- Nature Food/ ISSN 2662–1355. Adapted From: HLPE (2017). Nutrition and Food Systems. Lawrence Haddad and Jess Fanzo, World Bank, September 17,2020 https://olc. worldbank.org/system/files/Part%20 1_%20Food%20Systems%20 Dashboard.pdf

1.2 Concept of Stop Food Waste Day. Potato peels are one of the most commonly discarded items during food prep. By **Татьяна Креминская** dreamstime.com, https://www. dreamstime.com/photos-images/ food-loss-waste-reduction-leftovers-meal.html

1.3 Feeditforward.ca website, Chef Jagger Gordon

1.4 Feeditforward.ca website, Chef Jagger Gordon

1.5 Stock.Adobe.com_298907964, by Simon

1.6 USDA, Economic Research Service, Food Dollar Series, Marketing Bill Series, 2020, https://www.ers.usda.gov/ data-products/food-dollar-series/ documentation.aspx

1.7 Stock.adobe.com_310581123, by Yulia

1.8 Earth-Org, Why Environmental Impact Should Influence Your Diet, Poore & Nemeck (2018), Science. Animal and food comparison, November 17, 2020, https://earth.org/data_visualization/ why-environmental-impact-should-influence-your-diet/

1.9 USDA-NASS and Livestock Marketing Information Center U.S. Beef Cow Inventory (1970 to 2021) https://www. nass.usda.gov/Charts_and_Maps/ Cattle/bcow.php

1.10 Stock.adobe.com_434529448, by mvdiduk

1.11 goodneswetwork.org, The Largest Urban Rooftop Farm in the World is Now Bearing Fruit (and more) in Paris. pdf, July 17 2020, photos by Agripolis, https://www.goodnewsnetwork.org/ the-largest-urban-rooftop-farm-in-the-world-is-now-bearing-fruit-and-more-in-paris/

1.12   Douglas A. Munro Coast Guard Headquarters Building, photograph provided by Perkins&Will (architect)- Roof Garden

1.13   Stock.adobe.com_ 328694654, by sompong_tom

1.14   Vertical Harvest, Jackson Hole Wyoming, May 22, 2018, Author's personal collection.

1.15   Stock.adobe.com_409972127, by Halfpoint

1.16   Stock.adobe.com_446077995, by Sadia

1.17   EAT, Summary Report of the Eat-Lancet Commission, July 2021, page 13, thelancet.com/commissions/EAT.

1.18   SMART Studio- The salmon you buy in the future may be farmed on land - BBC News by Dan Gibson April 26 2021, https://www.bbc.com/news/business-56829129

1.19   Feeditforward.ca website, Chef Jagger Gordon

2. RENEWABLE ENERGY

2.1   National Energy Renewable Laboratory (NREL) Office of Energy Efficiency & Renewable Energy, Wind Turbines: the Bigger, the Better, August 16, 2022, https://www.energy.gov/eere/articles/wind-turbines-bigger-better

2.2   Stock.adobe.com_442758132, by Stefan_E

2.3   Aerial view of wind turbines at sea, North Holland, Netherlands, By pkawasaki

2.4   Ocean Grazer Wind Storage, February 17,2022, https://innovationorigins.com/en/ocean-grazer-to-test-storage-system-for-wind-energy-in-sand-quarry/

2.5   U.S. Department of Energy, Office of Energy Efficiency & Renewable Energy-Solar Land Use, Solar Futures Study Fact Sheet, September 2021, https://www.energy.gov/sites/default/files/2021-09/Solar_Futures_Study_Fact_Sheet.pdf

2.6   Stock.adobe.com_402938090, by trekandphoto

2.7   World Economic Forum, image by Sungrow Power Supply, June 2, 2017, https://www.weforum.org/agenda/2017/06/china-worlds-largest-floating-solar-power/

2.8   Next2Sun Mounting Systems- Vertical PV Panels, French-German alliance for vertical PV, March 30, 2020, https://www.pv-magazine.com/2020/03/30/french-german-alliance-for-vertical-pv/

2.9   Stock.adobe.com_ 470713279, by bilanol,

2.10   Stock.adobe.com_29442294, by Pavlo Glazkov,

2.11   Stock.adobe.com_459298030, by Negro Elkha,

2.12   Stock.adobe.com_264874699, by Felix Mizioznikov

2.13   Alabama News Center- Hurricane

2.14   Stock.adobe.com_248626760, by malp

2.15   Economist- deaths easy to re-create, How Safe is Nuclear, July 19, 2022, https://www.economist.com/graphic-detail/2022/07/19/how-safe-is-nuclear-energy

2.16   National Energy Renewable Laboratory (NREL), February 22, 2018 https://www.nrel.gov/gis/assets/images/geothermal-identified-hydrothermal-and-egs.jpg

2.17   Stock.adobe.com_291920946, by Thinapob

3. TRANSPORTATION

3.1   Stock.adobe.com_515400977, by Jetcityimage

3.2   Energy.gov.ev, Vehicle Technologies Office, June 14 2021, Electric Vehicles Have Lower Scheduled Maintenance Costs than Other Light-Duty Vehicles, https://www.energy.gov/eere/vehicles/articles/fotw-1190-june-14-2021-battery-electric-vehicles-have-lower-scheduled

3.3   Motor 1.com, Next Fully Electric Mercedes eSprinter Will Be Built In The US, By: Jacob Oliva, March 30 2021, https://www.motor1.com/photo/5366623/next-gen-mercedes-benz-esprinter-electric-versatility-platform/

3.4   Urb-i http://www.urb-i.com/before-after by Yuval Fogelson

3.5   Urb-i http://www.urb-i.com/before-after by Yuval Fogelson

3.6   Urb-i http://www.urb-i.com/before-after by Yuval Fogelson

3.7   designboom, ambitious plans by MX3D to 3D print metal bridge modeled by joris laarman, https://www.designboom.com/technology/mx3d-heijmans-3dprint-bridge-06-14-2015/ Joris Laarman Lab- image courtesy of joris laarman for MX3D

3.8   newstorycharity.org, Introducing the world's first community of 3D printed homes. https://newstorycharity.org/3d-community/

3.9   Stock.adobe.com_505230609, by Dmitrii

4. CITIES

4.1   68% of the world population projected to live in urban areas by 2050, May 16, 2018, photo: Greardo Pesantez/World Bank, UN image, https://www.un.org/development/desa/en/news/population/2018-revision-of-world-urbanization-prospects.html

4.2   United Nations Development Goals; https://www.unicefusa.org/mission/sustainable-developmentgoals?

4.3   Stock.adobe.com_508404816, by Whale Design

4.4 Development Asia, What the World's First Bus Rapid Transit Can Teach Us, May 18 2016, https://development.asia/case-study/what-worlds-first-bus-rapid-transit-system-can-teach-us

4.5 Ecologist, Curitiba: The Greenest city on Earth, March 15 2014, https://theecologist.org/2014/mar/15/curitiba-greenest-city-earth

4.6 City Plan by Doug Farr, FAIA

4.7 Community Sharing Living Building Center, Life Cycle Building Center.org, Shannon Goodman, https://www.lifecyclebuildingcenter.org

4.8 Perkins&Will- CIRS project

4.9 Stock.adobe.com_525310111, by hiv360

4.10 ResearchGate, Different Nature-Based Solutions Can Work Together Across Landscapes to Build Resilience, https://www.researchgate.net/figure/How-different-nature-based-solutions-can-work-together-across-landscapes-to-build_fig2_350715205

4.11 Boston.com; Boston no flood: How the rising sea levels will affect the city; created by Nickolay Lamm, from StorageFront.com, http://archive.boston.com/yourtown/specials/boston_under_water/

4.12 Boston.com; Boston underwater: How the rising sea levels will affect the city; created by Nickolay Lamm, from StorageFront.com, http://archive.boston.com/yourtown/specials/boston_under_water/

4.13 openknowledge.worldbank.org, Investing in Climate Adaption Delivers High Returns, GCA 2019, page 7, https://openknowledge.worldbank.org/bitstream/handle/10986/35203/Enabling-Private-Investment-in-Climate-Adaptation-and-Resilience-Current-Status-Barriers-to-Investment-and-Blueprint-for-Action.pdf?sequence=5

4.14 What does a Tesla charging station look like, centro-innato.com, https://www.google.com/search?client=safari&rls=en&q=Tesla+Supercharging+stations+images&ie=UTF-8&oe=UTF-8#imgrc=EFiWGjtO_RhBLM

4.15 Green Dream: How Future Cities Can Outsmart Nature?Sun Lillies – home.pdf, by Winy Maas, Pirjo Haikola, Ulf Hackauf, John Thackara, pages 389, August 13, 2014

4.16 Green Dream: How Future Cities Can Outsmart Nature? Barcelona– home.pdf, by Winy Maas, Pirjo Haikola, Ulf Hackauf, John Thackara, pages 348August 13, 2014

5. BUILDINGS

5.1 Architecture 2030, Embodied Carbon, Edward Mazria, mazria@architecture2030.org, https://architecture2030.org

5.2 Perkins&Will. Wood, concrete, steel

5.3 Architecture 2030, Different-layers-of-the-building-and-their-expected-time, Edward Mazria, mazria@architecture2030.org, https://architecture2030.org

5.4 Perkins&Will - Engineered Wood

5.5 Perkins&Will - Construction Time

5.6 carboncure.com, Media Kit, Media Library, infographic options

5.7 Mighty Earth's original analysis: U.S. EPA Greenhouse Gas Equivalencies Calculator

5.8 Architecture 2030, Steel, Edward Mazria, mazria@architecture2030.org, https://architecture2030.org

5.9 Architecture 2030, Net Zero Codes, Edward Mazria, mazria@architecture2030.org, https://architecture2030.org

5.10 Emily Higbee of Redwood Energy, Residential Natural Gas Methane System Leakage to California Residences: 2.7%- 5.2%, https://ww2.energy.ca.gov/2018publications/CEC-500-2018-021/CEC-500-2018-021.pdf

5.11 Architecture 2030, Data Source: IEA Energy Technology Perspectives 2020, February 2021 Revised Edition, Edward Mazria, mazria@architecture2030.org, https://architecture2030.org

5.12 Stock.adobe.com_444752042, by dizain

5.13 the5gexchange.com, Avoiding IoT pitfalls in the 5G era, by Jakob-Owens, by Blogs & Opinions 3/3/2022

5.14 Author photograph

5.15 Architecture 2030- Insulation, Edward Mazria, mazria@architecture2030.org, https://architecture2030.org

5.16 Architecture 2030, Water Systems Diagram, Edward Mazria, mazria@architecture2030.org, https://architecture2030.org

5.17 Living Building Challenge, Red List, Living Building's Red List aims to transform materials market, Portland Business Journal, by Christina Williams, June 20 2014

5.18 Bureau Door/ Courtesy Energiesprong

5.19 Bureau Door/ Courtesy Energiesprong

5.20 RMI

5.21 Bureau Door/ Courtesy Energiesprong

5.22 Chart by Author

6. CARBON SEQUESTRATION

6.1 World Economic Forum, Nature Risk Rising: Why the Crisis Engulfing Nature Matters for Business and Economy, January 2020, page 9, https://www3.weforum.org/docs/WEF_New_Nature_Economy_Report_2020.pdf

6.2 Stock.adobe.com _294857615, by Kotangens

6.3   Getty Images- Plant Trees Farm Blue Sky, Chris VanLennep

6.4   REUTERS, photo by Denis Balibouse

6.5   Conservation International, How an accidental forest saved a village from a storm for the ages, by Lynn Tang

6.6   Underwater360, 10 Things You Need To Know About Mangrove Forests, https://www.uw360.asia/10-things-you-need-to-know-about-mangrove-forests, October 27 2018

6.7   Stock.adobe.com_439710319, by Ray Dukin

6.8   Stock.adobe.com_402831716, by karunyapas

6.9   Alternative Crop and Soil Practices Can Improve Water Absorption During Heavy Rainfall,

6.10   USDA-NRCS, Five Ways Agroforestry Can Grow Forest Products and Benefit Your Land, Your Pockets & Wildlife, by Jim Robinson, https://www.usda.gov/media/blog/2016/10/19/five-ways-agroforestry-can-grow-forest-products-and-benefit-your-land-your

6.11   Hillel 1998; Rockstrom et al 2009

6.12   USDA, Five Ways Agroforestry Can Grow Forest Products and Benefit Your Land, Your Pockets & Wildlife, by Ben Fertig, February 21 2017, https://www.usda.gov/media/blog/2016/10/19/five-ways-agroforestry-can-grow-forest-products-and-benefit-your-land-your

6.13   NCAT, Learn How Massachusetts Farmers Harvest the Sun Twice During The Agrisolar Clearinghouse 'Follow The Sun' Tour, https://www.ncat.org/learn-how-massachusetts-farmers-harvest-the-sun-twice-during-the-agrisolar-clearinghouse-follow-the-sun-tour/

6.14   Stock.Adobe.com_240836452.jpg, by rbkelle

6.15   XCEL spreadsheet by author

6.16   Stock.adobe.com_462557017, by VectorMine

6.17   Environmental Defense Fund; Carbon capture: reversing climate pollution, By Joanna Foster, March 18, 2022, Photo illustrations by Tink Tank Studio

6.18   Stock.adobe.com_490696318.jpeg, by Pro_Vector

7. GOVERNMENT

Unsplash.com, o0kbc907i20, by Katie Moum

7.1   Statista.com, Percentage distribution of household income in the United States in 2021, September 2022, https://www.statista.com/statistics/203183/percentage-distribution-of-household-income-in-the-us/

7.2   Spreadsheet by author

7.3   Organization of Economic Cooperation and Development (OECD), https://sgp.fas.org/crs/misc/R44283.pdf

8. BUSINESSES

Unsplash.com, nC6CyrVBtkU, by Damir Kopezhanov

8.1   Photo by author

8.2   Spreadsheet by author

8.3   Gruber et al (2018, based on visualization by Tupy (2012)

8.4   U.S. Department of Energy;

9. CITIZENS

Unsplash.com, IBaVuZsJJTo, by Ryoji Iwata

9.1   EPA, https://www.google.com/url?sa=i&url=http%3A%2F%2Froperld.com%2Fscience%2FCarbonDioxideEmissionsGlobal.htm&psig=AOvVaw1eQVdNDGbtj9A-bJvia8PW&ust=1665620270934000&source=images&cd=vfe&ved=0CA0QjhxqFwoTCIjE-ra12foCFQAAAAdAAAAABAj

9.2   Bill & Melinda Gates Foundation, Gates Notes, Gates Foundation Spending, by Bill Gates, July 13 2022, https://www.gatesnotes.com/About-Bill-Gates/Commitment-to-the-Gates-Foundation

9.3   Spreadsheet by author

9.4   World Central Kitchen, www.wck.com, credit: National Geographic/ Sebastian Lindstrom, https://www.google.com/url?sa=i&url=https%3A%2F%2Fdcist.com%2Fstory%2F22%2F04%2F27%2Fnew-documentary-we-feed-people-jose-andres-world-central-kitchen%2F&psig=AOvVaw3dOEh7xUMZ4r4DIB1CAxSZ&ust=1665621035241000&source=images&cd=vfe&ved=0CA0QjhxqFwoTCIDO5KG42foCFQAAAAdAAAAABAG

10. GLOBAL

10.1   Roslan Rahman/ Getty Images

10.2   Asian Disaster Reduction Center (ADRC)

10.3   Eurostat, Coal Bonanza: Alliance Resource Partners/ Seeking Alpha, author Stephen Cross, August 24, 2022, https://seekingalpha.com/article/4536651-coal-bonanza-alliance-resource-partners

10.4   Getty Images, Rainforest

10.5   greatgreenwall.org, https://www.greatgreenwall.org/about-great-green-wall

10.6   Stock.Adobe_480612196, by Rhett A. Butler

10.7   Grid Arendal, https://www.grida.no/resources/12546

10.8   SolarImpulse.com

10.9   SolarImpulse.com, SafeWaterAfrica
        Autonomous and decentralized water
        purification system for rural Africa,
        https://solarimpulse.com
        /solutions-explorer/safewaterafrica?
        queryID=3f4d96622b55452f7204c325
        8d274686

10.10 International Energy Agency (IEA),
        IT'S THE END OF OIL: Blockbuster
        IEA Report Urges No New Fossil
        Development, May 19 2021, Primary
        Author: Mitchell Beer @mitchellbeer,
        https://www.iea.org

11. SUMMARY

Unsplash.com, yZygONrUBe8, by NASA

11.1   INNOVATION GROUP- J.Walter
        Thompson Intelligence, Cover
        image of the J. Walter Thompson
        Intelligence 'Trend Report' on 'The New
        Sustainability: Regeneration'(2018),
        by Daniel Christian Wahl, November 1
        2018, https://designforsustainability.
        medium.com/regeneration-hits-the-
        mainstream-but-what-about-the-
        deeper-practice-746c4aa7ea1b

Endorsements

ED MAZRIA, FAIA, FRAIC
Executive Director Architecture 2030 and AIA Gold Medal 2021

The title says it all – AFFORDABLE SOLUTIONS FOR CLIMATE CHANGE. Dan Watch provides us with the solutions and policies that effectively address climate change at scale TODAY. His book is essential reading that supports individuals, businesses, and governments in making smart, financially feasible and timely decisions to reach zero carbon emissions in buildings and cities to transportation and energy systems.

OTTO VAN GEET P.E., LEED AP
Principal Engineer, National Renewable Energy Laboratory (NREL)

Affordable Solutions for Climate Change is an informative, easy to read book. The book explains in simple terms how fossil fuel energy use in our buildings and transportation is driving climate change, and the actions that citizens and policy makers can take to reduce fossil fuel use and the associated carbon emissions. Climate change is the biggest challenge that humanity is facing, this book provides affordable solutions.

KEVIN HYDES
Past chair USGBC and WorldGBC, founder Integral Group

Mr. Watch has been pursuing and perfecting the integration of architecture natural systems and man-made ones to minimize the environmental footprint of our buildings... this is a must read.

Author

DANIEL WATCH, **FAIA, NCARB, LEED AP**

He has written over 50 articles, spoken at over 100 conferences globally and authored four books. His work, advocating sustainability, writing, and lecturing have educated thousands.

Mr. Watch has 25+ years of experience leading complex large-scale sustainability projects and teams. Dan's teams have designed and built over 13,000,000 gross square feet of research space in nine countries. He has traveled outside the U.S. over 250 times to China, Singapore, Brazil and several countries in the Middle East and Europe.

Dan has spoken at several universities in U.S., China and in the Middle East on sustainable design issues. Dan presents many of his latest ideas at Harvard University annually to 40 international developers who are most interested in the latest innovations that make financial sense and support a better, more sustainable world.

He is very happy to share his research with others.

dan.watch@4globalgood.org